VOLOGDA

VYATKA

PERM

SVERDLOVSK

KOSTROMA

YAROSLAVL

(Nizhnii Novgorod)
GORKI   *Volga*   KAZAN   *Kama*   *Belaya*   UFA

VLADIMIR

Kama

COLOMNA
RYAZAN

ULYANOVSK
(Simbursk)

R   S   S   I   A   *Ural*

SAMARA

KOZLOV
PENZA   *Volga*   ORENBURG

TAMBOV

S.   S.   S.   R.

VORONEZH   SARATOV   URAL.K

Volga

STALINGRAD

Don

ROSTOV

ASTRAKHAN   CASPIAN
SEA

STAVROPOL   *Kuma*

RASNODAR

Terek

Caucasus   NALCHIK
SUKHUM   VLADIKAVKAZ

KUTAIS   *Mts.*
TIFLIS

BATUM

A MAP of RUSSIA in EUROPE
(THE U.S.S.R.)

To Illustrate Places
mentioned by
WALTER DURANTY
in
"I WRITE AS I PLEASE"

L.V FARROW

WALTER DURANTY

I WRITE AS I PLEASE

New York · SIMON and SCHUSTER · 1935

CONTENTS

vii

CONTENTS

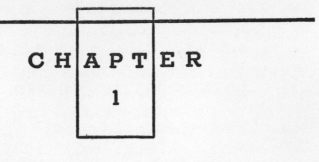

CHAPTER 1

BAPTISM OF BLOOD

I FIRST became aware of Russia at the age of four. Perhaps it was symbolic that what I heard, or rather saw, was strange and bloody, and untrue.

My nurse took me to a show entitled *Herr Parizer's Penny Novelties* at an English country fair. There were three principal items. First, a stout woman in a white night-gown wore a golden crown slightly askew and sang *Rock of Ages Cleft for Me*, while the screen bore a colored picture of another woman —or was it, I wonder, the same woman—clinging to a black rock surmounted by a white cross in the midst of raging waters.

The second scene was acted. We saw the Squire and his Lady at dinner, attended by a minion in a red waistcoat. Its climax was the hasty consumption by the minion of a mass of broken bread behind his master's back. The Squire turned and caught him, whereupon, in confusion, he regurgitated everything upon a silver tray. This repulsive playlet roused the audience to roars of enthusiasm, fully shared by me.

Having thus purged our souls, as Aristotle said, by religion and laughter, the Parizer genius next produced tragedy, a grim picture—or rather a series of colored "stills," entitled, with appalling subtlety, *A Russian Ride*. One of the cleverest officers in the Intelligence Department at French headquarters told me

3

in 1918 that what really brought America into the War and
saved the Allies from disaster was Alphonse Daudet's story,
The Last Lesson, about the French schoolmaster in Alsace on
the eve of its cession to Germany in 1871. "The best piece of
propaganda ever written," he said. "They used it in the First
Reader in America, and it left its mark upon their minds."
Looking backwards, I believe that Herr Parizer's *Russian
Ride* was an expression, conscious or not, of Anglo-Russian
rivalry, parallel to and contemporary with the:

> *We do not want to fight, but by jingo if we do*
> *We've got the men, we've got the ships, we've got the money*
>   *too;*
> *And the Russians shall not have Constantinople.*

The first picture showed the Russian family—father, mother
and five babies of tender years—going off for a sleigh ride
across the snowbound steppe. In the second appeared a wolf-
pack, hundreds of hungry beasts with slavering jaws and fiery
eyes. In the third picture, captioned "Pursuit," the wolves were
gaining. The fourth picture was shocking. The wolf-pack leaders
were abreast of the foam-flecked horses, which the driver, erect,
was lashing with all his strength. In the fifth, which froze our
blood, the father tossed a baby to the wolves. Sixth, ditto;
seventh, ditto; eighth, ditto. In each the driver stood erect and
flogged his foaming horses, while the wolf-pack surged around
them. The ninth and last picture let us breathe again. "Saved"
was the title in large black letters. The sleigh was at rest before
a wooden building, and the breath of the panting team smoked
in the frosty air. The driver sat huddled on his seat, and behind
him the distracted parents embraced their surviving child. In
the background a squad of soldiers fired a volley at the wolf-
pack.

The implications of this story, which, be it noted, also found its way into the First Readers of Great Britain, are obvious enough: Russia was a wild and barbarous country where savage animals still could menace Man; Russians, through callousness or necessity, do not hesitate to sacrifice lives of others, however dear to them, to save their own; in short, good advance propaganda for the decisive struggle between Lion and Bear which seemed imminent in the latter part of the nineteenth century.

It makes little difference that Vilhjalmur Stefansson, who knows more about the North than any living man, will stake his reputation on the two facts: (*a*) that wolves do not run in packs —never more than sire and dam and four or five growing pups; (*b*) that wolves never dare to attack an adult human being unless the human is wounded or prostrate from cold or hunger. Stefansson's contention is supported by everyone who knows the ways of wolves. He makes it his business to follow up all stories that are published about trappers or miners or postal couriers being devoured by wolves, and has never yet found one that stood the test of investigation. But the wolf-pack legend persists, and for all that I know the *Russian Ride* is still being handed out to British children, to mark their minds, as it marked mine, with error and prejudice about Russia.

. . . .

From that night until 1919 Russia was no more to me than a name on the map and in history books, save thrice. The first time—I think it was in 1912—was when my friend Arthur Ransome told me at the Café Versailles in Paris that he was going to Russia on a tutoring job and said, "Why don't you do that?" (I was rather at a loose end at the time.) "They pay your trip out and ten pounds a week—that's twice what you'd get in England—and it's quite easy to find a job if you want one."

Then, six years later, in the tragic month of March, 1918, when it seemed that the Allied cause was lost, a high official of the French War Department cried furiously, "It's the Russians who did this to us. While we fought the Marne they lost the Battle of Tannenberg through treachery, when they should have driven through against Berlin. Now they've made a separate peace and released a million Germans more to break our front."

And thirdly, a phrase which Alphonso, King of Spain, quoted from his mother, the shrewd Queen Isabella, to the French Military Attaché, General Devigne, when the latter talked in the early spring of '17 about a combined Allied attack on Eastern and Western Fronts, which should crush the German Empire in gigantic pincers. "I don't know about the Western Front," said Alphonso, "but I feel sure the Russians will fail you in the East. My mother always told me never to trust a Russian. 'He is like a cat,' she said, 'which jumps where it pleases and obeys no orders.' "

. . . .

At French headquarters, where I spent the last year of the War, it was an axiom that the Bolsheviks were enemies of God and Man, and sold to Germany—a loathsome union of anti-Christ and Judas. The matter touched me slightly, but I suppose I shared this view. Then, eighteen months later, I went myself to Russia, or what had been Russia—Finland and the Baltic Provinces.

It was October, 1919, and the American Government had just appointed a High Commissioner, Commander Gade, to the Baltic States, with headquarters at the Latvian capital, Riga. Conditions in the Baltic were so chaotic what with starvation, typhus, transport shot to pieces, and military and political confusion, that the only sensible route was by sea from Brest to Riga. It was announced that Mr. Gade, who was formerly a naval officer and presumably used to destroyers, would travel in one to his new post.

The New York Times suggested to C. H. Grasty, then a roving correspondent in Europe, that he might accompany the new Commissioner. I imagine that a string or two was pulled in Washington because the U.S.A. had suddenly realized that the Baltic States might be important either as bridge or barrier to the Soviet Union, which obstinately refused to fulfill the prophecies of the State Department and the French and British Foreign Offices, by collapsing. What's more, the British and, to a lesser degree, the French, were exceedingly busy in the Baltic States with important military and political missions, so the State Department doubtless felt it should follow their example. Grasty, who was Treasurer of *The New York Times* and no longer young, felt little eagerness to tempt the Baltic in winter in a destroyer, so the assignment was transferred to me. I was nothing loath because I found work as "second man" in the Paris office dreary after the excitement and independence of my job as war correspondent.

For all my ignorance of Russia, I believe that I was better equipped for it than I realized. The war in France had taught me a measure of indifference to blood and squalor, and fear and pity. Sudden death had become a commonplace, and vermin a joke.

Once I lunched with a group of young Frenchmen in the tank corps, and five hours later saw the bodies of three of them after a shell hit their tank and fired the gasoline, black and incredibly shriveled, like three little faceless nigger boys. Even Russia has never shown me worse than that, and the horror of it struck deeper because I had tried to share their fatal ride. They had driven me up in the tank that morning to an advance post behind the lines, and after lunch we all thought it would be fun to go on together to a point in the front trench from which they were to attack next morning. The officer commanding the advance post objected, not because he thought there was any danger— there was not much shelling that afternoon—but he said the

Germans might start something in the evening and I would get stuck up there and miss my car back to headquarters and not be able to write my story. So they went and I stayed and talked with the rest of the tank detachment. They were full of stories, because the tank corps "saw life," as they say in the Marines— and death. I do not know about the other armies, but with the French it was not considered tactful to ask after friends in any tank or battle-plane outfit who were not around when you came to visit. They might be on leave or just sick or slightly wounded, but the odds were they were dead. The tanks lost sixty per cent killed of their effectives in the French Army, which is the highest mortality for any branch of any fighting service in the War.

While we were talking, there came a phone message from the line ahead saying that a stray shell had hit one of the tanks, which had gone up in flames. The commanding officer said quietly, "That's too bad . . . I wonder which it was. Can you get the number?" Five minutes later they phoned again to say it was number seventeen, which was the one I had ridden in, and that they were sending back the bodies because there was not much firing, just an occasional shell or so. So I saw them and felt sick. There were other things I saw in the War which won't bear telling, but after a time you became hardened or callous or maybe a little crazy for the rest of your life.

All of this was preparation for Russia, where foreigners are apt to suffer from æsthetic or sentimental shell-shock and get their perspectives distorted. If they escape that, they are upset by Bolshevik doctrines and the Bolshevik desire to destroy Capitalism and all its works, among which are generally included what foreigners mean by Civilization and Patriotism and Respect for Institutions and Duty to the Flag. Other foreigners in Russia grow worried at being spied upon and followed and having their letters opened. I had been so bitterly scared by real dangers—air-raids, shells, bullets—that these intangible perils did not bulk large any more.

. . . .

Grasty might have accompanied Mr. Gade because, as it happened, he did not go on a destroyer but on a big cruiser, from Brest to Copenhagen, then across to Reval, the Esthonian capital, named Tallin nowadays, and so to Riga. I did not accompany him either because a few days before the party sailed I came down with *grippe*.

I had not seen much of the *grippe* epidemic, which hit the French Armies less than the Americans, but I had heard of men dying like flies on transports between New York and the French ports in '18. And once in Brussels, just after the Armistice, I had met a young English captain who had gone through the whole War with nothing worse than a slight flesh wound in the first Somme battle. We were sitting in a café drinking champagne, talking about the War and friends in England, all excited because the War was over and the King of the Belgians was making a triumphal entry the next day. The place was full of girls and officers dancing, and the atmosphere thick with smoke. Suddenly the Englishman said, "Lord, it's hot in here, isn't it? I feel terribly hot. I can't stand any more of it; I'm going home."

I said, "Oh, wait, it's only two o'clock; you don't have to go yet."

He said, "It's too hot in here; I'm going. We'll meet here tomorrow after the parade about 7.30 for dinner. I can't stay now. I'm so terribly hot."

The next afternoon he was not there, but a few minutes later a friend of his came in who had been with him the night before. I asked, "Where's Bill? I wanted to see him again. Why did he rush off so suddenly last night?" His friend said, "He went home because he had *grippe*, and he died at three o'clock this afternoon. Isn't that bad luck, after going through the whole show since '14? Well, let's drink to his ashes, but isn't it damn bad luck?"

That incident rather shook me, so when I got *grippe* myself a year later I went to bed quick and stayed there until the fever dropped, and missed the cruiser at Brest. I thought it might be possible to catch it at Copenhagen, so I suggested that to my office and they agreed. I had to travel up through Germany to Hamburg, and take the train-ferry across to Denmark and on to Copenhagen. It should have been about forty-eight hours from Paris, which gave me plenty of time, but when I got to Cologne I found the Germans had ordered a "stillstand" on all railroads. The reason given was conservation of coal, but the British in Cologne said there was danger of revolution or something. I managed to board the last train to Hamburg, but there was no connection beyond to the train-ferry.

Although I did not know it yet, that journey was a good introduction to my stay in the Baltic States—the most fantastic three months I have ever known, a sort of "Mad Hatter's Tea-party"—and for that matter to subsequent years in the Soviet Union. There was a Danish-American on the train, and the next day we drove in a car from Hamburg to Lübeck, where there might be a small coasting boat to Copenhagen. In Lübeck I got a real idea of what the Allied Hunger Blockade had done to Germany. The Rhineland was bad enough the year before when our troops went in after the Armistice, but in Lübeck the people were almost starving. There was one woman, a relative by marriage of my Danish friend, who owned a nice house with a garden in the better section of the town. Her husband had been a Colonel in the army, killed in the War, and she and her three servants were living on potatoes they had planted that summer, and black bread. They had no meat or butter or milk or eggs, but sometimes a small fish, not very fresh. Everything was stringently rationed on a card system, and the woman said she was liable to a fine for hoarding her own potatoes.

One of the city doctors told me that ninety per cent of the children were anæmic or below weight, and that more than half of them had rickets or T.B. They reminded me of a so-called fairy-tale from my childhood. I don't know where it came from, but it was one of those moral and improving tales where children who are naughty get punished frightfully. In those days people believed in punishing children in England. I remember once when I lied to my grandmother she put my finger, just a touch, of course, on a hot bar in the fire grate, and when I yelled, she said, "Liars go to hell, and in hell it burns like that for ever." My grandmother was a woman of rigid virtue and a pillar of the Presbyterian Church, and generous withal, but I never really loved her after that. The punishment in the story was that the children were lost in a fog and wandered aimlessly ever afterwards, hungry and lost in the fog. A sort of foggy hell, I suppose it was, to punish naughty children. There was an illustration of a small boy, about my own age, which may have been five or six. I have forgotten his name, but I can see his face now, and it brings up in my heart the same flow of sympathy and friendship as it did then. I felt that this boy was a friend of mine and I hated to think of him lost for ever in the fog.

Lübeck on the North German coast was foggy too in October. In the central square there I met a group of tiny pale-faced children going home through the fog from school. So sad and silent and pale, as if they were lost and hungry. In Lübeck all food was rationed; you couldn't buy it for any amount of money. I think that the foggy hell of my "fairy-tale" may be a good place for some of the French and British politicians who maintained the Hunger Blockade upon Germany for twelve months after the War was over.

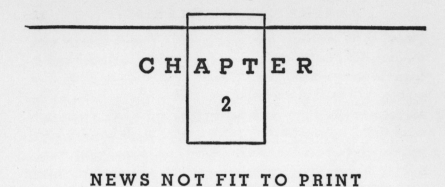

CHAPTER 2

NEWS NOT FIT TO PRINT

WHEN at last we reached Copenhagen, the American cruiser had left for Reval, so I decided to make the overland trip through Sweden and Finland to Esthonia. In the meantime I had an interview with the Danish Foreign Minister, and talked with Russian refugees and Red Cross officials of various nations, thus getting my first glimpse of what the Russian Revolution meant.

I went to Stockholm quickly, arrived in the morning and caught a boat the same night for Åbo in Finland. We hove to for six hours in the darkness west of the Åland Islands because there were reports, subsequently denied as it happened, that a Bolshevik submarine had laid mines in the channel. But it was as well to take no chances. Once, about a month or so before the end of the War, I had traveled in a French torpedo boat from Dunkirk to Ostend, which the Germans had just evacuated, although you couldn't yet reach it by road. The Germans did indeed put mines in the channel, and I saw a British tanker or coal boat hit one. It made a loud impressive noise, and she sank in three minutes.

This disaster threw light for me on a phase of human psychology which I had not known before. That is what makes life interesting to me, going places and learning new things about people and the way their minds work. On our way back from

12

Ostend in the evening I was talking with a French Colonel who was one of the heroes of the War. He had been in the thick of it from the start, wounded half a dozen times and won every decoration the French Army could give. There was no doubt about his courage—he'd proved it during four and a half years, and mind you, it takes courage to go back again to the trenches after you have been wounded once or twice. Lots of people can stand it up to the first wound, or even the second, then their nerve begins to break. To go back again after three or four wounds you've got to be a glutton for punishment.

The sea was calm and there was not a cloud in the sky, and the shelling had stopped. The Germans had run from Ostend but it seems they had a battery of twelve-inch guns farther up the coast at Knocke near the Dutch border, which was getting rid of its ammunition before they left that town. All afternoon they had been throwing twelve-inch shells at intervals of about ten minutes in the general direction of Ostend. One of them set a big munitions dump on fire, and it went on blazing and exploding throughout our trip back to Dunkirk. Those big shells had worried me all day, and I was glad when they stopped and we were safely aboard the steamer running back to Dunkirk. Suddenly the Colonel tapped me on the shoulder. "Excuse me," he said, "do you happen to have a flask with you? I need a drink." I had a flask half full of brandy and gave it to him. His hand was shaking as he drank it. "Thanks," he said, "that's better. Do you know, I'm nervous as a cat? I don't know what I'd have done without that drink."

"What do you mean?" I asked. "Nervous about what?"

"Mines," he said. "You saw that ship this morning, and when I think what would happen if this little boat hit one, it makes me cold down the back. If I hadn't had that drink, I don't know what I'd have done."

That to me was interesting, because this man had not been

scared by real immediate danger in the trenches, but he was not afraid to admit that an impalpable danger made him jittery. I am just the opposite; the thing that frightens me is noise. When a shell bursts or bullets zip past, then I'm scared. But the risk that we might hit a mine and get blown sky-high failed to distress me unduly.

The point seems to lie in the difference between the fact of danger and the thought of danger. The bursting shell or the bullet is a present fact, whereas the potential effect of a mine or torpedo is thought. I somehow feel that I can control my thoughts better than extraneous facts, although I noticed later in Russia that people who had gone through the War and faced real danger without dismay, which I don't think I could have done, could scare themselves, as I said before, into something like shell-shock about the menace of the Gay-pay-oo, even when they were not doing anything for which the Gay-pay-oo might jump them.

.   .   .   .

At Åbo I first came into direct contact with the Soviet Revolution, or rather with its effects, and for the first time set foot on soil that had formerly been part of the Russian Empire. It seemed like getting back to war-time, with heavy display of uniformed troops at dock and Customs and the railroad station. Everywhere tall blond soldiers in German helmets with Mauser automatic pistols on their hips. This was the famous White Guard of Finland, which had broken the Red Revolution after far bloodier fighting, at least *pro rata* of population, than occurred anywhere in Russia proper. The Reds were mostly Russian soldiers or Finns of native stock, while the Whites were higher-class Russians or "Finlanders" of Swedish blood. With the help of German troops from the Baltic Provinces the Whites finally won, but the fighting and executions on both sides had left bitter hatred between the two factions.

The Government was Finnish *bourgeois* for the most part, but the real power was still in the hands of the White Guard, whose officers were nearly all of Swedish, German or Russian origin. I found that a military pass was needed to travel on the train to Helsingfors, Finland's capital, and the fact that I had been a war correspondent with the French Armies and had a khaki uniform with me did not win much favor in the eyes of an ex-officer of the German Army wearing the Iron Cross, who commanded the depot. I should never have secured a place if it had not been for a diplomatic courier of one of the Scandinavian countries, who took me into his reserved coupé. This shrewd and amiable citizen, with whom I had made friends on the boat from Stockholm, afterwards showed me a new racket, which was then popular in Eastern Europe. A man with nerve, some pull and a little money could, it seemed, get a courier job in some of the smaller countries and carry official mail at his own risk and peril. He would also take a suit-case full of silk stockings, underwear, cosmetics, vanilla extract, and so forth, and if he was sufficiently unscrupulous, cocaine or heroin. He would sell his "cargo" on reaching his goal, then buy jewels or furs or *objets d'art* or even platinum, which had leaked out of Russia. On both transactions there was a profit of five hundred per cent or more, and I knew a case where such a "courier" made the equivalent of $60,000, without smuggling dope, in little more than half a year, then prudently retired and bought a place in the country to live happily ever after.

· · · · · · · · · ·

There was much excitement in Helsingfors at that time about the recent attack on Petrograd by the White general, Yuden-ich, which appeared to have come within an ace of success. Indeed, one of the more enterprising British correspondents claimed to have seen, or that someone had seen, a white flag hoisted over the Red stronghold of Kronstadt, and for a day or two the Western world believed in a White victory.

The Yudenich affair showed me how anti-Bolshevik efforts were rotted by incompetence and jealousy, or worse. Yudenich, who won fame in the War as conqueror of the Turkish fortress of Erzeroum, had a force of some 25,000 men, largely equipped and trained by the British and French, in the northeast corner of Esthonia near Narva. The campaign plans, which had been drawn up with British assistance, provided for a combined attack of the Russian and Esthonian forces—the latter on a wide front between Narva and Pskov—while a British monitor, the *Erebus,* should support Yudenich's left wing by shelling the Russian fort of Krasnaya Garka from the sea with twelve-inch guns. In addition, there were three vessels loaded with 10,000 tons of foodstuffs at the British naval base of Bjorki on the Finnish side of the gulf, ready to be rushed to Petrograd after its occupation by the Whites. These supplies belonged to the American Red Cross, whose energetic representatives in the Baltic States wore uniforms and military titles and played quite a political rôle in those days, not always to the delight of the British and French Missions. There was thus some justification for Litvinov's statement at Riga in '21 during the negotiations between the Soviet and the American Relief Administration that "Food is a weapon." Yes, and a strong one in a land of starvation and hunger-typhus.

Unfortunately the campaign plan was better on paper than in practice. To begin with, the Esthonian forces took no part in the attack. Against Esthonian protests the Allies had allowed Yudenich to form a "Northwest Russian Government," which, if it had no territorial possessions outside its sector of the Front, was nevertheless able to issue its own paper money, and did so lavishly. Yudenich had two million pounds sterling, part of the old Imperial gold reserve, in a Stockholm bank, and a small group of insiders, including some foreigners, made a neat little killing by speculating in Exchange. The watermark on the larger bills of this currency was the Imperial double eagle, which displeased the Esthonians, and many of the White officers had said openly that after they took Petrograd they would come back and clean up Esthonia. So the Esthonians refused to coöperate. Nevertheless, Yudenich's vanguard, headed by four British whippet tanks, broke through the flimsy Red defense and occupied Gatchina, twenty-five miles from Petrograd. At this point the story may be continued by a young British officer commanding the White tank corps, whom I met a few days later in Reval.

"We were supposed to be no more than instructors, my colleague and I and a sergeant and ten men, for the picked group of Russian officers, about a hundred of them, who formed the Yudenich tank corps. We drilled them and trained them as best we could, but when the show came I thought we had better make certain of a good start, so we took the four whippets into action ourselves with a Russian or two in each tank, and the rest of them accompanied us on foot. There was some fighting the first day, but we soon broke that. The Reds had never seen tanks before, and we smashed right through them, and the second evening we occupied Gatchina, practically without resistance. There had been good progress all along the Front and it seemed plain sailing, so I turned the tanks over to the Russians for their attack early next morning and went to bed in the palace. We were sure that they would take Petrograd next day because the Reds were demoralized. About five they woke me and said that the Reds were advancing and the tanks were out of action. I couldn't believe it, but rushed out to the field about a mile beyond Gatchina where the tanks were. There was no firing on the Red side and that was lucky, because of the four tanks one had the engine smashed with a sledge-hammer and couldn't possibly run. From another they'd taken the magneto and hidden it in the snow; we found it and put it back. A third had the carburetor stuffed with cotton wadding; we soon fixed that. There was nothing wrong with the fourth except that all its fuel had been drained out. And mind you, this Russian tank outfit was supposed to be all ex-officers and hand-picked as well. By the time we had got the three tanks in order the Reds were beginning to attack, cautiously, and all our Russians had disappeared. We made a demonstration against the Reds and they ran away. Then we cruised along the Front and found the Reds were advancing everywhere with no sign of our people. So we turned round and caught up with the retreat about five miles west of Gatchina."

"How do you explain it?" I asked.

He shrugged his shoulders. "They're just rotten, for one thing. Sooner drink and talk than fight. But I did hear that the general commanding the attack had stolen the best girl of the general commanding the transport, and the latter had said publicly, 'If that son-of-a-bitch thinks he's going to get the credit for taking Petrograd, I'll have a word to say about it.' At least this I do know," the Englishman concluded, "that in the forty-eight hours of the advance not a single cartridge or ounce of food reached the front line from behind, so perhaps the transport commander made good his threat."

Be that as it may, the main body of Yudenich's force retired more or less unmolested to its lines near Narva, where a few weeks later it was destroyed by a typhus epidemic which killed 11,000 out of 15,000, in circumstances of despair, filth, starvation, misery and lack of medical aid so frightful that *The New York Times* would not print my account of it, which was taken from the report of the American Red Cross to Commissioner Gade.

. . . .

I need hardly say that General Yudenich and his staff did not share their army's shocking fate. They lived comfortably for some months in Reval, then withdrew to Stockholm, where their money was, and doubtless spent it cheerfully. The general died in his bed some years ago, but before leaving Reval he had one narrow shave, about six weeks after his attack on Petrograd had collapsed.

He and his staff were living at the Golden Eagle, Reval's best hotel. The old man had grown very heavy, and he and his personal aide had a small suite in the garden on the ground floor away from the rest of the staff. This, it seems, became known to a citizen named Balakhovich, an ex-officer of Cossacks, who was then commanding what he was pleased to call a "Green Band" in the No-Man's-Land between the Esthonians and the Reds. He had about 400 men and operated mostly in Red territory, dashing forth from the forests to raid in all directions. Later he moved down to the Polish Front, and took part in the Russo-Polish War in 1920. He lived to get away with his loot to Paris, where I think he was assassinated. Anyway, he deserved it. I met him once, an elegant young man in his close-cut Cossack uniform with its silver cartridge belt, and a blood-thirsty bandit he was.

One fine night this Balakhovich, with six of his merry men, rode up to the Golden Eagle—don't ask me how they managed it, but money talks in Esthonia and Yudenich was not popular—and yanked the general out of his bed, tied him on a horse and set off hell-for-leather back towards the Front. "We'll hang him face downwards over a slow fire till his eyes pop out or he signs an order for a million pounds on that bank in Stockholm, and keep him till we get the money," said Balakhovich to Yudenich's terrified aide-de-camp as he swung himself into the saddle.

He had done worse than that before, and the aide-de-camp knew it, so he lost no time in rushing round to the Esthonian Army Headquarters with his tale of woe. The Esthonian Army was annoyed at being roused from slumber by anything so triv-

ial. With soldierly bluntness they told the Russian to go to hell
or come back later in the morning, but anyway not to bother
them now at 2 A.M. Then the aide-de-camp appealed to the British, with little greater success. The British commander regretted
—"A most disgraceful outrage, but you must see, my dear fellow, it's not precisely in our province. I mean to say, it's a matter for the Esthonian authorities. I suggest you apply to them."

Meanwhile time was passing, and each tick of the clock took
the unhappy general a horse's length nearer to the frontier (that
is, to the Front and No-Man's-Land beyond it) and to the slow
fire that Balakhovich had promised. With relays of horses the
kidnapers might pass the Front in five or six hours, of which
two had already been wasted in fruitless appeals to Esthonians
and British. At this point the aide-de-camp had an inspiration.
Surely, he thought, the American Red Cross was his goal, its
diligent officials were always ready, nay, eager, to fish in any
waters, however troubled, and put their fingers in any pie, however hot. He rushed to the Red Cross building.

According to my informant (for this is a true story told me
under pledge of secrecy by an officer of one of the Foreign
Missions in Riga some months later) the Red Cross was not
even asleep. "Those guys sat up nights making trouble for
everyone," my informant said bitterly. "They never forgave the
rest of us for thinking that Red Cross military titles were outranked by the real army, and don't forget that they had lots of
money and food, at a time when food mattered enormously,
and were active, busy boys, who never missed a chance."

The Red Cross leapt to the rescue. Within fifteen minutes
their big Cadillac was hooting outside the Esthonian War Department like Joshua at the walls of Jericho. Again the exasperated Esthonians were roused from their slumbers, but this
time it was no pitiful White Russian aide but the Commander-
in-Chief of the American Red Cross, Baltic Division, in uni-

form complete with stripes and ribbons and with a line of talk that made the Esthonians' hair curl. "Don't you dumb-bells realize," said the Red Cross Colonel to the Esthonian General, "that it's your money that's being raped off there through the night towards the frontier? If they once get across with the old man, what chance do you have of getting that million dollars you're claiming from Yudenich for comfort and assistance to his army, and all the supplies you gave him and rent for his trenches up there near Narva? Do you think that there'll be anything left for you when Balakhovich has done with him?"

People say the Esthonians are slow of thought, with dull and sluggish minds, but no one has ever accused them of ignoring the value of money. The General's eyes blazed as he caught the Colonel's drift. *"Gott in Himmel,"* he shouted, "I never thought of that," and sprang immediately to action. There was hasty telephoning and swift telegrams, and before dawn the news came back that Balakhovich and his men had been caught a bare half-hour's ride from the border. The intrepid Cossack won freedom for himself and his men by the simple expedient of putting a pistol to Yudenich's head and saying to the Esthonian officer who had checked him, "If you won't guarantee us safe conduct over the border I'll blow his brains out now, and the fact that you shoot us afterwards won't help to explain away his death. Come now, I give you five seconds to decide."

The Esthonian also thought fast. Balakhovich went free and the General returned somewhat shattered to his bed in the Golden Eagle. The Commander-in-Chief of the American Red Cross bought drinks at lunch next day for the British Military Mission and patronized them in an urbane and intolerable manner, which mortified them to the quick, but they found no word to say. In the checkered annals of the American Red Cross in the Baltic this was indeed a famous victory, and recognized as such by friend and foe.

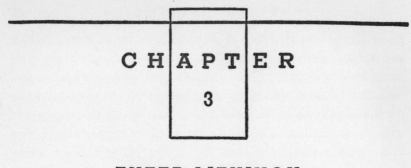

CHAPTER
3

ENTER LITVINOV

I HAD a lot of trouble getting from Helsingfors to Reval. There was no regular service, but someone told me that the British ran destroyers over every day or two; it was only a three hours' trip. So first I went round to see the British Naval Attaché, who was a big potato in Helsingfors at that time. He received me with unexpected warmth and said, "Why, of course, my dear fellow, any time you want. Let me see, there's one going to-morrow morning early. You'd better take that." I thanked him, and he sat down to write my permit. Then I made a big mistake. "Correspondent of *The Times*," he said, and I was fool enough to reply, "*The New York Times*," which made all the difference.

"*The New York Times?*" he asked. "I thought you were English."

"I am English, but I work for *The New York Times.*"

"I thought you worked for THE *Times*," he said reproachfully. "I mean this makes all the difference. *The Times* is one thing, but, you know, the navy is not a ferry-boat for American reporters." I argued in vain, but he was right; it wasn't.

Ultimately I found a small coasting vessel that would take me to Reval. I met aboard it a plump Dutchman who had been Dutch Consul in Libau for eleven years, under the Tsarist ré-

gime. He told me that he was going to Esthonia to meet Litvinov
and arrange for the release of a dozen Dutch citizens who were
being held in Soviet Russia. That was the first intimation I had
had that Litvinov was coming to Esthonia, but my Dutchman
explained that Esthonia and Finland were going to make peace
with the Reds, that an armistice had already been declared, and
that Litvinov would represent the Soviet in the peace negotiations at Dorpat.

All this was news to me, because I had not seen a newspaper
that I could read since I had left France. I was grateful to the
Dutchman and said so, whereupon he broached a more intimate
topic. He admired and coveted my coat. That showed his poor
taste because the coat was a shoddy pseudo-Burberry with a
kangaroo collar and a lining of rabbit dressed to look like seal-
skin. It had cost me forty dollars at the Galeries Lafayette in
Paris and was a popular line with second-rate French aviators.
It was flashy without dignity and pretentious without warmth.
But the Dutchman liked it, and wanted me to swap it for his
own fur coat, a modest job of plain blue serge and seal collar
with nutria lining, which had cost him, he said, 900 guilders or
450 dollars. The difference was that his coat looked seedy and
mine looked snappy. I said I would wait and see.

When we reached Reval about noon I lost the Dutchman and
spent my time hunting around to find out how I could get to
Riga and join Commander Gade, which, after all, was the chief
purpose of my trip. No one seemed to know anything, but
finally, like the Yudenich aide-de-camp, I betook me to the
American Red Cross. They knew everything, and wanted to help
me. They said that Litvinov would arrive at Dorpat the following
day and that I must certainly be present. It was an event in history, they told me, and they could arrange for me to witness it. I
thought that they were right.

They fixed me a pass on a military train which left at midnight, and suggested that I would be wise to wear uniform, the khaki uniform and riding-breeches of war correspondents at the French Front, because the trains were lousy and lice carry ty-phus, while breeches and puttees made it harder for lice to reach you. And uniform looked better on a military train.

I had an amusing dinner with two of the Red Cross people and the young British tank officer who told me about the Yuden-ich fiasco, and then boarded the train with my portable type-writer and one small bag. Just as we pulled out, the Englishman said to me, "These troops you're traveling with have been moved away from the Northern Front because they are supposed to be tinged with Bolshevism. You may have trouble on the way down. Have you got a gun?" I said no, I hadn't.

I shared a coupé with an Esthonian officer who had *grippe*. His head was burning and he did not know what he was talking about; I suppose he had a temperature of 103 at least. He knew a few words of English and French, which I knew well, and a lot of German, which I knew badly. But he could not talk any of them coherently; he was really sick. About two hours after we left Reval there came a lot of noise in the corridor outside our compartment and kicking at our door. They went on kicking and the noise got louder, and there was a note in it which I did not like, although of course I did not understand a word of what they said. I asked the Esthonian officer what it was all about and gathered from him that his troops were mutinous and looking for trouble. "Then go and tell them to shut up," I said, "because if you don't do something they'll kick this door in." He groaned and said he had *grippe*, which I knew already, and that anyway he didn't give a damn.

At this point they kicked the door more violently than ever, and by now there was no doubt for me about the threat in what they shouted. I was scared badly, and when I get scared it makes me cross. So I said to this Esthonian, "Damn your soul, can't you do something about it? I mean, you've got to do something because these fellows are getting nasty, and you've got to do something." He just groaned and said he didn't care what the hell they did. By this time I was really alarmed, so I grabbed his gun, a long old-fashioned Russian cavalry revolver and, opening the door suddenly, poked the gun into the stomach of the first man I met and said in English, "God damn you if you don't get away from here, I'll blow you to hell-and-gone." I was frightened enough to have done it, and I think he knew it, because he backed away down the corridor. I followed him, waving the gun and saying, still in English, "Get to hell out of here, and stay gone, damn you. Why can't you let me sleep? If you come back here any more I'll kill the first man who comes."

I think it is William Blake who says somewhere in one of his poems, "Beware of the rabbit in a rage." Well, that was exactly my position. I was a rabbit, that is to say I was terrified, but so terrified that I was furious enough to have lost all sense of fear, and to have started shooting at the least provocation. The soldiers backed down the corridor to their own car, and I followed them, waving the large, heavy pistol. As I bolted the door I told them, "Now don't forget, the first one who opens this door gets a bullet in the guts, so don't be silly. The best thing you can do is to go and sleep it off." Then I went back to bed myself. There was no more trouble, and two or three hours later I woke up in a big station called Tartu and went to sleep again. When I next woke it was at the frontier town of Walk.

The Esthonian officer was feeling better by this time, and grateful to me. He explained that Tartu was the new Esthonian name for Dorpat, but anyway I had saved his life, he said, and he would arrange for me to get the next train back to Tartu. Maybe I *had* saved his life, and my own for that matter, but anyway they put me on a train half an hour later and I got back to Dorpat just in time to meet Litvinov when he came in from the Soviet frontier under the direct and careful charge of the British Commissioner, Colonel Tallents.

It is rather significant that at the first official conference between the Bolsheviks and any Western State—in this case two States, Esthonia and Finland—seven of the eight foreign reporters represented American newspapers or agencies, and the eighth was a Japanese. There were no British, French or Germans, despite the fact that the British virtually ran the Baltic at that time and that Von der Goltz, with Bermont's German-trained White Russian army, was then making a last bid to hold Germany's earlier gains there by an attack on Riga.

Most of the newspaper men lived in a big apartment reserved for them by the Esthonian Government, but I, as a late-comer, stayed at the hotel. We had an interesting general interview with the Esthonian Foreign Minister, Doctor Piip—pronounced Peep—a cultivated and intelligent citizen who had been Esthonian envoy to London and spoke excellent English. He was evidently pleased with the interview because they gave us a banquet that night in the apartment and Doctor Piip sent round a huge carboy of pre-War vodka as a present. It was ninety per cent alcohol, so strong that when water was mixed with it, it turned milky like eau-de-Cologne. The Japanese and my colleague from the Hearst Press drank it neat, with disastrous results. The Japanese provided me with food for thought. In his cups he developed a grievance against a Japanese Colonel, who for some reason had attached himself to Tallents. "That son-of-a-bitch," said the Japanese reporter, "when we get home I show him. Here he high-hat me. . . . 'Go to hell, you dirty boy from newspaper.' He not know much, that damn fool. At home he salute me and say, 'Yes sir'; he just Colonel, but I General on Emperor's staff. I no tell him now, but one day soon I show him." Perhaps it was true; the Japanese are a funny people and I have noticed that their Oriental secretiveness is apt to vanish when they get tight, which they do with gusto. I have been to parties in Moscow where Japanese officers and diplomats made the most frank and extraordinary statements about their country's future and ambitions; like Kipling's story of the drunken Cossack officer with his "You little Western peoples, one day we shall eat you up." The fact of the matter is that both of them, Russians and Japanese, have an inordinate race-pride, which they conceal when sober, and are for the most part so ignorant of the Western world that they honestly believe that it is inferior to them. Nations are like individuals, they judge other people by themselves. I mean, to give an instance, a Russian said to me not long ago, "You Americans have been awfully clever to hide all news of the typhus epidemic in your country." "What on earth do you mean?" I asked in amazement. He smiled cunningly. "Oh, you can't fool me; ten million unemployed, or is it twelve, that's forty million souls on the verge of starvation, and we know what that means. There must be typhus, and lots of it, even if you do not mention it in your newspapers." Once upon a time I might have argued, but now I knew better. I got a picture of New York in *The Times* rotogravure section, taken from an aëroplane, and shoved it under his nose. "When you can build a city like that, you may talk about America. Until then, shut up." He shut up.

     .   .   .   .

Colonel Tallents had Litvinov so tightly held under his wing that none of us could get near him, and we finally decided that the only thing to do was to tackle the Colonel himself. He received us none too eagerly and gave us little satisfaction, but I recognized him as the boy I had sat next to for two terms at Harrow. His whole attitude changed when I told him who I was. The English are like that; when they know you or know people who know you, they are as friendly as can be; otherwise they are apt to be stiff. We chatted pleasantly for twenty minutes, although he did not tell me anything about Litvinov, for the good reason as I found out later, that he did not know himself, and asked me to lunch with him the following day.

That evening I had a stroke of luck. The little Dutchman I spoke of had all the perseverance of his race, and had set his heart upon my rather spurious coat. Some English statesman, I think it was Canning, once said about the Hollanders:

> *In matters of business the fault of the Dutch*
> *Is giving too little and asking too much.*

My man was just the opposite. He was like the warrior in the *Iliad*. The Greeks and Trojans were always fighting duels, and it was apparently the custom that if the duel was indecisive, that is, if neither party won outright by killing the other, they swapped armor as a token of mutual respect. In one case some excessively gilded Trojan fought such a duel with Diomedes who was one of the biggest and toughest Greek battlers. He was so big and tough that one day when Aphrodite joined the battle under the guise of a Trojan (the gods did it constantly in that war, which was rough on the mortals they encountered) Diomedes heaved a huge stone at her and knocked the goddess out. Anyway, this Trojan fought him to a draw, and probably felt grateful, because Homer says:

> *Zeus, king of gods, must have robbed Neoptolemus (or whatever his name was) of his wisdom, because he exchanged golden armor worth 3,000 cattle for the bronze armor of Diomedes worth 30.*

Perhaps Zeus had been working on my Dutchman, because nutria is worth a lot more cattle than rabbit.

In his eagerness to clinch the deal the Dutchman bought me a dinner, whereat he casually remarked that he had had a long conversation that afternoon with Litvinov about his fellow-countrymen detailed in Moscow, whose release he had secured. "Litvinov's all right," he continued. "Of course he hates the English and is rather restive at being shepherded by them here, but he talked quite freely—you understand that I speak Russian after all those years in Libau—and he told me his plans and asked my advice about them. I mean he is going from here to Stockholm and then perhaps to England, and he wanted to know what I thought of the general situation in Europe. Naturally enough the Bolsheviks have been terribly cut off from the outside world, and I think he realized that I was friendly and wouldn't lie to him."

"He did, did he?" said I with some interest. "Well now, look, Mynheer, I don't suppose you want to be quoted, but if you will tell me what Litvinov said, you can have that coat of mine and welcome."

The Dutchman glowed with delight. "You can quote me if you like," he said, "and here's the story." It was a story, and what is more it was true, as events proved later—just where Litvinov was going and when and for what purpose.

So I gave the Dutchman my flashy-looking bogus rabbit coat and took his seedy-looking genuine nutria one in exchange, and sat down and wrote a powerful piece about Litvinov's whys and wherefores.

As it happened, Piip gave us a news handout that evening, so I decided to hold up my Litvinov story for twenty-four hours. I knew it was exclusive because the Dutchman left Dorpat that night for points west, his mission being concluded.

At lunch next day with Tallents I made some reference to the Dutchman; in fact, I think I referred to Homer's line about swapping golden armor for bronze because Tallents was a classical scholar too, and added that he had given me a good story about Litvinov's plans. I thought, of course, that Tallents knew them; but he didn't. "Well," I said, "if you want the story, it's yours. We can send to my hotel and get it. I don't guarantee that it's fact, but it's what this Dutchman said, and I'm going to cable it to-night to New York." Tallents immediately sent an orderly for the story and read it with the greatest interest. "By Jove!" he said, "this is just what we want to know. Do you think it is authentic?" "I can't tell you," I replied, "but the Dutchman thought so, and it sounds reasonable enough. Anyway, I'm going to take a chance on it." "So shall I," said Tallents. And it *was* reasonable, and turned out to be correct.

Tallents was much pleased with this and said cheerily, "By the way, aren't you trying to get to Riga? I'm going there to-morrow morning because these peace negotiations are running along all right, and I've just received a message that the Von der Goltz-Bermont army is shelling Riga, and I suppose I ought to go back there to stiffen up the Letts a bit. Why don't you come with me? I'm afraid I can't put you up because we have no room, but you can be a member of our mess if you like and you won't have much trouble in getting lodgings in the town, if there's anything left of it by the time we get there."

Tallents talked lightly, but as a matter of fact he was the best type of English public servant, that small exclusive group of men who keep the Empire going. Neatly and unostentatiously he had done a marvelous job in Latvia. The Reds took Riga at Christmas, 1918, and held it for five months. In May, 1919, the Letts got sick of the Bolsheviks, who after all were Russians, and the Letts hated Russians. So they threw them out with the help of Von der Goltz, who was all that was left of German power in the Baltic. Tallents had no power, just a couple of destroyers in the river, but he had food, and the might of Britain behind him. He talked the Letts into replacing their pro-German

Government by pro-English, and he talked Von der Goltz out of Riga. Von der Goltz had with him a Russian adventurer who called himself Count Avalov-Bermont, with a White army. They withdrew to Mitau, twenty miles from Riga, set up a government of sorts and began printing money. That was the great Baltic racket, everyone printed money, even the Bolsheviks when they held Latvia. Von der Goltz and Bermont kept quiet all summer but refused to obey orders from Paris, where the Peace Conference was in session, to move back into Germany, and Paris had no means of enforcing its authority. They plotted with Germanophile elements in Latvia, where there had always been a strong German influence—the old Baltic Barons and their retainers descended from the Knights of the Sword who had conquered the country in the fifteenth century, and a big and more recent contingent of German business men. By the end of October they felt strong enough to make another drive at Riga. They did not actually attack the city or attempt to cross the river, but shelled it for some days from the southern bank. They used mostly light stuff, three-inch guns, with the idea rather of scaring the pro-Ally section of the Letts than doing any real damage. It was part of their plan that the Baltic Landeswehr, an anti-Bolshevik White-Guard corps of 2,500 men, largely composed of Baltic Barons and their henchmen, which the Germans had earlier formed and equipped, should coöperate by marching from its trenches on the Red Front near Jacobstadt, a hundred miles down the river near Dvinsk, to enter Riga on the right bank and proclaim a pro-German Government. The Landeswehr failed to march, for reasons I shall explain later, and after three days' shelling, which broke most of the glass in the city and panicked its large Jewish population but caused comparatively few casualties, the Von der Goltz-Bermont outfit retired again more or less unmolested to Mitau.

What fools the Germans were in 1918! General Hoffmann, who made the peace of Brest-Litovsk, told the Kaiser, "For God's sake, Your Imperial Highness, stand pat on the Western Front and hold what we won for you in the East. We have Poland and Galicia and Roumania with their oil and grain, and the Ukraine with its grain, coal and iron. We can make the German frontier from Riga to Odessa. For God's sake, Your Imperial Majesty, hold that and let the Entente Powers, and America too, break their heads against our Western wall." Hoffmann broke his own head by this direct appeal to the All-Highest across Ludendorff, his hierarchic superior. Ludendorff thought he could win the War in the West by pulling fresh troops back from Russia and smashing through the French and British junction-point in Artois, and nearly did it, but not quite. Ludendorff ruined Germany. He was just the opposite of the British Admiral Jellicoe, who might have won the battle of Jutland if he had cared to take a chance, but he did not take it because he knew better. There was no reason to take a chance at Jutland since the English held the seas whether chances were taken or not, and the fact that a German fleet might or might not be sunk at Jutland or retreat successfully to Kiel did not affect the issue of the War. Ludendorff was rasher. He played the fate of Germany on the card of Western victory. And lost, when he might have stood pat and kept his Eastern gains. It was Ludendorff himself who broke the German Front, not our attacks, because by the time the Germans were forced back to their impregnable entrenchments they were already on the run, and gallantly as some of them resisted, their rank and file had lost heart.

What a different story it would have been if the Germans had waited in those impregnable entrenchments for Allied plus American assault! I agree with General Hoffmann that we should have broken our heads, and finally there would have been peace on even terms. Perhaps the Germans would have yielded Belgium, even given autonomy to Alsace-Lorraine in return for their lost colonies; but they would have kept their Eastern frontier from Riga to Odessa. If you do not think I am right, ask Hitler, or Rosenberg; or wait and see.

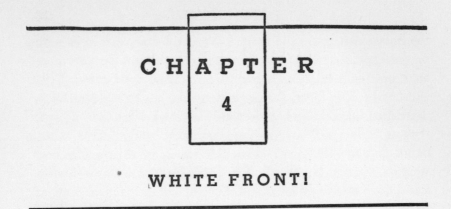

CHAPTER
4

WHITE FRONT!

I DROVE down to Riga with Tallents in his big Crossley car with the Lion and Unicorn of Great Britain flaring on its door. We went through Walk again, which was then the frontier town between Esthonia and Latvia, and a fine job those Baltic brothers were making of it. Both of them claimed the town outright, with the result that it was divided in the middle by a barbed-wire fence, across which Letts and Ests exchanged curses and occasionally a hand-grenade. The day we got there Tallents had to stop and fix up a fracas of this kind. Without him they would have been at each other's throats in no time.

It is hard to describe the muddle and confusion of the Baltic Provinces at that time. To begin with, there was the conflict between "Red" and "White," and there was still a lot of "Red" feeling among the workers and even in the armies. The population was on the verge of starvation, transport was so shattered that there were only five working locomotives in the whole of Latvia, and everywhere of course there was martial law and "curfew" after eight o'clock. You had to have a special pass to be out after eight in Riga itself, as I nearly got a bullet through the head some weeks later to remind me. I didn't hear the sentry's challenge and he only missed me by six inches.

Both the Letts and the Esthonians were nominally at war with the Bolsheviks, but while there was an armistice, as I have said, on the Esthonian Front, and peace negotiations in Dorpat, there were continual skirmishes and raids between the Letts and the Bolsheviks. The Letts claimed a province on their eastern border called Lettgalen, which was still in Bolshevik hands. It was, they said, the cradle of their race, or words to that effect, as its name showed. The Russians wouldn't hear of this, so the war went on. No regular "line" as in France, and a wide No-Man's-Land, four or five miles across. Each side had fortified posts at intervals along the Front and raided the other, usually by night. The Letts did most of the raiding.

The Germans, the Von der Goltz-Bermont army, held all Lithuania and part of Latvia. They were desperate, because pressure from Paris made their departure only a matter of time, but they were meanwhile the strongest military force in the Baltic, and knew it.

Then there were the Foreign Missions, French and British, military and civil, not to mention the American Red Cross and the Hoover Relief. Theoretically, these worthy foreigners had common aims and common enemies, but in practice they carried on an internecine warfare amongst themselves, and with each other. I mean that the British or French Political Missions were rarely reluctant to spike each other's guns, but got much more fun and pleasure from spiking the game of their respective military outfits. And the military felt the same way.

The Hoover Relief sawed wood and fed babies, who needed feeding, Lord knows, but it wasn't above an occasional crack at the American Red Cross when it got the chance. The Red Cross was simply tremendous; having no official standing, it worked day and night to show that its standing was superofficial. It had no official support and didn't need it. It was powerful, intelligent, pervasive, rich and busy, and above all, a hundred per cent American, which meant that it disapproved thoroughly of

the French and British, disliked the Germans, despised the Letts
and Esthonians, and was willing to play all these against one an·
other for its own glory.

There were three outstanding personalities among the foreigners: Tallents for the British; the French Comte de Martel,
a direct descendant of Charles Martel, "The Hammer" they
called him, who smashed the Saracens at Tours in the eighth
century or thereabouts and saved Europe for Christendom; and
Colonel Ryan of the American Red Cross, who had gone through
the typhus epidemic in Serbia (he died later of malaria in
Persia) and, having looked death close in the face, no longer
cared for hell or high water. I didn't know then, but I know now,
what it means to dwell awhile on Death's doorstep. What it
means is that "the bitterness of death is past" or, if not past,
discounted. To human beings death is the End. One may think
one believes in a life after death, but it is generally a vague sort
of belief, rather a hope than a belief, and death is the End. If
you come very near to death and get familiar so to speak with
death, you begin to feel that you have reached ultimate issues
and that you don't give a damn.

Colonel Ryan, I imagine, learnt that lesson from the Serbian
typhus epidemic, and it stood him in good stead in Riga. Tallents had seen the War, in the Irish Guards, when they went into
battle full strength, at Delville Wood on the Somme in '16, and
came back a few hundred living. Martel, to the best of my
knowledge, had not been in the War or faced death nearly, but
he was a natural-born tough Frenchman, incredibly intelligent
and utterly cynical. He was the cleverest of the three, but he had
less backing from his government than Tallents, and neither the
money nor the supplies of the Red Cross. It amused him—I use
the word advisedly—to upset other people's apple carts, which
he did.

The result of all this was that life in the Baltic was a series of alarms and excursions. Storms in teacups for the most part, but full of salt and variety. Everyone had schemes, chiefly or at least nominally for their country's benefit, but also for their own. There was a British General, one of the War Office Generals rather than a fighting General, whose pet scheme was a combined anti-Bolshevik Front, the Finns, Yudenich, the Ests and Letts and Lits, and Bermont and the Germans, and the Poles as well. What a salad that would have been, because most of them detested each other more than they disliked the Bolsheviks! But the General spent a lot of time, money, talk and gasoline rushing up and down to connect his strange bedfellows and hurl them eastwards in three sections, one drive against Petrograd, another at Moscow and a third at Kiev. Tallents had a much sounder scheme, on an economic basis, which would have established British financial hegemony over Latvia and probably Esthonia too. He proposed to float a Lettish loan in England—Latvia had practically no money at that time—of ten million pounds, using Lettish flax as collateral. The money, of course, would be spent in England for equipment, munitions and supplies, everything from shoes and shells to rolling-stock and cocoa. The price of the flax was very high, but England needed it and the deal nearly went through. Unfortunately the representative of a large British bank who came to Riga to settle the final details did not hit it off with the Letts, and negotiations dragged on until one fine day the bottom fell out of the flax market. I think the Letts finally sold their flax for three million pounds or less, and there were some awkward questions in Parliament which distressed the British Foreign Office. Tallents was recalled not long afterwards, although he personally was in no way to blame, and if his scheme had succeeded, British prestige and business in the Baltic would have profited enormously.

My first impressions of Riga, which we reached about 6 P.M., pitch-dark, of course, at that time of year, November, were mournful enough. The streets were littered with broken glass from the Von der Goltz-Bermont shelling, and the lamps were unlighted. It was a fine modern city, much more German than Russian in appearance, but there seemed to be nobody about save a few soldiers. I heard afterwards that two-thirds of the population had fled to surrounding villages during the four days' bombardment.

The British Political Mission had most comfortable quarters in the old town at the "Ritter-House," which had formerly been the headquarters of the Baltic Barons, something similar to the Nobles' Clubs in Moscow and Russian provincial capitals. We found the Mission in a state of excitement. The Germans, they told us, were in full retreat. According to the latest information they had evacuated Mitau, after setting the palace there and its celebrated library on fire, and were moving southwards towards Kovno and the German border. Tallents was delighted. His right-hand man, Captain Dewhurst, had arranged for a couple of the Mission cars to go to Mitau that night and see what was happening, and they said I could go too.

I had an idea that I ought to get in touch with Commander Gade without delay, but this was too good a chance to be missed. It was terribly cold, but they fixed me up with aviators' boots reaching right up to the thigh, tanned sheepskin outside and wool inside with heavy rubber soles. They were part of the British Army supplies for the Murmansk and Archangel expeditions, and were simply marvelous. I wore them all the time on my trips to the Lettish Front. In the train coming back from Walk on my second day in Esthonia I had lost my British warm, army coat, so had to wear the Dutchman's blue fur coat over a khaki uniform. It looked most unmilitary and provoked a lot of sarcastic comment, but it was warm and, as I told them, I was a reporter, not a warrior, and anyway who cared? On my trips to the Front, however, I borrowed a British warm from a friend in the Military Mission.

The trip to Mitau was a gay adventure. None of us knew whether the Germans were really retreating or not and whether we might not be suddenly met by shells or a burst of machine-gun fire. I rode with Dewhurst, who was a "big bad wolf," if ever I met one. Like myself, he came from Lancashire, which was a bond between us. He had been in the ranks in the British Army in India, then graduated to Intelligence work—at one time he was in charge of the Red Light district of Lahore, or perhaps Allahabad; as Kipling says, the "oldest profession in the world" is always fertile soil for espionage and intrigue, and some of the stories Dewhurst told made Kipling read like prunes and prisms. From India Dewhurst was sent to Saloniki (I think he already had a commission by then) and did splendidly in that other hotbed of intrigue. He had about a dozen of the narrowest possible escapes from assassination and won British, French and Greek decorations. He was a typical British North-countryman, tall, burly and slow-speaking, with a deceptive naïveté of manner which concealed a shrewd and ruthless brain. I liked him very much and we became good friends.

Sure enough, the palace at Mitau was flaming beyond hope of succor and the German-Bermont army had disappeared. The Lettish troops were advancing rather cautiously because they were badly outnumbered, most of their forces being further east on the Red Front. There had not been much fighting; indeed I gathered that the German retirement had been a surprise to the Lettish Command. We spent that night in Mitau in a literally lousy hotel, and the next morning I had a talk with the Lettish Military Commander of the city, who showed me evidence of a nasty little atrocity the Germans committed before leaving.

They had captured four Lettish soldiers. Perhaps the latter were spies, or at least snoopers. The Germans took them along a road to a big field which was separated from the road by a six-foot ditch. Across the field about a hundred yards away there was a wood. The Germans said to the Letts, "Now, you bastards, we'll give you a chance. At the word of command you jump the ditch and run for your lives. We shall give you ten seconds, then start shooting." In short, revolver practice with human targets. One Lett fell less than a dozen yards beyond the ditch with the back of his head blown off. The second was shot through the heart about twenty yards farther, and the third took a bullet in the spine a moment later, which killed him too. I saw the bodies of these three still lying in the snow. The fourth man was winged, but reached the shelter of the wood, and lived to tell the tale. I talked with him in the hospital.

The next day on my return to Riga I heard another atrocity story. Four or five nights before, during the bombardment, the Bermont troops had caught a Lettish spy, or a man they thought was a spy. They tied him up in barbed wire, then cut a hole in the ice on the river and dipped him through for five seconds, to make him confess. They would pull him out and a film of ice would immediately form over him. There were thirteen such films on his body when the Letts found it, so one presumes he died hard and slowly; but he didn't talk. The Letts are not always excessively quick on the uptake but they are loyal as steel, and damn tough. I like the Letts and admire them. Half of their troops there in Mitau were barefoot, or next to it, with the temperature ten degrees below zero, but they kept going. Good tough peasant soldiers, a hundred per cent loyal and intensely patriotic.

I encountered what might have been a most unpleasant sequel to these atrocity stories, a few months later at Duisburg in the Rhineland. It was in March of 1920, just after the abortive Kapp *putsch,* and there was a Communist rebellion in the "Ruhrgebiet"—Alten-Essen was the Communist headquarters—with some ugly fighting. I had been sent from Paris to cover the story, and somewhere in the Ruhr ran into my friend Ryall of the *Manchester Guardian,* who afterwards made a big hit in America under the name of William Bolitho, which was, indeed, his name—William Bolitho Ryall. He had been in Alten-Essen, but we had heard that things were hot in Duisburg, so we decided to go there. He was a little uncertain lest the Germans there might find out he had been playing with the Reds, but news is news, so we thought we would take a chance. Instead of that it was I who got into trouble. Of course we were picked up by a White German patrol after we had been in the town ten minutes—we expected that—and taken to the Military Commander, Major von Stamm or some such name, a big, hard-faced Prussian who, it appeared, had been with Von der Goltz in Latvia. Anyhow the first thing he said to me when I showed him my credentials was, "Oh, yes, I know you, Duranty. You're the man who wrote filthy lying stories about atrocities we committed in the Baltic. And what have you got to say for yourself now?" he added, giving me no friendly look.

I was frightened, and as I said before, when I am frightened I get cross, which was lucky in this case. I said, "Damn it all, sir, it wasn't lies; I saw the bodies and talked to the survivor. The men may have been spies, and personally I'd far sooner, if I were a spy, be a target for revolver practice and have a chance for my life than be stood up against a wall and shot."

"Did you really see the bodies?" he asked me roughly.

"I'm telling you so," I replied, and I had; it was true.

"All right," he said, after a minute, "and what do you want here?"

"We want you to tell us what's going on and give us a pass to circulate and see for ourselves what's going on."

He grinned and gave us the pass, and shook hands as he showed us out. You can say what you like about the Germans, they're brutal and rough at times, but they've got sense and understanding. I mean that Major von Stamm understood that I had my job and was trying to do it, just as he had his. This story, strangely enough, had a parallel in Riga itself—that is to say I got myself into an awkward position of rather the same kind, although more ludicrous, with another warrior, as I shall explain further on in this chapter.

.   .   .   .

I went back to Riga in the evening after twenty-four hours in Mitau, and spent most of the night at the "Ritter-House" writing my stories. It was like old times at the French Front when stories wrote themselves, all full of color and fire. I had grown tired of the Peace Conference in Paris with everyone pulling their own strings and talking about their noble motives, while the small group of high-minded men who were trying to make a fair peace were being bluffed and buffaloed by tough expert nationalists, alert and eager to stamp on the faces of their beaten foes.

The next morning I went to see the Americans, and found them comfortably lodged but slightly dazed. Mr. Gade had already received advice from his compatriots representing the Red Cross and the Hoover Relief respectively, and from both effusive offers of help. Unfortunately the advice of both parties differed diametrically, and each took occasion to warn him against listening to the other. The French had also paid a visit, or rather two visits, one military and one political, and here again there was discord and some confusion of views. With the British, it seemed, there had arisen a hitch. Tallents was senior in Riga standing, but he was only a Lieutenant-Colonel in the army, whereas Gade as a Naval Commander outranked him, or thought he did. I think that was the reason for strained relations, but maybe I am wrong. Anyway the breach, if one might call it that, was bridged without delay and for the rest of the winter Americans and British played cards together and drank each other's liquor in good fellowship. I had been assigned by the Letts a magnificent furnished apartment of ten rooms with two or three baths and a huge *salon*, which they requisitioned from some recalcitrant Baltic German who had played too closely with Von der Goltz and Bermont. Amply supplied with comforts from the British political canteen, I was able to give Anglo-American parties which "joined hands across the sea" in a free and cordial manner.

Tallents helped me to get an interview with the Lettish Commander-in-Chief, Colonel Ballod, a large, red-faced citizen with a deep, booming voice who combined the tough native shrewdness of Latvia with no small strategic ability. He talked frankly about the difficulty of fighting on two fronts with ill-equipped forces and crippled mechanical transport. He was no less outspoken about the remnants of Bolshevism in Latvia, which he said were being rapidly "liquidated"—I was to hear that word later in Russia—in the Lettish Army, but still existed amongst the civil population, especially the workers. Colonel Ballod showed me on his staff maps the exact position of the retreating Germans and outlined the Letto-Bolshevik Front with candid estimates of numbers and military strength, in short, a most satisfactory interview. I wrote it up as high as I could, and amongst other things remarked, using Bunyan's phrase, that Colonel Ballod had "set his face like a flint" against Bolshevism in the Lettish Army.

I showed my dispatch to Tallents, who wholly approved it, and on the strength of a telephone message from him it was passed without hesitation by the Lettish military censor, who, be it said, gave me no trouble whatever during my stay in Latvia. But trouble there was, and big trouble, six weeks later in connection with my Ballod interview, and Bunyan's pungent phrase.

One morning I was lunching at the British Mission, when

Dewhurst, who was then in charge because Tallents had gone to London to further the banking scheme, said to me cheerfully, "What have you been doing? General Ballod (the Commander-in-Chief had been "promoted") is roaring for your blood. He came round here an hour ago, swearing that you had insulted him and would be expelled from Latvia immediately. From the way he shouted I think you will probably be shot within twenty-four hours." Dewhurst had an English penchant for practical jokes, so I only laughed, but when that afternoon I visited Mr. Gade, I had reason to think differently.

"I'm afraid you have got yourself into trouble," said the American Commissioner seriously. "General Ballod visited me this morning in a state of the utmost indignation. He claims that you have insulted him personally in the grossest manner. I don't know what it's all about, and the General shouted so loud that my interpreter became confused. I think that you had better look into the matter without delay."

I rushed back to the British Mission and found the young Lettish officer, Lieutenant Students, who had interpreted for me in my interview with his Generalissimo. That was the only piece I had written about Ballod, of that I was certain.

Students could not understand why the General should be cross and said spontaneously, "But, Mr. Duranty, Colonel Tallents himself saw the story, and I know that he told the General that it was excellent. I don't understand this at all."

"Well," I said, "in any case you'd better ring up headquarters and find out—I thought Dewhurst was kidding, but I know Mr. Gade was serious."

Students telephoned the staff, and his face lengthened. "My God!" he said, "something terrible has happened. The General says that you wrote in the interview that he has a face like a red brick and is supporting Bolshevism in the Lettish Army."

It required formal orders from Dewhurst as acting chief of

the British Mission to induce Students, as liaison officer between the Mission and the Lettish Staff, to accompany me to head-quarters. He didn't like it, he said. I was a foreigner, on good terms with the British and American Missions, but why should he put his head in the lion's mouth on my behalf? Ballod, wrath-ful, he said, was worse than any lion, and Ballod, he said, was very wrathful indeed.

By this time, however, I had guessed what the trouble was, so when we bearded the General in his den I told Students at once to explain that there had doubtless been an error in the transla-tion of my dispatch, that I had used the phrase of a famous English writer to express the General's hostility to Bolshevism in his army, but that I feared this phrase had not been fully un-derstood. I added, meekly, that the General must know that Colonel Tallents would never have approved anything deroga-tory to him or the glorious Lettish Army.

Students breathed more freely and the General's voice sof-tened. He sent for his Chief of Staff who talked fluent French, and there followed a lot of Lettish conversation. Then the Chief of Staff produced a copy of my dispatch, like a rabbit from a hat, and drew my notice to the Bunyan quotation. Again I ex-plained, and the Chief of Staff hastily translated to the General, who banged his fist upon the desk and bellowed Homeric laugh-ter. Even Students laughed, who had been in no laughing mood, so I seized the occasion to tell the General that I wanted nothing better than to report the exploits of his troops in their war against the Reds, and would he kindly give me a really power-ful pass that would be good for every section of the Front. He did, and it *was* good. In fact, it was so good, that for two or three years to come, I received the "courtesy of the port" from every Lettish customs officer to whom I showed it, and obtained sleep-ing-car accommodations pronto when they said the train was full. As Students and I walked down the corridor after exchang-

ing warm handshakes and salaams with the General, his loud
voice again boomed forth and Students blanched.

"What is that?" I said. "We are all right, aren't we?"

"*We* are quite all right, but *that* is the General calling for the
interpreter who made the mistake in translation of your piece. I
would not be in his shoes for ten thousand pounds."

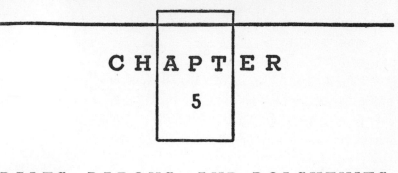

CHAPTER
5

BALTS, BARONS, AND BOLSHEVIKS

I USUALLY took lunch and pre-lunch cocktail at the British Mission, and one day, about a week after my arrival in Riga, I found sitting by the fire in the big club-room, a young British officer in khaki uniform with the insignia of a Colonel, but wearing Russian high boots; beside him there was a gray astrakhan cap, of the type worn in the Cossack regiments. This was Lieutenant-Colonel Alexander, a regular officer in the Irish Guards, now detached by special order to command the Baltic Landeswehr, the White-Guard German-trained corps of which I spoke before. Alex, as everyone called him, was the most charming and picturesque person I have ever met, and one of the two soldiers I have known who derived a strong, positive, and permanent exhilaration from the worst of danger. The other was Colonel Charles Sweeney of the Foreign Legion, and later of the American Army.

After seeing a lot of soldiers in various armies I have come to the conclusion that about seventy per cent of them are frightened of danger, but "stick it out" with the help of discipline and nerve and pride and *esprit de corps*. They can thus be honestly ranked as courageous, because one must not forget the old story about the group of Napoleon's veterans who were arguing which was the bravest among them. One said he had done this, another that he had done that, and a third that he did not know what fear meant. Finally an old sergeant said quietly, "You hot-blooded youngsters won your red ribbons from the Emperor and perhaps enjoyed winning them, but I have won one too and I tell you frankly that I have never been into action without being scared. But I went into action none the less, and that's what I call courage." Some men in an army are what one terms cowards, that is they can't control their fear and their nerves break sooner or later. They try to run or hide in the first shell-hole, or shoot themselves in hand or foot and, in extreme cases, deliberately seek the death they fear by putting their heads over the top of a trench; I've known that to happen. Then there is a larger group, whose nerves are dull. They don't much fear danger, or grow used to it, and carry on calmly with more interest most of the time in how they are fed and clothed and paid, and whether the trenches are damp or dry, and what the girls and eats and drinks will be like in their next period of rest behind the line, than in the enemy's shelling or their own fears. Finally there are the exceptional men, one in ten thousand or more, like Alexander and Sweeney, who get a real kick from danger, and the greater the danger the greater the kick.

Alexander fought all through the War without serious injury —I think he was wounded once, not dangerously—and had the British D.S.O. and the French Legion of Honor. He got the D.S.O. for what might well have won him the Victoria Cross, in the first Somme battle in 1916. His battalion was hammered to pieces; I believe there were only eighty or so alive out of a thousand when the time came for them to be relieved, and he was the only surviving officer. As they staggered back from hell, most of them wounded, they met the troops ordered to take their place, which after one look at them decided almost unanimously that they would stay where they were. This was rank mutiny but the soldiers knew that at worst not more than one in ten of them would be shot for it, whereas at the front-line the odds were nearly ten to one against the life of everyone. Their officers stormed and pleaded, vainly; the men refused to budge.

Then Alex said, "God knows it's bad enough up there, but you can't disgrace Ireland like this. If you'll march I'll go back with you." One of the sergeants said the same, and a corporal and five men. That shamed the others, who agreed to advance, without insisting that Alex and his comrades should share their lot; and, as it happened, the second battalion spent its full fort-night in the welter of shell-torn earth that was labeled front-line trenches with total casualties of little more than a hundred, say forty killed and sixty wounded or thereabouts. Alex slept for twenty-four hours and had a week in Amiens, with the D.S.O. and a fortnight's leave at home.

When Tallents talked Von der Goltz out of Riga in May, 1919, and established a pro-Ally government, the question arose what was to be done with the Baltic Landeswehr who were all of German stock, that is Baltic-German blood, although most of them were Russian citizens. Latvia was still pretty "Red" and the Landeswehr was the surest "White" unit and moreover the best-equipped and trained. It was finally decided that if the Landeswehr would accept an Allied Commander, they need not be disbanded, with the added proviso that they would not be called upon to fight Von der Goltz or Bermont's White Russians, but should serve on the Bolshevik Front. They agreed, and Tallents got hold of Alexander, who had been his brother officer in the Irish Guards. There could have been no happier choice because Alex was the second son of the Earl of Caledon, an Irish peer, who was descended from one of Cromwell's officers in Ireland, and his family thus had, for centuries, been noble landlords in a conquered country, exactly like the Baltic Barons descended from the Teutonic Knights of the Sword, who conquered the Baltic Provinces in the fifteenth century and had lived there ever since with their retainers, as feudal overlords amongst the Letts and other Baltic races.

Within a month of his taking command, the Landeswehr was devoted to Alexander, who combined the qualities of a first-class soldier with those virtues of aristocracy, courage, honor, and *noblesse oblige*, which had reached a fine flower amongst the Baltic Barons. It was he, quite unconsciously, who prevented them from marching on Riga to complete the Von der Goltz-Bermont plans that autumn. As one of them told me, "We wanted to march on Riga and perhaps we ought to have done it in our own interests, because these damned Letts have seized our estates and it is not likely that the British or French will do much for us to get them back, as the Germans would have done. But in that case we should have had to knock Alexander on the head, and we liked him far too much, so we stayed quiet in our trenches, and Von der Goltz retreated."

.   .   .   .

Alexander suggested that I should go back with him to visit the Landeswehr Front near Jacobstadt. "Nothing much is happening at present except some raiding, but I am sure it would interest you, if only by contrast with the war in France; and a lot of my people have stories about the Bolshevik Revolution in Latvia."

His headquarters were a big, comfortable, wooden house, which had formerly belonged to the manager of Prince Lieven's estate. Lieven was the great Baltic landlord in that neighborhood, but his own *château* was on the Bolshevik side of the Line. Most of the staff spoke English, and there was probably no corps in the world which had such a high type of men physically, intellectually, and for that matter, socially. The Landeswehr was organized like a division, although it was only twenty-five hundred strong, and, as I have said, consisted almost wholly of Baltic Barons and their retainers, the majority of whom had done their duty as subjects of the Tsar and served in the Russian Army, although a few had followed the call of their blood and fought for Germany. The "division" had its own artillery, transport, and a cavalry detachment of some two hundred men, all of whom, officers and troopers, were of noble birth and provided their own horses, though their uniforms were ragged and there were holes in their riding-boots.

Amongst them was a young baron who had joined the Russian Army at the beginning of the War, taking with him as soldier-servant a retainer, seventeen generations of whose family had served the baron's family in military campaigns. This officer, whose name I have forgotten, was either captured or badly wounded in the War and never rose above the rank of Captain, but his servant, who came of no less good fighting stock, was promoted for gallantry in action, received the order of St. George, and ended the War as a full Colonel. In the Landeswehr this experienced soldier was a Major, whereas his hereditary lord was only a Sergeant. They handled this anomalous position in a typical Baltic way. Once a week the Major would come to the dugout which his lord shared with three other Sergeants. All four of the subordinates saluted. The officer returned the salute, then said punctiliously, "Herr Baron, your boots need cleaning." The baron sat down on a bench, his ex-servant pulled off his lord's boots, cleaned them and put them on again. Then he in turn saluted, saying, "My respects, Herr Baron," and the ceremony was over.

There was another interesting fellow whose name I did not forget but won't mention here, who later won renown as "the gold courier." After establishment of diplomatic relations between the Soviet and the Baltic States, this man secured an appointment as official courier making weekly trips to and from Moscow. He had formerly had high connections at the Court of the Tsar and somehow located a cache of gold, which doubtless

belonged to one of his friends, I think in Moscow, but it may
have been Leningrad. It was said to amount to over a million
dollars, that's nearly a ton of gold, and he got most of it out in
parcels of fifty to a hundred pounds weight before the Gay-
pay-oo discovered it. Then there was a big fuss and official protests by the Soviet Government and some people were shot in
Leningrad, but the Balt got clear with the money. He could
doubtless use it because when I met him on the Landeswehr
Front his toes were sticking out through his boots and it was cold
weather. His family's estates were all on Soviet territory and
utterly lost. Not that the Balts who had property in Latvia or
Esthonia were much better off; their land was all confiscated
too, and most of it never returned, but some of them received a
small compensation or were allowed to keep their *châteaux* and
the surrounding parks, say fifty to a hundred acres.

Speaking of gold caches, there was a remarkable find in Moscow in 1924 or 1925, in the cellar of a house which had been
occupied during the famine years by the Food Packet and
Transport Sections of the American Relief Administration. It
was a huge neo-Gothic mansion in incredibly bad taste, which
formerly belonged to Sava Morosov, the head of a tremendous
textile combine and the richest man in Russia, second, of course,
to the Tsar. In 1916, what with War orders and so forth, his fortune was said to be a billion dollars gold, which was more than
Rockefeller's. He shot himself before the Revolution, apparently in a fit of insanity, in his country house at Gorki, where
Lenin died, which is now Stalin's summer residence.

Another of the big War profiteers, Vtorov, who built the
pseudo-marble palace which was allotted to Ambassador Bullitt
after American recognition, had even worse luck than Morosov.
He was the Lipton of Russia, and made fifty or sixty million
dollars supplying food for the Tsar's army. He was said to be a
friend of Rasputin, which may have helped his contracts but

doubtless cost him a slice of the profits. Anyhow, he had plenty left and spent two or three million of it on a house which he never lived to enjoy. He was not killed by the Bolsheviks, but by his own illegitimate son, who came and demanded that the father take steps for his legal recognition, either by adoption or by some form of declaration. Old Vtorov refused, so the youngster shot him dead, and escaped with a comparatively short term of imprisonment.

Curiously enough, there was a similar case in England a few years later with William Whiteley—the "universal provider" they called him—who had the biggest department store in London. He also had an illegitimate son who felt aggrieved by his equivocal status and demanded legal recognition. This boy also met refusal and shot his father dead, but British law brooks no trifling with murder, and he was promptly tried and hanged.

London and William Whiteley are a long way from the hidden treasure of the Morosov house in Moscow. After the American Relief had gone home, the place was occupied by the representatives of one of the Central Asian Republics, Uzbekistan or Turkmenistan. It became necessary to make some repairs to the drains, during which time the workmen found that there was a false wall in the wine-cellar and that a space existed beyond what appeared to be the cellar's end. They broke down the wall and uncovered a safe containing several million dollars' worth of jewels and gold, and about ten million dollars' worth of Tsarist paper currency, which, of course, had no value. I wrote that story for the *N.Y.T.* when the treasure was found, and learnt later that it caused acute mortification to some of the boys in the American Relief, who hated to think that they had worked and slept for eighteen months or more within easy reach of all that money.

This reminds me of one of their men who was feeding babies somewhere on the Volga. He was a Southerner of good family,

which had been ruined by "The War"; he didn't mean the
World War. It was, it seems, his custom, perhaps to keep his
memory of "The War" alive, to carry in his wallet a few twenty-
dollar bills of Confederate issue. To his delight and amazement the "black bourse" money-changers of his region—those
were the early days of N.E.P. and money-changing flourished
like a green bay tree—proved willing to accept his Confederate dollars at their face value as American currency. The
young man uttered a scream of joy. "My God!" he cried, "with
this I can buy back the old plantation," and immediately cabled
in "clear" through the A.R.A. headquarters in Moscow, to his
family to send him the trunkful of Confederate bills which lay
up in the attic, as proof of the loyalty to Dixie of Grandfather
Sylvester. I have rarely known anything funnier than the fury
and bewilderment of this youth when he was summoned to Moscow and not only fired from the A.R.A. without benefit of
clergy, but ordered to recompense the N.E.P.-men speculators
for the worthless Confederate money. To him, it was a cruel
echo of the guns of Grant and Sherman, and a final injustice to
the South.

I ought to get back to the Baltic Front, but there is a story
about another Southerner with the American Relief in Russia
which should not be omitted. This worthy came from Tennessee,
and was one of the hardest drinkers I have ever met; and mind
you, newspaper men meet a lot of hearty drinkers, and sometimes drink themselves. He was stationed on the Volga, and was
a friend of mine, so when I called on him once he took me upstairs, mysteriously, to his bedroom. "Hush," he said, "don't
make a sound. Sit down there quietly and don't dare to breathe
or the bloodhound will hear you." "What do you mean," I whispered, "what bloodhound? What do you mean?"

"The bloodhound next door," he replied. "Don't make a
sound. It's the last bottle left, and he's a real bloodhound."

Then with infinite stealth he drew a suitcase from under his bed and took from it a bottle of whisky. "The last bottle in Simbirsk," he whispered. "For you and me, unless the bloodhound smells it, so don't make a sound." He uncorked the bottle so softly that I couldn't hear a pop, put two glasses delicately on the table, and was about to pour the whisky when the door opened noisily and a loud, cheerful voice exclaimed, "What's this?—whisky—my God, man, I thought it was all finished. This *really* is good news."

My poor host gasped feebly, "The bloodhound! I told you he'd smell it," and surrendered the bottle. Our visitor poured out a full tumbler and drank it quick. He was a confirmed alcoholic, that one. A few weeks later he drank all the medical alcohol, or maybe methylated spirit, belonging to the A.R.A. sanitary outfit in Simbirsk. He didn't die of it but got delirium tremens and had to be sent home.

. . . .

The Baltic Barons and the Landeswehr were mostly young, reckless and desperate. They had had a high place in society, and a share in or expectation of, great possessions, and had seen those possessions seized and their society crumble to pieces about their ears. It was not only the loss of wealth, as with Insull or Ivar Kreuger, but the total collapse of an ancient, settled, hereditary system. These Barons had been masters in the Baltic for five hundred years, and are one of the rare instances of an aristocracy which grew neither fat nor slothful. They kept themselves fit by riding and hunting, and went to war whenever the occasion offered. They didn't think much of the Russians, and married among themselves or with the noble families of Eastern Germany. They despised the Letts and Esthonians as hewers of wood and drawers of water. As landlords they were enlightened; there was little of the "absenteeism" which was the curse of Russia, and the Baltic landlords freed their serfs many years before Alexander II decided to free them in the rest of Russia in 1863. The first tractors and agricultural combines ever seen in Europe were used on the estate of a thickset young man whom I met on the Landeswehr Front. He had obtained them a year or two before the War, when tractors were little known in America itself. And when the Baltic went Red in the winter of 1918, the Balts, unlike their fellow-aristocrats in Russia, did not yield tamely to mob law, but fought back.

There was one man in the Landeswehr, who had cut notches on the wooden grip of his Mauser automatic for each Red he killed. He talked about this the night I met him at Alexander's headquarters, because, he said, he was so pleased that he had just reached the score of fifty. There had only been forty-seven until two nights ago when he had commanded a raid into the Red Lines and made it up to the half-century. He was a naïve, simple soul, as delighted with his notched gun as a little boy with a new drum. I asked him when he began making the notches, and this is what he told me. He was lunching, he said, with his wife and her mother in the dining-room of his *château* in Latvia, twenty miles from Riga, in the fall of 1918. It was not the big dining-room on the ground floor, but the little private dining-room to the left at the top of the carved oak staircase. There had been some talk of Bolshevik agitators and a revolutionary movement amongst the Letts, but the Baron had paid it small attention. His family had won their estate by the sword, and held it ever since by force of arms and courage, so he refused to let rumors of uprisings disturb him. Suddenly, however, his lunch was interrupted by a rush of Lettish peasants who came piling up the staircase, headed by a Bolshevik agitator in person. They burst into the room, and told the Baron that his reign was ended. "The land belongs to the people," the agitator shouted, "and you we shall shoot. I order you to come downstairs, so that we may shoot you in the court-yard, in front of everybody, but if you resist, we shall shoot you here." The Baron thought quick. "Wait a minute," he said, "don't you want some money? I've got ten thousand roubles here in gold in this drawer. You had better take that before you shoot me," and without waiting for them to answer he ran to the sideboard and took from the drawer no handfuls of Tsarist gold pieces, but his Mauser automatic, and wheeled round and opened fire. He killed the Bolshevik agitator and five of the others, then chased them down the stairs, still firing. "I had ten bullets in the gun," he told me, "and only missed once. Those were my first nine notches." He hurried round to the stables and ordered the coach-man to harness four horses to his coach, then dashed upstairs to tell his wife and her mother and the butler to pack quick and be ready to leave in half an hour. He got away with them and his jewels, and the family silver, and his genealogical tree as big as a picture, which dated back to Charlemagne, and the hoof of a horse he once owned which had won the Russian Derby, and a stag's head with fourteen-point antlers, and one of the English collapsible opera-hats which fold up flat ("Why I took that I can't tell you," he said), and a jeweled saber that had been given to his great-grandfather by Tsar Nicholas I. They piled all this and his wife and mother-in-law and the butler into the coach, and drove to Riga hell-for-leather, getting clear away. From that time forward, said the Baron, he had vowed a hate against the Bolsheviks and shot them whenever possible. There were fifty notches on his gun and he hoped to reach a hundred.

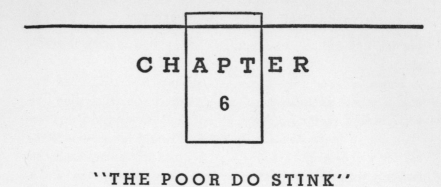

CHAPTER
6

"THE POOR DO STINK"

ALEXANDER sent me back from the Front to Jacobstadt, which was the rail head, in one of his cars with an officer of his staff, to get me a place on the train to Riga. The officer made all arrangements and told me that the train would be leaving in an hour. Then he went away and I waited, reading a book near a metal stove—it was well below zero outside—in a small room adjoining the offices of the Station Commandant. An hour passed, then another, and no sign of the train. It was nearly 2 A.M. by this time and I grew restive, so I went into the Commandant's office to see what was happening. To my dismay, I found that they had "changed the guard" at midnight and a new Pharaoh had taken command who knew not Joseph, nor for that matter any language of which I had the faintest knowledge. In such a case there is one invariable rule to be followed—and I may say Americans and the English invariably follow it—namely, to talk one's own language louder and louder. Fortunately, I was wearing my French Front correspondent's uniform which was that of a British officer, with Sam Browne belt and all, except that it had no "tabs" or other ornaments denoting rank. Thus I might have been anything from a second lieutenant to a commanding general. I felt, and doubtless looked, like the former, but tried to imitate the latter, and demanded a train immediately.

There followed a lot of conversation, but it seemed I had created a certain effect, because they produced a small civilian like a frightened rabbit who talked English. He explained that the train would leave at 4 A.M. but that it would be composed exclusively of "hard" cars, that is to say something like American box-cars with tiers of wooden shelves one above the other and a corridor at one side. No private compartments of any kind. "Of course," he said, "a shelf will be reserved for you." "An upper shelf," I corrected. And they replied, "Of course an upper shelf," and the train would leave promptly at four.

At 4.30 the Commandant and his chief subordinate and I had a hearty Lettish meal of sausage, black bread, cold goose and vodka (contributed by them) and canned *pâté de foie gras,* English porter and cold baked beans (contributed by me). We found that the vodka and porter made a wonderful mixture, and, as they say, "a good time was had by all."

Once during the War, in the Parc Monceau in Paris I saw a big kilted Scottish soldier sitting on a bench with his little French girl friend. They appeared on the best of terms and were talking together cheerfully, each in his own language, without understanding a word of what the other said. I happen to know this definitely because the Scotchman asked me the time, and when I had told him he said, "Will ye explain to the little gurrl that I haf to meet a mon at this address," he showed me a scrap of paper, "and she's to come, and we'll all have dinner with his gurrl too."

While we talked, the little girl looked at him with eyes of love.

"Don't you understand *anything?*" I asked her. "*Pas un mot,*" she replied, "*mais il est si gentil.*"

Well, that was how it was with me and the Letts, and if it was

not a love-feast, I can at least say that porter, well laced with
vodka, is a big help to mutual understanding.

. . . .

Finally, about six, the train pulled out crowded to the limit
with people sleeping in the corridors and on the floor between
the bunks. I had an upper berth with a young Lettish officer opposite me, and settled down as best I could for a long and uncomfortable journey. There was no light, heat or ventilation,
and the atmosphere was terrible. "The poor do stink," as Dr.
Johnson said, I believe it was Dr. Johnson, and Latvia at that
time was desperately poor. And, it must be remembered, in the
winter of 1919–20 there was hardly a cake of soap in the whole
area from the Baltic Sea to Vladivostok, including Eastern Germany, Poland and the Ukraine. A lot has been said and written
about famine mortality caused by war and blockade, but the
shortage of fats produced an even greater shortage of soap, and
this in turn was responsible for much of the typhus which rav-
aged Eastern Europe then and for several years later. Cleanli-
ness may or may not be next to godliness, but dirt certainly be-
gets disease.

I am sensitive to smells, perhaps because I have met so many
bad ones in the last twenty years, and I noticed long ago that
what Kipling said about smell being associated with memory is
true in my case. Whenever, for instance, I smell French *caporal*
tobacco I think at once of the racecourses near Paris, and there
echoes in my ears the monotonous cry of the tobacco venders:
"*Cigares, Cigarettes, Allumettes, Tabac,*" and I see the green
sweep of the Longchamps with the trees in the background, the
white posts marking the course, the crowd on the *pelouse* surg-
ing around the *pari-mutuel* booths, and the flowers and beautiful mannequins on the *pesage* side, and the horses like burnished
satin, prancing as if on springs round the inner ring before each
race.

There was another time when a smell reminded me of something I would gladly have forgotten, if that was the true explanation of a most strange and terrifying experience. It was in Athens in the summer of 1933, and to escape the heat I decided to spend a few days on the coast, some miles away, at a rather nice hotel where I had had lunch three or four times. They gave me a little suite, bedroom, bathroom, sitting-room and balcony, overlooking the sea, on the second floor of the annex at the right of the hotel. The way into it was through the main restaurant which opened on to a terrace. It was about eleven at night when I got there, and for some reason the lights downstairs were not functioning, so the porter took me with a candle down a short passage from the restaurant, then across the ground floor, where the lights were working. I said to him, "I thought you told me there was no one in the other apartment" (there were only two in the annex), and he said, "No, there isn't." That was all. Thinking it over afterwards, it seems to me that the only reason I made this remark must have been that I heard some kind of noise. It was a clean, modern hotel, and apparently perfectly all right in every way. When the porter left me, I sat down by the open window of the sitting-room near the balcony and began to read an amusing, but not especially thrilling, detective story. They were burning some refuse outside, somewhere near, and there came a whiff of rank smoke from time to time. I read for about half an hour, then suddenly was seized by a paroxysm of utter terror, bodily terror, and in my nostrils there was a dreadful smell of carrion. Mechanically I put my sleeve to my nose and sniffed at it, and sure enough it smelled of corpses, which I think was the key to the whole story.

I shall come to that later, but for the moment there I was in this Greek hotel, paralyzed by physical fear and the odor of death. When I say physical fear I mean that I had no dread of anything supernatural; I *knew* that "They" were waiting to kill me unless I acted immediately. My first thought was to jump from the balcony, but it was too high. At last I managed to tip-toe to the door of the apartment and look out on the landing. There was no sound, but I knew "They" were lurking some-where in the shadows. My body was dripping with sweat and my only light was a little cigarette-lighter. I was in a state of unreasoning fright, the true "panic" terror, as the Greeks called it—the word is derived from the God Pan, who I suppose symbolizes Nature, and they meant by "panic" the sum-total of man's atavistic fears in a dark and cruel world.

Going downstairs and across the hallway leading to the corri-dor I said aloud in as natural a tone as I could muster, "How stupid of me not to have told the porter I wanted breakfast at nine o'clock. Now I've got to go back and tell him. It's very tiresome; they really should have a telephone in every room." I thought somehow that by my saying this "They" would think I was coming back, that I would fool "Them" into waiting. With my small flickering light, I shuffled across the wide floor of the restaurant and reached the door. Thank God the key was there! I turned it as quietly as possible and hurried out across the ter-race.

I can't run because I got my left leg cut off in a train wreck in France, and one cannot run with a wooden leg, but I limped along as fast as I could to the roadway between the terrace and the sea and turned to the right in the direction of Athens. Fifty yards further I met a uniformed policeman and asked him where I could get a taxi; it was still only eleven-thirty or there-abouts. "Round there," he said, pointing. For a moment I thought of asking him to come back with me to deal with "Them," then I knew I did not dare to, and hurried on to the taxi. Fifteen minutes later I was back in the Grande Bretagne Hotel in Athens, and slept soundly until morning. The next day I sent my chauffeur to the hotel on the coast to get my bag and typewriter, pay the bill and tell them I had changed my mind because some friends of mine had suddenly arrived in Athens. I did not care to go back again myself.

Is that or is it not an utterly silly story? I mean, do you believe in presentiments and so forth, or don't you? Personally I do not, any more than I believe in ghosts—I have tried hard enough to find them—but there are some things in life which are not easy to explain. In my case I think the clew was that instinctive sniff at my sleeve, for the following reason. In the summer of 1918 when the Germans were retreating from the Marne I came one day to a village just north of the river where four French batteries had caught a German battalion and blown it to hell-and-gone. The place was a horror, torn bodies of men and horses all sprawled anyhow where the shells had hit them, and stinking to high heaven, because they had been there for several days and the weather was hot. I got back to the Press *château* at headquarters only a few minutes before dinner, and just had time to wash hurriedly and to change my riding-breeches for a pair of slacks. When I sat down to the table the man on my right said, "Good God, where have you been; you stink like a polecat." I put my sleeve to my nose, just as I did that night in the hotel, and sniffed. Sure enough, the cloth was impregnated with the smell of carrion. I rushed upstairs and changed the tunic, which had to be fumigated; but my appetite had gone.

Now, I believe that in that Greek hotel I dozed over my book without realizing it, and had a very brief nightmare and forgot it, as one sometimes does with dreams, but woke in the full bewilderment of terror that nightmares often bring. It must have had something to do with corpses, and was possibly suggested by the smell of a dead rat that was being burnt amidst the refuse outside. That explains my sniffing at my sleeve, and I can make a guess at what the nightmare was about. I was alone in a strange hostelry in a foreign country, and Europe is full of old legends of "murder-inns" where travelers are robbed and slain and their bodies hidden in a "murder-cellar." In the flash of time that dreams may take, this fate had threatened me.

That is a logical, rational explanation, and I shrink from any other, but I did make inquiries about the reputation of the hotel and its personnel, to find that both were excellent, that furthermore it had only been built a few years, and that to the best of general knowledge no tragedy had ever occurred there, nor any hidden corpse been discovered. Yet there may have been some murderous vagabond lurking in the other apartment.

. . . .

I have rarely had a more uncomfortable journey than that train ride back to Riga, which took nearly thirty hours. They said at the time that there were only five working locomotives in the whole of Latvia, and whether this was true or not, one thing was certain, that at every station where we stopped the engine went off and did shunting work for three or four hours. It was bitterly cold, the atmosphere in the car was horrible, I had finished my book and run out of food and drink, and soon got tired of exchanging scraps of German with the Lettish officer in the bunk opposite. I thought the second night would never end, and to make it worse there was a sick man on the shelf below me —they had put him in at one of the intermediate stations—who groaned continuously in a most distressing way.

Finally, about nine-thirty on the second morning, we pulled into Riga, and I dropped down from my bunk thinking eagerly about bath and breakfast. The Lettish officer was bending over the passenger below me who had been groaning. He turned round with a gesture that I later came to know well, a flick of the right hand across the throat, signifying finish.

"Dead," he said curtly. "Spotty typhus." I nodded. There was no need to tell me that; the man was well-dressed and wore a good fur coat, but was a most unpleasant sight. The Lett grinned. "Lucky it hard car," he said. "In hard car lice stay with him, they no like wood. In soft car they come bite rest of us, then we have typhus too. That no good for us, but—him," he jerked his thumb at the body contemptuously. "Hell to him, him Russian or German."

The Letts had virtually been slaves for centuries to their Baltic-German and Russian masters, and hated both, with reason. I saw a place in northern Latvia which reminded me of some of the villages on the Somme during the War. I mean it was smashed to pieces, utterly flattened. There was nothing left of it save brick foundations and a few charred beams, and I said to my Lettish interpreter, "Good Lord, I didn't know there was any fighting as far north as this; what happened?"

He smiled, the curious, cruel smile of a subject people which has been downtrodden for generations and has at last defeated its oppressors.

"Oh," he replied, "that wasn't the War, that was the 'punitive expeditions' in the spring of 1906. You see, we revolted then against the Tsar and against our Baltic landlords, the Tsar's *gendarmes*, the bloody German landlords and mercenaries who killed our Lettish peasants in the name of the Tsar, to hold the land for themselves. And in any village where there had been one single revolutionary, the 'punitive expeditions' came to the village and burnt it flat, like this one you see here. They didn't shoot anyone, unless there was a resistance; they just burnt the village flat and took the cattle and horses and the farm tools, and destroyed the rest. It was a lesson, they said, to teach the Letts not to revolt again."

I wonder whether such lessons are clever, whether they really teach what they are meant to teach. There was the case of the Tsar Nicholas II and his wife, the Tsarina, and the little son and their four daughters, in Ekaterinburg on the Ural border

between Europe and Asia. The Tsar and his family were held
there in a big house, living comfortably enough, but under
guard. It was August, 1918, and the Whites were advancing
from the East. The question arose what should be done with the
Imperial family; send them back Westward or let the Whites
rescue them, or what? There had been revolts in the Urals too,
in the winter of 1905–06 and in Siberia, and there too came
"punitive expeditions," General Rennenkampf with his Cossacks,
the Cossacks with their whips. General Rennenkampf was accused of betraying his master, the Tsar Nicholas II, eight years
later, at the Battle of Tannenberg, when he had 300,000 men
on Hindenburg's flank, and never moved a man of them. The
estimable General Rennenkampf was reputed to have killed
70,000 men, women and children in Siberia and the Urals on
his "punitive expedition" in the spring of 1906, in the name of
the Tsar. This did not please the population of the Urals, just
as the Letts were not pleased by similar proceedings, and the
population of the Urals no longer revered the name of the Tsar
or thought of him as their "Little Father." They were simple-
minded, those Ural peasants and workers, and primitive. In
their simple primitive way they thought that the Tsar was a
murderer, and that if ever they had a chance they would deal
with the Tsar as Rennenkampf and his Cossacks had dealt with
them. In August, 1918, they got that chance and did so deal
with the Tsar and his wife and children—root and branch—
"hew Agag in pieces before the Lord, an eye for an eye and a
tooth for a tooth." It is said that Lenin, in Moscow, tried to
save the Tsar and his family, but they were doomed when they
reached Ekaterinburg.

.   .   .   .

The Poles, also, had their share of Tsarist oppression, which
may affect history that is yet to be written. I once knew a "Left"
Polish Deputy in 1923, who was so "Left" that he was shortly

afterwards clapped into jail. He told me in Warsaw, "I am a Revolutionary and a Marxist. In the troubles here in the winter of 1905–06 I was a student at the University, and went out with the others to demonstrate. My sister went with me, who was about sixteen, a pretty blonde girl, romantic as girls are at that age, but sweet and pretty, and I loved her very much. Then the Cossacks came and rode us down in the square where stood the Russian Cathedral—do you wonder why we pulled that Cathedral to bits and flattened out the place where it had been so that no one would know there ever was a Cathedral there?—the Russian Cathedral. And one of the Cossacks took his whip, you know the Cossack whips, *nagaikas* they call them, rawhide leather thongs with bits of lead tied to them, and he slashed my sister across the face, and there was nothing I could do about it. It spoilt her beauty, and it spoilt the rest of her life, and there was nothing I could do about it; that was what hurt most. Now I tell you, I am a Marxist and a Revolutionary, but if any God-Damn Russian tells me that those sons-of-bitches of Cossacks are my comrades and brothers, I say No, and No, and No. If the Third International was Swiss or French or Jewish or Japanese I wouldn't mind it, but don't let anyone tell me that *Cossacks* are *my* brothers. The only good Cossack is what they used to say in America about Indians, namely, dead. There are *no* good Cossacks. at least not to Poles, there aren't, because they have used their *nagaikas* too often in this country."

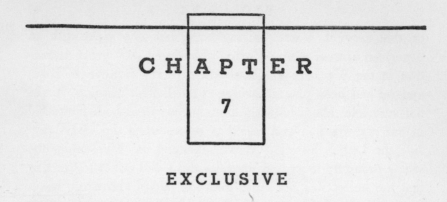

CHAPTER
7

EXCLUSIVE

WHEN I returned to Riga about the 10th of December, I found that everyone was looking forward eagerly to the holidays, which were to be celebrated doubly that year for two reasons, first, because the country had at last emerged from the darkness of war, starvation and misery, and the future was bright with hope; second, the 21st of December (December 6th according to the Russian calendar) was a great feast of the Russian Church, the anniversary of St. Nicholas the Wonder-Worker, and "name-day" of the Tsar. The large Russian colony, which included many charming ladies, was resolved to hold a grand three days' "wake" for its martyred Emperor, so as to coincide with a round of Christmas parties given by the foreign Missions.

The city was still under martial law, and there was a "curfew" rule that no one was allowed on the streets after 8 P.M. without a pass. If people went to a theater or to visit friends, or what not, they had to stay out all night. In the case of foreigners it was different; one received a pass without difficulty or simply didn't bother. I, myself, for instance, never had a pass all the time I was there. I just said, "English Mission" if I was challenged, and generally that was enough without even showing a passport, although once I nearly got a bullet through the head on that account. I was walking home late one night with an American airman named Curtis, who served with great distinction in the War. He was Assistant Military Attaché in Riga, and we had been playing bridge at the British Mission. It was not very late, about half-past one, but we were both interested in our conversation and failed to notice when the sentry outside the Lettish Foreign Office challenged us. Whereupon the sentry promptly loosed off his rifle, and I will swear to this day that the bullet was not more than six inches above my head. Automatically I threw myself flat on my face in the snow, but Curtis was made of sterner stuff. He ran across the road to the sentry, cursing furiously in English. The sentry did not fire again, so I scrambled up and somewhat sheepishly followed. The sentry spoke nothing but Lettish, but he seemed to think he had made a mistake, so everything ended happily and we went on home.

When I told this story to my friends in the Mission the next day, they shouted with laughter and said it was all nonsense, that the sentry had not aimed at us at all; just fired a shot over our heads to halt us, and that it would have amused them very much to see me dive across the snow. That was all very well, but a few nights later, two of those humorous young Englishmen came back with a different story. On the way home from the theater they had found the body of an elderly man lying in the street with the back of his head blown off. They made inquiries and learnt that he too had been challenged by a sentry and had paid no attention; it turned out later that he had a pass but was almost totally deaf. So the sentry shot at him, and aimed better than the lad Curtis and I had encountered; that was all.

A funny parallel to this occurred in Moscow some years later, at the beginning of 1923. The Russians had given some sort of party at the Hermitage Restaurant, for the American

Relief people, and amongst the Americans there were two youngsters who had only landed in Moscow the day before, and had doubtless been told all sorts of stories about the risks of life in Russia. They went home together from the party in a little one-horse sleigh, whose driver had been told where to take them. Half-way down the Boulevard the sleigh was halted by a patrol of uniformed police, who were checking up on documents of people on the street at night. There was no curfew law in Moscow, but check-ups of that kind were frequent in those days. The American boys did not know that, and thought they had run into a hold-up by bandits, or Lord knows what. Being unarmed, there was nothing they could do but flee, and flee they did. Each of them leapt out of the sleigh on opposite sides and fled like the wind. The Russian police jumped to the natural conclusion that they were dangerous malefactors and gave chase, shooting. One American who, like myself, had seen the War, dived, like me, into the nearest snowdrift, where according to his story, he dug himself in so swiftly and successfully that nothing was visible to the pursuers save his boots, which they failed to notice. The chase swept on, past him, after the other citizen. The latter rushed down the nearest side-street, with bullets whistling round him, and one of them took off the heel of his right boot and inflicted a small flesh-wound on his foot. That checked him—I think he said it knocked him over. Anyhow, there was an open doorway right there. He plunged in, scrambled upstairs, and began banging on the door of the first apartment he came to, shouting, "Help, help, bandits!" The door was opened—miraculously, because Muscovites have learnt caution—and he fell inside exhausted and bleeding, followed a moment later by the police, hot as any "wolf-pack" on his trail.

The confusion that ensued must have passed all limits. The young man said that everyone talked for hours at the top of their voices, women had hysterics and children roused from sleep threw fits. Ultimately he had a bright thought and waved the address of the A.R.A. house where he lived (which had been written on a piece of paper in case the sleigh-driver forgot his instructions) under the nose of the nearest policeman, who of course could not read it. But someone else could, and they finally understood that he was not a malefactor, but an American Relief worker, while he understood that they were not bandits, but devoted guardians of the peace.

In the meantime, the other boy dragged himself out of the snowdrift and set out on his homeward path. But he did not know the address, his friend had that, as I have said, and all he could say was that it was "The Brown House." (I must explain that the A.R.A. in Moscow named its various living-quarters by colors—the Brown House, the Pink House, the White House, and so forth.) "The Brown House"—in English —naturally meant nothing to any Russian, so the American wandered about in despair until somewhere he saw a large building with lights, and entered it. It was a Red Army barracks, and what followed was an illustration of the essential friendliness of Russians and their kindness to forlorn strangers. They may be cruel and suspicious, but withal they have that sense of hospitality which Classical Greece rated as the noblest of human sentiments. They gave him hot tea with vodka, half and half, and sat him next to a big warm stove. Remember, he still thought that he had been the victim of a bandit outrage. In short, his worst fears and all the dreadful stories that the boy had heard about Moscow were horribly confirmed; but here suddenly he found a refuge, with tea and vodka (which at that time was illegal because they still had partial prohibition), and bread and salted fish. Next morning someone came along who understood enough English to get in touch with the A.R.A., and the young man reached home about noon, "tight as a tick," to employ a Britannic vulgarism. The wounded American had an easier, if less pleasant, passage. One of the policemen telephoned the Gay-pay-oo, and the Gay-pay-oo sent a car with a doctor, who bandaged the boy's heel and took him back to "The Brown House."

The next day, as it happened, the Acting Chief of the A.R.A. (Colonel Haskell, who was the Chief, was then away) was lunching with me, and he told me this story, but not, he said, for publication. "What do you mean?" I asked. "Of course it must be published at once, to take the curse off it. I mean that if I write it now, just as it happened, as a joke, there will be no trouble anywhere, but if it isn't written now, sooner or later it will leak out to Riga, and one of the bright anti-Bolshevik reporters there will write a dreadful story about a pogrom by the Red Army against the A.R.A. in Moscow, with headlines 'Soviet Soldiers Shoot American Relief Worker,' or something of the kind. Let me write it, and I'll take the curse off it."

He agreed and I wrote the story, in a somewhat jocular vein, and cabled it that night after a little discussion with the censor; it was published the next day with the headline, "SOVIET SOLDIERS SHOOT AMERICAN RELIEF WORKER," which did not win me any good marks with my friend in charge of the A.R.A., when he heard about it. But no foreign correspondent is responsible for headlines, thank God, and the story was clear enough, if anyone cared to read it.

There is an interesting point of newspaper etiquette involved here. One point of view is that news is news no matter how you get it, and if and when you get it you write it and let the devil take the consequences. That may be all right at home—the tabloids do it, and some others, and seem to get away with it— but it surely is a mistake in foreign service. A foreign correspondent has to play fair with his sources. If he is given a story with a string to it, that it is not for publication, or anyway not before a certain date, he makes a big practical mistake if he ignores the restriction and sends the story. Some competitor may get hold of it, without any strings attached to it, and send it and the first correspondent gets a snooty cable from his office and feels sick. That has happened to me, and more than once. But I still say that the answer is invariable; if you are given a story in confidence, or with restrictions, you *must* respect that confidence and observe these restrictions. And even if you are beaten in consequence, it will pay you in the long run. At least that is what I think, and what I do.

In this case, of course, there was none of that, because the Acting Chief of the A.R.A. gave me permission to use the story. And it was a good story and did no harm to anyone, despite the headline. But the American boy who had dug himself into the snow-drift was very cross about it. He thought, and said, that I had made him look ridiculous, which was true enough, and that if ever he met me, he would knock me for a loop. But he was sent somewhere down in the Volga and I don't think we ever did meet, or if we did, he had forgotten his wrath by that time.

.   .   .   .

My gay and care-free enjoyment of the double Christmas-New Year celebrations in Riga was facilitated and enhanced by disaster, imprisonment, and ultimately death, which overtook a man doubtless worthier than I. This citizen was a courier of the Third International on his way from Moscow to New York, who was captured by the Letts in Libau, betrayed, if I remember, by some girl with whom he had unwisely slept.

He was as authentic and picturesque a secret agent as any reporter could desire. The Letts found $8,000 worth of diamonds in his boot heels and a marvelous seventeenth-century miniature surrounded by diamonds, worth another $4,000 or $5,000, sewn into the seam of his pants, and last but not least, his little sailor's wooden box had a false bottom filled with documents of the most seditious nature from the Comintern to the American Communist Party.

To me the effects of this capture were delightful. Most reporters know cases when they were handed a cracker-jack story on a plate, so to speak, but in this instance, it was not one story but a dozen, at a time when nothing was happening in Latvia, and when the United States was in the throes of a fantastic anti-Red scare. And the story was genuine; this was no "Zinoviev letter" stuff; I saw the diamonds and the miniature and the original documents and the citizen himself. It meant that my work for the next two weeks during those violent and protracted festivities was confined to hitting a typewriter for half an hour daily to transcribe one of the documents, with the certainty that it was an exclusive front-page story.

In twenty years of newspaper work that was the best break I ever had, and I think I must be right in saying so because it was the only occasion on which I ever received a bonus from *The New York Times*. Some newspapers or agencies make a practice of bonuses, large or small. I think the idea was first put generally into practice by Joseph Pulitzer, the proprietor and publisher of *The New York World*. According to legend, any reporter on *The World* might suddenly find a check for $1,000 or a 300 guinea fur coat beside his typewriter when he came to the office some morning, in reward for a story he had written the day before. Other newspapers have a simpler and less expensive technique. They give their worthy hireling loud words of glowing praise, written in a formal note if it is home service, or by cable if the man is abroad. This is supposed to cheer and encourage the hireling, but, as Anita Loos said, a kiss on the wrist makes a girl feel good, but an emerald bracelet lasts longer, or words to that effect.

The New York Times, however, maintains a dignified aloof-

ness. It is sparse with praise and blame, and apparently thinks
that the salaries it pays and the honor of working for it are
sufficient for its employees. And I think that it is right. I do not
mean to imply, of course, that the former Managing Editor,
Van Anda, who in my opinion was the greatest newspaper man
America ever knew, did not have a gift for reprimanding foreign correspondents in terms that singed their hair off. I know
that to my cost, and am prematurely bald in consequence. Sometimes a message of approval made one feel good for weeks, but
there were almost never bonuses or anything of that kind. So
that I think I am right in believing that my "Red International
Documents" series must have pleased my home office very
much.

It was simply pie for me, and what is more, killed two birds
with one stone. You see the Letts caught this fellow and put him
in jail and turned his documents over to the British, although
the documents had nothing to do with the British whatever.
They exclusively concerned America and were silly, inflam-
matory stuff, telling American Communists to work on American troops as they came home from France and induce them to
kill their officers, or anyway refuse to turn in their rifles and
ammunition. I imagine the Russians thought that the demobi-
lization process in the United States would be something like
what happened in Russia when the defeated forces of the Tsar
left the Front *en masse* during the Kerensky period, and came
home all ripe and ready for a revolutionary movement.

As it happened, the American Commissioner, Commander
Gade, had gone to Scandinavia for Christmas, which perhaps
was why the Lettish authorities didn't hand the documents to
the Americans; or perhaps they thought the British were more
important, which at that time was true enough in the Baltic.
Anyhow, I went to the Mission for lunch a day or two after my
return from Alexander's Front, and Dewhurst told me the story

about the Bolshevik courier and said, "It might interest you to have copies of these documents, and here they are." Interest me! Of course it interested me! Diamonds and miniatures and secret agents and seditious documents; it would have interested Edgar Wallace. I blazed with excitement and couldn't eat until Dewhurst had arranged for me to interview the courier in prison. He was a stocky, sullen fellow, the first Russian Communist I had met, by the way, but brave and loyal. He would not "talk" at all to me or anyone else, no matter how they treated him, as he declared with what seemed to me unnecessary emphasis—I didn't know then what means of pressure had been current in Latvia in the old days. And he knew, it seems, that he was going to be shot; the Letts shot Communists on principle, but that is a story I shall come to later. As an interview it was not a great success, but there was color in it, and they showed me the diamonds and the miniature, and the courier admitted the facts readily enough, so that it was a good story. A curious feature of many of the documents was their similarity in manner, and even in phrasing, to the Epistles of St. Paul, when he was "exhorting the churches" in the first Christian communities of Greece and Asia Minor, reproving back sliders and warning against schism. There was one sentence which might have been taken verbatim from the Epistles: "Some so-called Party members cannot really make up their minds whether they are Communists or not; they are no good to the Party and must be expelled." St. Paul's wording was, "There be those amongst you that blow neither hot nor cold, like the Laodiceans; ye shall spew them out."

I wrote the general story and my interview with the prisoner the first day, then followed with a document a day for the next two weeks or more. The third day something gratifying happened, in the shape of a cable from Washington to the acting head of the American Mission, asking him how it came that he had not reported the big Courier-Spy-Document story that was being brandished across the front page of *The New York Times*. The chief reason was that he did not know about it. The British might have told him, but I had asked them not to; and I might have told him, but I didn't because one night at a party he had grabbed away a nice girl I had invited. Girls were scarce in Riga, and it made me cross. He was a tall handsome citizen (I am neither) and danced like Fred Astaire, which I do not. He was the kind of man who would never have any trouble about any girls, so why grab mine?

I thought of the story of Nathan the Prophet and King David (which is one of the greatest stories in the world and marvelously written). After David had taken Bath-sheba, the wife of Uriah the Hittite, he commanded the captain of the host that Uriah be put in the forefront of the battle, which was duly done. Uriah died in battle, and David kept Bath-sheba. But Nathan, the Prophet of the Lord, came to David and told him the parable of the rich man, who had many flocks and herds, and the poor man, who had only one ewe lamb and nursed it in his bosom, and "it was to him as a daughter." "And there came," said Nathan, "a wayfarer to visit the rich man, and for the wayfarer's dinner the rich man took and gave him the poor man's one ewe lamb." When King David heard this story, he was furious, and said, "Who is this rich man that doeth such wrong in Israel? He shall surely die."

And Nathan said to him, "Thou art the man," which I think is the most terrific line in literature. These are words to wring every heart.

The American *chargé d'affaires* summoned me to his presence and said he had had a cable, and asked why I hadn't told him about the courier. I said, "Can't you guess?" He looked as if he did guess. "Yes," I added, "and I hope that the cable you received from Washington was the kind of cable Van Anda sometimes sends me, I mean the sort of cable that makes you think you've been scalped by a troop of Indians." He said it was, which made me feel better; and he said he was sorry, which made me feel better still. He said, too, "If you've got any more of this stuff, will you let me see it?" So I let him see it; the hatchet was buried, and I felt magnanimous. But the girl always danced with him at parties, and gave me only a pleasant smile.

CHAPTER 8

THE BRAVE MAN DIES BUT ONCE

FOREIGNERS in Riga were just recovering from their New Year's holiday when they were startled by the news that Latvia, wearying of the fruitless attempt to obtain from the Soviet the Province of Lettgalen by negotiation, had decided to seize it by force. On the morning of January 3rd, 1920, a surprise attack was launched in an easterly direction on a front of about a hundred miles, from Lake Luban in the north to the Landeswehr position facing Dvinsk in the south. The attack was supported by the Poles, who moved small forces on a narrow front northeastwards against Dvinsk. (When I speak of "front" the word must not be understood in the sense of a continuous line, as it was used in France, but a series of parallel attacks at various points more or less in touch with each other, each group being fairly well supported by artillery, cavalry and tanks.)

The secret had been well kept, and a curious feature of the action was that between the Lettish right and the Polish left there was a small section of line, ten miles or so in length, held by the Lithuanians, who were not even informed that an attack was contemplated. The Letts and Poles, or their foreign military advisers, suspected Lithuanian sympathy for the Bolsheviks, and wished to run no risk of leakage. So the attack was made in converging directions, with the result that the Poles and Letts joined hands at a point a few miles in front of the Lithuanian section. The Bolsheviks were completely surprised and the Letts advanced fifteen or twenty miles the first day without great resistance, capturing a large number of prisoners. The Lettish troops may have totaled as many as 30,000 or 40,000 men, including the Landeswehr, but it was difficult to estimate because, as I have said of the Landeswehr, there were "divisions" with no greater strength than 3,000 or 4,000, so that there may not have been more than 25,000 men in all. The Poles, whose strength was not more than a full brigade, drove straight at Dvinsk, took it with little difficulty, and promptly announced they would keep it. They thought that Dvinsk and Vilna, which were both important railroad junctions, might be useful to Poland in the future. The Letts did not see that at all, and the Lettish High Command gave the Poles two hours to evacuate Dvinsk or take the consequences. The Letts were undoubtedly prepared to halt their attack on the Bolsheviks and swing back against the Poles at Dvinsk. The Poles retired, sullen and grumbling, and took no further part in that campaign. This untoward incident, which, however, had no serious consequences, illustrates and explains the whole failure of Allied intervention against the Bolsheviks, which cost so heavily in Russian lives, both Red and White, and involved no small expenditure of foreign blood and treasure. There was never any genuine coöperation or practical coördination of time and place between the various "intervening" forces.

In this connection unexpected evidence about the state of the White armies was provided by the documents seized by the Letts from the Comintern courier I mentioned before. It consisted of three letters from an officer on Denikin's staff to a friend in the *entourage* of Kolchak. These letters, written in the summer of 1919, when Denikin's army was still advancing, but Kolchak's vanguard had already been beaten near Samara (although the writer did not know that), had been intercepted by the Bolsheviks, probably as a result of that White defeat, and were being sent to New York, for use, no doubt, as anti-intervention propaganda. I gave them better and bigger publicity in *The New York Times* than any Communist group in America could have secured. The writer said frankly that Denikin was surrounded by a gang of crooks and grafters who cared nothing for the White cause, if only they might fill their own pockets and have a good time. He said that clothing and supplies intended for the troops were being sold openly in the rear areas and never reached the Front at all. Carloads of munitions, guns and machine-guns stood idle in the rear depots, to permit the transport of champagne and other luxuries for officers and their women. Weapons, even including cannon and tanks, were being sold to middle-men who were acting for the Reds. In some cases war material had been sold to the Reds direct. Meanwhile there was no attempt to conciliate the civil population. The property of peasants and others was looted scandalously by the White troops, and if they protested, they were shot as Reds. There were cases, the writer declared, of inhuman cruelty towards alleged Bolsheviks or their sympathizers. All this, he concluded, was alienating the civil population and undoubtedly preparing for catastrophe.

He appealed to his friend on the staff of Kolchak, "who," he said, "has the reputation of being a firm and honorable leader," to beg Kolchak as supreme White Commander to send immediately a trusted group of officers to investigate conditions in Denikin's Staff and make the necessary changes. "R—— in particular is our evil genius," he said. "The General (Denikin) is well-meaning and, I believe, honest, but he trusts R—— implicitly and is completely under his influence. There is no time to be lost; unless R—— be speedily removed, our cause is ruined."

Needless to say the letters were never delivered and Kolchak took no action. Indeed, the news of his own execution at Irkutsk

reached Riga a few weeks after the letters came to my notice
Some months later the chief of Denikin's staff, named Colonel
R——, was shot on the steps of a hotel in Nice by one of his former subordinates. The assassin justified his act by the assertion
that Colonel R—— had betrayed the White cause in order to
enrich himself, and therefore deserved death. He was tried by a
French court a few months later and, I believe, acquitted.

Left to their own devices after "liquidating" the Dvinsk incident, the Letts advanced steadily with trifling losses. Their northern force met little opposition until it reached the railroad junction of Marienhausen and began to threaten Pskov, which was an
old Russian town outside the limits of Lettgalen. Here they met
stiffer resistance and decided to halt. In the center, along the
railroad leading to Regitsa, the capital of Lettgalen, there was
sharper fighting, but the Soviet left flank was turned by a north-
easterly advance of the Landeswehr, which Alexander had trained
in the Western tactics of indirect fire by machine-guns, with
which he was fairly well supplied although he had little artillery. This gave him an enormous advantage, as the following
figures show. In less than three weeks the Landeswehr inflicted
casualties of at least 3,000 killed and wounded, took over 2,000
prisoners and eighty villages or towns. Its own total losses were
less than a hundred killed and wounded. Outflanked by the
Landeswehr, the Reds abandoned Regitsa in such a hurry that
they left behind four huge American locomotives built for and
captured from Kolchak. It was a great disappointment to the
Letts that when their General and a picked body of troops returned victorious to Riga after the armistice early in February,
those ponderous steel elephants could not grace their triumph.
There was hardly a bridge or culvert in Latvia that could bear
their weight without months of work.

By the end of January all Lettgalen had been occupied, although there was no real fighting after the 20th. True to their

original intention, the Letts advanced no further and thus was ended the only successful campaign against the Bolsheviks in the whole history of Intervention and the Civil War. The Letts kept their heads, too, during the peace negotiations which followed and did not ask too much. A treaty was signed at Riga on August 11th, 1920, which guaranteed the full independence of Latvia, including Lettgalen, and the return to Latvia of archives and other property which had been removed by the Tsarist Government, or during the Red occupation of 1918–19. The question of indemnities was not raised by either side.

• • • • • • • • • • • •

During the first week I covered the "War" from Riga, despite the all-embracing pass I had received from the Lettish Commander-in-Chief. For two good reasons, first, that it would have taken two or three days to reach the Front, had a train been available, which was doubtful, as all the locomotives save one were being used behind the lines of advance. Second, that through the courtesy of the Lettish General Staff and my British friends, I was getting full information two or three hours before the short Lettish *communiqués* were issued, and was thus able to write a good running story every day. For some curious reason there were practically no other newspaper men in Riga at that time. They naturally supposed that the peace negotiations between the Soviet, Esthonia and Finland, which had now been resumed in Dorpat, were the central interest in the Baltic. None of them foresaw, any more than I did, the sudden resumption of hostilities by the Letts. As far as I remember none of them had come to Riga by the time I left for the northern front, on a troop train in company with the American flying officer, Major Curtis, whom I mentioned before when telling how the Lett sentry had shot at us in the street. We were to have a much narrower escape on this journey, though of a different character. The troop train made such good time, since the engine was not al-

lowed to be removed *en route* for shunting, that we arrived at
midnight instead of 8 A.M. at the way station from which we
were to drive to headquarters. The station Commandant had prepared food and a room for us, but I have rarely spent a less
pleasant night. The place was alive with vermin, amongst which
the gray typhus louse was all too prominent. Typhus was epidemic throughout the region and at that very time the unfortunate remnant of Yudenich's army was dying like flies in Narva.
Curtis and I had smeared ourselves liberally with oil of anise,
the specific used by the German Army on the Eastern Front,
whose smell is supposed to deter the hungry cootie. Everything
we ate or drank reeked of it, but I doubt whether it was much
protection, as we were plentifully bitten, with no worse results,
however, than a day or two's discomfort. But the thought that
each fresh bite might be injecting deadly germs was not comforting for a long and sleepless night.

We received a warm welcome at headquarters, and I had an
excellent interview with the Commanding Officer, who not only
explained in detail what had happened and the subsequent objectives, but offered us his private sleigh, and an aide-de-camp to
act as interpreter, to take us up to the Front, which was now
about fifty kilometers eastwards along the main railroad line
running south from the Russian town of Pskov to Dvinsk. The
General said that the Letts had that morning captured the important junction of Marienhausen, and that we should probably
find Divisional Headquarters somewhere in that neighborhood. I
sent my story by military courier, who was returning to Riga the
next morning, and at 7 A.M. we set out in pitch darkness in a big
two-horse sleigh. We drove all day without seeing a soul, along
a narrow trail not more than five yards wide through dense pine
forest. The Lettish advance had been so rapid, our interpreter
said, that the woods were still full of Red stragglers, and until

they were rounded up the civil population would lie low at home. We were to find out later how true this was.

About three o'clock we met a train of peasant sleighs and moved out of the track to let them pass. It was a convoy of prisoners, eight or ten of them wounded, lying on the sleighs, the rest, about twenty, marching on foot, under the guard of four Lettish soldiers and a Sergeant with rifles. On the last sleigh, the Sergeant told us, was a "Bolshevik Commissar," who had only a slight flesh wound in the arm but who had the privilege of riding because of his superior rank. I gathered later that although he wore uniform, he must have been one of the trusted civilian Communists then attached to military units of the Red Army to keep an eye on the officers, many of whom were ex-Whites of doubtful loyalty. Owing to the shortage of officer material of their own, the Reds commonly used White officers in this way during the Civil War, but found it necessary to supplement them by civilian "guardians" called Commissars. We offered the man some brandy and began to talk to him. He spat back at us like an infuriated cat. "Tell him there is no need to be so rude about it," I said to the young aide-de-camp. "We wish him no harm and it won't hurt him to be polite." Again the Commissar replied with a burst of Russian expletive. "He says you can go to hell," said the interpreter. "He knows he is going to be shot, so why should he satisfy your curiosity? He says to hell with America too, and all the other stinking rotten capitalists." Meanwhile the rest of the prisoners watched with mildly curious faces.

As we went on, I said to the aide-de-camp, "What's that the Commissar said about being shot? What did he mean?"

"Oh, yes," he replied cheerfully, "they'll all be shot, that lot. They're all Communists, and we can't keep them, you know; they make trouble in the prison camps and start rebellions, and so on. So now we always shoot them. That lot is going back to head-

quarters for examination—of course they never tell anything,
Communists don't, but one or two might be stupid and give away
some useful information—then we'll have to shoot them. Of
course we don't shoot prisoners," he added hastily, "but Communists are different. They *always* make trouble, so we have no
choice." "But do they know that?" I persisted. "I mean not only
the Commissar, but the others?" "I expect so, they all heard
what he said, didn't they?"

Now that was a curious example of Russian temperament.
These men were such devoted Communists that they would not
speak to save their lives and would not rest quiet in prison
camps. Yet here were twenty of them unwounded on a narrow
trail through trackless woods, and only four guards, or five with
the Sergeant, armed with rifles. If the prisoners had broken away
in a body, it is doubtful whether the guards would have had time
to shoot any of them. Mind you, they were not chained or bound
in any way. There were Red soldiers a-plenty in the forest, and
a group of determined men could undoubtedly have found their
way back through the loose Lettish lines to the Red outposts. But
no, they trudged on apathetically to their fate. To Curtis and
me it was incomprehensible.

Two days later, at the Lettish Division Headquarters near
Marienhausen, I had a further example of Russian indifference
to death. Three Communists were to be executed; they were so
tough and recalcitrant that it wasn't any good sending them back
to Army Headquarters. I saw them stroll out towards a fence
about a quarter of a mile from where I was standing. They were
accompanied by a Lettish Sergeant with a big cavalry revolver.
I watched through my glasses, without the least compunction or
pity because at that time I regarded the Bolsheviks as enemies
of God and man, and the Sergeant later told me what happened.
The Russians, it seemed, had one cigarette among them. When
they lined up with their backs to the fence the first man said,

"Do you mind if I smoke three puffs of the cigarette?" I may add that they were not bound or blindfolded. The Sergeant nodded assent, whereupon the man lit his cigarette, cursing the while because two or three of his matches failed to light, drew three or four puffs of smoke, then, passing it on to his comrade on the right, slightly bent his head to receive the Lett's bullet. The same performance was repeated with the second Communist, whereupon the third said, "You may as well let me finish the cigarette." Again the Sergeant nodded, then this man also took a bullet in the brain and died.

At the moment the most interesting thing to me was the fact that all of them received a bullet of the same caliber under the left ear, but all died different ways. The first man fell flat on his back as if he had been hit with a club, kicked his heels for a minute, then lay still. The second stood swaying a moment, then fell forward on his face and flopped his hands twice in the snow. The third staggered a step backwards as the bullet hit him, then a step forward, putting out his hands as if to save himself from falling, then slumped down in a heap without a movement of hand or foot. They were all men of about the same physique and I couldn't understand this difference until it was explained to me by an American nerve specialist who visited Moscow in 1933 or 1934. "It is a matter of muscular tension," he said. "The first man was limp when the bullet hit him, so it knocked him backwards. The second and third were braced as if to jump forward, but the muscular bracing of the second was greater than that of the third." Which sounds reasonable when you come to think of it.

But what puzzled Curtis and me was that one of the three, or all of them together, did not take a swing at the Lettish Sergeant and run for it. The edge of the forest was only a hundred yards away and they would have had at least an even chance of getting clear instead of smoking a cigarette and dying like sheep.

Curtis and I spent the night at Advance Headquarters where they told us that a Lettish armored train would be in action the next day, and said that if we cared to be at the Marienhausen railroad station at 6.30 A.M. we could accompany it. We were both delighted because this was a form of warfare that was unknown in France, and there was some prospect, it seemed, of a battle with a Red armored train which was operating in the neighborhood of Pskov, a little further north. If this occurred the Letts were confident of victory because, in addition to two cars mounting three-inch cannon and machine-guns, they had a third car with an old British 4.7 naval gun which would outweigh anything the Reds might have.

We set off in a minor blizzard at 2 A.M. the next morning to drive twenty-five miles across the frozen steppe to Marienhausen. It was dark as pitch and desperately cold, but the driver knew the road and was quite sure that we should arrive on time. About half-way, going through a patch of forest, we were suddenly startled by a shot that sailed over the horses' heads. They broke into a gallop and there came two more shots, fortunately both high, although the range was short. The horses kicked and plunged and broke a trace. The sleigh stopped. Our interpreter, the aide-de-camp, cried, "It's Red stragglers; they probably want the horses for food." He seized a rifle, threw himself down in the snow, and began firing off to the right where he'd seen the two last flashes. Curtis got out of the sleigh and set coolly about helping the driver fix the trace. He stood on the right side of the team, but I thought it more prudent to move over to the left, where I had the bodies of both horses between me and the enemy rifles. No more shots, however, were fired and in ten minutes we resumed our journey.

About half-past five we saw lights a mile ahead—it had stopped snowing—and the driver pointed forward, "Marienhausen," he said. There had evidently been a sharp skirmish before the junction was taken because we saw a score or more of dead Russians half hidden by the snow on both sides of the lighted track that led to the station yard. Although it was not yet six o'clock, we were disgusted to learn that the armored train had left the station a few minutes before, on receipt of a report that the Red train was advancing southwards along the railroad. "How unlucky!" I said to the interpreter. "If those damned stragglers hadn't shot at us we wouldn't have missed it." The driver of the sleigh evidently caught my meaning, for he burst into a flood of excited Lettish and ended by crossing himself, then, pointing to the rest of us, made the sign of the cross in our direction, too. "What does he say?" I asked. The interpreter shrugged his shoulders. "He's crazy," he said. "He claims that this has been a stroke of good luck for us somehow. He says that we escaped a danger; he's a stupid fellow." "Kipling once said the Finns were warlocks and could tell the future," I replied laughing, "but I didn't know your people had the same gift." Later that afternoon we saw from a hill-top the two armored trains about three miles apart banging away at each other for all they were worth. Neither side made good practice, as during the ten minutes we could see them there were no hits at all, although shells were bursting near them both. It was exciting without much danger apparently, and Curtis and I were furious to have missed this chance. When we got back to headquarters, we had reason to think differently. Just before dusk the old British naval gun on the Lettish train burst and killed everyone in that car, the Lettish Colonel commanding, an artillery officer, and the gun crew, nine persons in all. The effects of the explosion in that narrow steel box were terrific; they said the place was a shambles dripping with blood and torn fragments of humanity. We should almost certainly have been in that car with the commanding officer.

I told this story in Paris to my friend Bolitho, who seemed

less skeptical about the Lettish driver than I had expected. "I knew a curious case in the War," he said, "and I've never been able to decide whether it was accident or coincidence, or really a case of second sight." This was the story he told.

At the beginning of the War, Bolitho, who was then about eighteen, worked his way to England from South Africa, where he was born, and enlisted in the British Army. Early in 1916 he was a junior Lieutenant on the Front in France, in the Ypres Salient I think it was, but anyway some hot spot where the British losses were heavy. In his battalion there was an Irish Captain, a dark saturnine fellow from Ulster, who was not popular with his brother officers on general grounds and for one reason in particular, although he was a good soldier and the men liked him well enough. At "mess" he was sarcastic and cantankerous, but if anyone took umbrage at his manner he had a nasty way of closing the dispute by saying, "Ye're not worth it for me to argue with, but I'll tell yer this, yer name's in me little black book."

As Bolitho said, they were being badly hammered, so that perhaps it was only a coincidence that on three or four occasions when the Captain made this remark the other party to the dispute was killed within forty-eight hours. But the British were under a strain in the Salient those days, and the feeling crept round that this Captain had the evil eye and that to be listed in his little black book, which by the way no one ever saw or knew if it existed, was the same as a sentence of death. Before long most of the officers dodged away when they saw him coming and hardly dared speak to him at "mess." Which shows what shell-fire does to human nerves.

At last the battalion was relieved, after losing half its effectives, and sent back to a rear area on the coast to rest and be raised again to full strength and smartened up for the coming Battle of the Somme. No English leave was allowed, but most of the officers got a week or two in Paris, the Irishman amongst them.

"Here I am compelled," Bolitho interrupted himself, "to make a digression about the barbarous customs of the English. They had a hospital at Havre for venereal diseases, and there's nothing wrong in that because armies catch them with avidity. But there was a dreadful and cruel rule that any man sent back to Havre with such a disease must wear a big yellow label round his neck with the number of that hospital and the nature of his malady in large black letters. In addition he lost seniority during the time he was absent from duty and it was deducted from his next leave. But all that was nothing. What really counted was that his parents or his wife, if he was married, were given specific information on the subject. That was too damnable for words, especially when home leave was canceled and men had to go to Paris or the towns behind the Front. As a matter of fact, they dropped all that in the last year of the War, but at the time I'm speaking of it was still in force."

Well, this Irish Captain spent his leave in Paris, and although he was recently married and dearly loved his wife, or perhaps because he loved and missed her, he went with other girls, which is one of the things women never understand. I mean that when a woman loves a man, really loves his body with her body, she almost never wants other men, won't let another man touch her unless she has to, and even then tries to deceive herself into believing that it's the man she loves. But men are different. If a man loves and longs for a woman and can't get her, it makes him take the next best, or the third best, or the worst, or anything that comes along. Especially if he's just been a month or so in the Ypres Salient.

So the Irishman did what other soldiers have done on leave in Paris and joined his battalion at a rest camp a few days later, where it was being made ready for the new butchery on the

Somme. One morning he went to the surgeon and explained something and added lightly, "It's lucky we're not up in the Line, but here yer can just put it down as *grippe* or intestinal catarrh or what not." Now the surgeon had had a friend, a good friend whom he liked well, and this friend had quarreled once with the Captain, who had said, "Yer name's in me little black book," and a large hot piece of shell had ripped across his stomach the next evening, and he died like a Japanese doing *hara-kiri*. The surgeon looked at the Captain and said in a cold voice, "You ask me to put my name to a lie? Oh, no indeed, Captain, you will go at once to Havre." The man's dark face paled until even his lips were gray, but he said nothing nor tried to plead for mercy, and went off that night to Havre with his yellow ticket, and they duly told his wife the reason why.

The battalion was in the line again when he came back from Havre. The Somme battle had been postponed, it was reported, or maybe someone higher up thought it would be a good idea to "blood" the new levies in a fairly quiet sector. The Captain came into the big dugout where the officers messed just as they were finishing their evening meal. He saluted the Colonel and nodded to the others, then sat down without speaking. But the surgeon was implacable. "Any more names in your little black book, Captain?" he asked in a casual tone, as if making conversation. The other stared at him in silence, then said slowly, "Yes, there's one name." He paused and added, "Me own," again a pause, then with a small bitter smile, "Yer see, I've read me mail from home."

The next day soon after it was light he went out in the trench and stood on a kerosene can, with his head and shoulders in full view of the enemy 200 yards away, and a bullet promptly greeted him between the eyes. It was a quiet sector, but snipers watched for their quarry like Indians hunting scalps.

CHAPTER
9

FROM BOLITHO TO LENIN

I LEFT the Baltic at the beginning of March, 1920, and the last thing my friends in the British and French Missions told me was to be sure and come back in the early summer because the Poles were getting ready to attack the Bolsheviks, and this time it would be a real war.

Not long after my arrival in Paris, there occurred the abortive Kapp *putsch* in Berlin, a "Right" movement of what now would be called a Nazi-Militarist type, which was crushed by the threat of a general strike. It provoked, however, a sharp reaction from the extreme "Left" in the industrial and mining centers of the Ruhr, where they formed workers' and miners' soviets, raised the Red flag, and broke into open rebellion against the Social-Democratic Government. There was sharp fighting at several points, notably just north of Düsseldorf, where a White battalion was cut to pieces by the Reds, and the latter were in turn destroyed by the Erhardt Naval Brigade, which had been part of the Bermont-Von der Goltz army in the Baltic and was savagely anti-Red.

There was a fine historic irony in this affair, because the Naval Brigade had also supported Kapp in the *putsch* I spoke of earlier. The Government used the labor unions to beat Kapp and the Naval Brigade. Then when the labor extremists got out of hand and thought to seize power for themselves, the Government used the Naval Brigade to beat them, a piece of work for which the Social-Democratic leader, Scheidemann, was chiefly responsible. It was he, too, who tricked the most desperate section of the Reds in the final stage of the rebellion. Their headquarters were at Alten-Essen, not far from the great Krupp works at Essen proper, and their position was still strong, both physically and politically. They had plenty of machine-guns and some artillery and a not ill-organized "Red Army" with regular commissariat, transport and Red Cross services. The White troops had the upper hand in most of the Ruhr, but the situation was still uncertain, and the Scheidemann Government knew quite well that the more moderate central mass of the labor unions did not look with favor upon any ruthless White action to crush the last stand of the Reds.

Bolitho, then *Manchester Guardian* correspondent, was at Alten-Essen with the Reds. He was quick to see that they had a trump card in their hands if they dared to play it. They could dynamite the mines and factories. Bolitho spent all one night with the Red leaders trying to persuade them that this was their only chance. "The net is closing round you," he told them, "but you still have forty-eight hours in which to act. Send Scheidemann an ultimatum at once that unless he agrees to certain economic and political terms, and of course guarantees a free pardon for all of you, you will blow up every mine and factory in the area you control. And then, without waiting for his answer, blow up a small mine or plant immediately, to show you mean business."

"Do you think they'd do it?" said Bolitho disgustedly, when I met him two days later at Düsseldorf. "Of course not. There'll never be a Red revolution in Germany because they have too high a regard for property. Why, these fellows kept repeating—mind you the knife was at their throats and they knew it

—that if they blew the mines they wouldn't have any places to work at afterwards. I couldn't make them see they didn't have to blow them all; one or two would have been enough, and they'd have bluffed Scheidemann off his perch. But they wouldn't do it, they preferred to take Scheidemann's word that he would give them fair treatment. Fair treatment!" he added bitterly, "they were shooting some of those ducks by drum-head court-martial before I left town. But isn't this a comic rebellion when the trolley-cars go on functioning! I just hopped aboard a car with two little 'Red' Red Cross girls and their brother who'd been slightly wounded in the fighting—he was a Red too—and we came through to Düsseldorf entirely unmolested; they never even asked for our papers."

Bolitho afterwards wrote a play about that episode in the Ruhr, but died before he had finished it. It was produced by Marc Connelly, under the title of *Overture,* but it was still rough and unpolished and had no more than a moderate *succès d'estime.*

Of all the people I have met in the last twenty years, and there have been some high-sounding names amongst them, I think Bolitho had the finest intellect. Under forty when he died, he had already made his name as a forceful and original writer, but his mental range went far beyond the limits of literature. He possessed to a remarkable degree the same quality which proved the key to Lenin's success, namely, the gift of making a quick and accurate summary of facts and drawing therefrom the right, logical and inevitable conclusions. The matter of dynamiting the Ruhr mines was only one of a score of incidents I have known of his brilliant political insight and flair for the underlying realities of any situation. Unlike most people, he never blindly accepted the opinion of others, but always thought things out for himself, and never ceased to impress on me the necessity of doing that at all times.

"Don't forget," he used to say, "that the majority of people and the majority of opinions are nearly always wrong about everything, not always, but nearly always, and if you ever are in doubt and can't make up your mind, and have to make it up, there are long odds in favor of your being right if you take the opposite view from the majority. All this talk of Democracy and the 'Sovereign Peepul' and *vox populi* being *vox Dei* is just a trick by cunning demagogues to kid the masses. Read Gustave Le Bon on the psychology of crowds and you'll know the true value of so-called public opinion."

Bolitho and I worked together pretty consistently in 1918, 1920 and 1921, while he was *Manchester Guardian* correspondent in Paris, and he taught me nearly all about the newspaper business that is worth knowing. I have never met anyone who could see further through a brick wall than he could, or who was better, to use a newspaper phrase, at "doping out the inside facts" of any situation. I shall never cease to regret that death prevented him from keeping his promise to visit me in Moscow in the fall of 1929. If the Bolsheviks' sphinx has indeed a Riddle, which I am sometimes inclined to doubt, Bolitho was the man, perhaps the only man, who might have solved it. The trouble with most people is that they think with their hopes or fears or wishes rather than with their minds; or else they take a certain line, either of thought or conduct, and then see facts or twist facts in accordance with that line. Bolitho, however, like Lenin, thought objectively and dispassionately and judged things as they were, irrespective of his own personal line or interests. To me, of course, his death was a heavy personal blow, but I believe it was also a grievous loss to humanity.

. . . .

The Polish War began according to schedule in May, and at first the Poles carried all before them and occupied Kiev and the Western Ukraine. It was said in Paris that Marshal Pilsudski planned to "recover" all the territory Poland had occupied at the time of its greatest expansion in the fifteenth and sixteenth centuries, including most of the Ukraine and Odessa; but in military circles many doubts were expressed about the issue of the campaign. I was unable to cover it on the spot, as I had hoped, because the chief of the Paris Bureau of *The New York Times* was absent in America and I had to take his place, with the result that I tried to cover the War from Paris with the help of what I had learned the previous winter about the Polish and Soviet Armies and the probable Polish objectives. And a pretty poor job I made of it, partly because the French Press, from which I got most of my information, was unduly prejudiced in favor of Poland, partly owing to the fact that I was unaware that the Red Army had been radically reorganized after the Civil War.

About midsummer the Soviet cavalry leader, Budyonny, worked round the Polish flank in the Southern Ukraine, while simultaneously the Polish center further north was shattered by a frontal attack conducted by the brilliant young General Tukhachevsky, who at the age of twenty-six was appointed Field Commander of the Soviet Armies fighting Poland. The Poles were forced to retreat, and the retreat became a rout. The Red Armies advanced like huge pincers, their right wing parallel to the German border almost as far west as Thorn, while the extreme left, Budyonny's cavalry, was instructed to swing up northwards past Lwow. The Red center pressed forward almost to the gates of Warsaw without meeting resistance, and so confident were the Bolsheviks of victory that they set up a Polish Soviet Government, headed bv Djerzhinsky, the founder and chief of the Cheka, with Karl Radek and other Bolsheviks of Polish origin. I was afterwards told in Russia that the Soviet military authorities thought the drive on Warsaw too hazardous, but that Lenin overruled them on the grounds that a Sovietized

Poland would be a bridge to Germany, some of whose provinces, notably Saxony, Thuringia and Bavaria, were strongly
tinged with Red sentiment, and to Hungary, where Bela Kun's
Proletarian Dictatorship had been overthrown only the year
before.

The news reached Paris that the Polish Government was prepared to evacuate Warsaw. France immediately sent Foch's
Chief of Staff, General Weygand, with a picked group of advisers to try and save the situation, and it is a fact that when he
reached Warsaw he found a special train ready to move the
Government westwards. Marshal Pilsudski, however, was of
tougher fiber and refused to despair. With the coöperation of
Weygand he worked out a surprise attack which cut through
a gap in the Soviet center and completely turned the tables. In
forty-eight hours the Red Armies were retreating as fast as they
had advanced. A large part of the Red right wing fled into German territory, where it gave up its arms and was allowed to
return to Russia. The rest of the Red forces made good their
escape. I was told in Moscow that responsibility for the defeat
lay chiefly on Budyonny, who moved straight forward against
Lwow instead of swinging northwards, as ordered, to close the
ring that was tightening around Warsaw.

A curious feature of this war was that in its most exciting
period during the rapid Red advance and retreat, there was
practically no fighting at all. It was said in Paris that Sir Mau-
rice Hankey, who was sent by Lloyd George to Warsaw shortly
before Weygand's arrival, reported that despite newspaper
stories of thousands of Polish wounded arriving by trainloads
in Warsaw the only casualty he could swear to was a too gallant
Polish officer who had jumped from a balcony when the girl's
husband came home unexpectedly. This was probably untrue,
but an American newspaper man told me a few months later
that he and a group of colleagues were taken out to view the

graves of the brave warriors who had died to save Warsaw from the Red hordes. They were shown two mounds surmounted by flags and crosses, and one of them said incautiously, "I suppose all the dead buried here will later be disinterred and placed in separate graves as they did in France." Their Polish guide showed surprise and answered, "These *are* the graves, Lieutenant X—— and Sergeant Y——." From Soviet sources, too, I was able to confirm the bloodless nature of the struggle in the latter part of the campaign. The fact was that the Reds had utterly outrun their supplies of food and munitions and that their Front was absurdly over-extended and ill-coördinated. Nevertheless, the "battle" of Warsaw was one of the decisive engagements of the world, because it marked the end of Soviet plans for the speedy revolutionizing of Europe. Indeed it inaugurated one of the periodic swings from West to East and *vice versa* that have been a feature of Russian history for the past two hundred years. After this check in the West, the Soviet turned its attention to China, where Red advisers, both military and civil, contributed greatly to the success of the so-called Nationalist Movement. At one time, in the winter of 1926–27, there seemed a possibility that the Nationalists might go "Left," and bring most of China under a régime not dissimilar to that of Russia. By the spring of 1927, however, it was clear that the pendulum had swung the other way. Chiang Kai-shek and the Nationalist leaders preferred the fleshpots of Shanghai, with its wealthy native and foreign capitalists, to the Spartan fare of Bolshevism. The Soviet advisers were forced to flee homewards, and the eastern expansion of Bolshevism thus shared the fate of its western predecessor, which no doubt gave strength to Stalin's less adventurous policy that the U.S.S.R. should henceforth "cultivate its own garden," and that the best means of revolutionary "propaganda" would be the establishment of a prosperous Socialist Republic where everyone could be happy and comfortable but no man might exploit another.

.   .   .   .

Undismayed by my faulty handling of the Polish War story I still believed that my three months in the Baltic made me an authority on the Russian problem. The only justification for this, and it is a poor one, is that most other people knew even less than I did, and that the "real experts," that is the foreigners whether civil or military who had known Russia in the old days, were so utterly discredited by being consistently wrong during the whole three years of the Soviet Government's existence that I had some reason to think my guesses were as good as theirs, or better. It is one of the strangest things about Russia, and is true to this day, that nine out of ten of the foreigners who go there immediately feel that they, and only they, know all about it. Fully half of them, it seems, rush straight into print to express their new-found knowledge, and what is still more remarkable, most of the books they write are no worse than the maturer conclusions of more seasoned or less hasty observers.

As Paul Sheffer, who for three or four years was the best of the foreign correspondents in Moscow, once remarked, "To know about the Soviet Union properly you must stay here ten days or ten years." This was more than a mere *boutade* or wise-crack, because first impressions are unusually sharp in the U.S.S.R., whose great and startling differences from life in Capitalist countries are at once apparent on the surface. It is only when the visitor begins to go deeper that he gets lost in a maze of paradox and contradiction. As time passes, too, his sympathies become involved on this side or on that, to the detriment of his critical faculty. And his judgment is warped by the myriad discomforts and minor annoyances of Moscow life, which a newly arrived foreigner either expects, and so discounts, or ignores in the novelty and interest of what he does and sees. Unfortunately, Sheffer himself did not complete his ten years' stay because he took up the cudgels for the Right opposition and peasant individualism against Stalin and the Collective Farm Movement. As he had previously espoused with equal warmth the cause of Trotzky and the "Left" opposition, the authorities decided that he was prejudiced and refused him permission to return to Moscow after a vacation at the end of his fifth or sixth year in the U.S.S.R.

I spent the twelve months following June, 1920, to 1921, in Paris and found life dull. I have always thought that a foreign correspondent's office ought to be under his hat, with a cubby-hole somewhere to park the hat and a typewriter, and meet people on occasion. A desk and a telephone and one or two assistants and a good man for night work—that's all an American newspaper really needs in any European capital. The upkeep would be trifling and the paper could spend its money on salaries and cable tolls. Actually the practice was just the opposite. The American newspapers were full of money after the War, and Paris—for that matter all Europe—was full of American newspaper men who had been covering the War, with the result that the big papers took showy, expensive offices, and filled them with reporters who trod on each other's feet, stenographers, filing clerks, messengers and attendants, and then introduced a bookkeeping department to take care of the whole show. The work, of course, was done by three or four men, the boss and two assistants and a night man, and the rest of them just used up money. In the big Paris bureaus the overhead, what with rent and all, must have averaged $2,000 a month, without counting the salaries of the men who really did the work. The head of the bureau became an executive instead of a reporter, and half his time was taken up with office detail. Most of the bureau heads seemed to like it, because they felt it increased their shadow to have a fat staff and a lot of space, and, of all things, a reading-room for people who come in and grumble that the files are not kept right, and plague you with fool questions. I say that a foreign reporter does not need an office like that, that he ought to be running about instead of sitting at a desk, and as for increasing my shadow with a lot of incumbrances, I'd prefer an increase in salary. Some people say it advertises the paper, but *The New York Times*, for instance, doesn't need to be advertised in Paris, or anywhere else.

The worst of all this show business was that one was expected to keep regular office hours, though what there was to do when you got there except sit and chew the rag I never could find out. A foreign correspondent is, or ought to be, on the job any hour in the twenty-four, that is to say meeting people and seeing things and keeping his ears open, but the actual "work" he does —desk work—is only the forty minutes or so it takes to write his story. I know it is gratifying for the big shots of the home office to come and find large expensive premises in the center of town, and an air of bustling activity, but you'd think they would see that from a business point of view it is mostly wasted motion and wasted money.

So I began pestering New York to give me a job in the field somewhere, and finally got from them a promise that if and when Russia opened up I could have the job. Several of us American reporters had tackled Litvinov on the subject at Dorpat in October, 1919, but he wouldn't hear of it. He said that the Soviet did not want *bourgeois* reporters, that it had suffered enough already from lies and slander in the Capitalist Press. I replied that that was just the reason for having correspondents in Moscow, where they could see the truth for themselves, instead of forcing them to stay outside and get their information about the Soviet from its bitterest enemies—Riga, Warsaw, Helsingfors, and so forth. But Litvinov was impervious to argument, although he had the grace subsequently to admit that I was right. Not that he has really changed his mind much; in 1919 he thought the foreign Press was an unnecessary nuisance and later admitted it was a necessary nuisance, but he has always thought it was a nuisance.

At last in July, 1921, luck broke my way in the shape of the great Russian famine, which then threatened to cost about 30,000,000 lives, and probably did cost 5,000,000 or 6,000,000 including deaths from disease. The Russians appealed for foreign help, and Hoover's American Relief, which had done magnificent work during the War in Belgium and afterwards in Eastern Europe, stepped forward to meet the emergency on the scale it warranted. Many hard things have been said about Mr. Hoover—some of them by me as far as that is concerned— but I take off my hat with a low bow to his Relief Administration.

From every point of view they were a splendid set of men, efficient, honest, friendly and intensely loyal to each other and to The Chief, as they called him. The original crowd were all hand-picked, and although later when the A.R.A. (American Relief Administration) expanded in Russia, one or two black or wandering sheep slipped into the organization, they did not last long, and never interfered with its smooth and competent functioning. From its start in Belgium in the winter of 1914–15 to its finish in Moscow in the summer of 1923, the A.R.A. did its job, often in circumstances of great delicacy, difficulty, and actual danger, with a maximum of success and minimum of cost. Its overhead was cut to the bone, and the management was so good and economical that ninety-eight and a half cents of every dollar subscribed reached the recipients of relief in the form of food or supplies. As the A.R.A. bought wholesale in immense quantities, any American youngster who subscribed a dollar could legitimately reckon that some Belgian or Polish or Russian child would get for that dollar as much food as he himself could have bought for a dollar and a quarter in America.

The A.R.A., represented by one of Hoover's chief Lieuten-
ants, Walter Lyman Brown, negotiated a regular treaty with the
Soviet Government, represented by Litvinov, in August, 1921.
I had received a cable at the end of July to go to Riga to cover
the negotiations, which lasted about three weeks, and be prepared to enter Russia when they were concluded. The A.R.A.
had stipulated that American *bourgeois* correspondents should
be allowed to report the Relief work.

On the American side the chief point at issue was to make
sure that no food should anywhere be diverted from famine
sufferers. There was a fear in America, which proved to be
groundless, that somehow or other the Red Army or the Cheka
would get the food, and the children be left to starve. Litvinov,
on the other hand, was chiefly concerned lest the A.R.A. should
use its food supplies for political purposes, not to mention the
possibility of espionage by American Relief workers, although
what there was for them to spy out, except in literal truth the
"nakedness of the land," we were at a loss to imagine. He
startled Brown one day by saying explosively, "You do not
understand that food is a weapon." As a matter of fact there
was truth in this remark, as the Bolsheviks had reason to know,
because the head of the A.R.A. in Budapest, one Captain Gregory, had undoubtedly made political use of his food supplies
against Bela Kun's Red Government. I do not say that this was
the prime cause of Bela Kun's downfall, but it contributed no
little, and to make matters worse Gregory published a series of
articles, I think in the *World's Work*, saying so proudly, at the
very time when the Riga negotiations were in progress. However, an accord was reached in the last week of August, and to
the credit of both sides be it said that it operated smoothly and
effectively throughout the two years of A.R.A. work on Russian
soil. There were, of course, minor cases of friction, but the

only serious trouble that occurred, in the spring and early summer of 1922, was due to transport difficulties, complicated by
Soviet red tape, rather than to any defect in the "treaty" itself.

The Soviet had a permanent "Mission" in Riga by this time,
what we should call a legation, although as a matter of fact the
Bolsheviks make no distinction between legations and embassies
in their Foreign Service, and instead of being called Minister
or Ambassador their representative is always entitled Plenipotentiary. I made friends with the Press officer, a bright young
man named Markov, who had been born and educated in England. He was the first real Bolshevik I had talked to in a
friendly way, and I liked him very much. He had served with
distinction in the Civil War, and had courage, loyalty and
brains. He told me at first that I had small chance of getting
into Russia no matter what the outcome of the A.R.A.-Litvinov
negotiations, because of the stuff I had written from Riga two
years before about the Comintern courier. But Markov proved
more amenable to my arguments than Litvinov had been, and
finally understood not merely that I had written the courier
story in good faith and that the documents were perfectly genuine, but, more important, that any self-respecting reporter tries
to write the truth as he sees it, and that, although like most
foreigners I had been prejudiced against the Bolsheviks, this
did not necessarily mean that I would send untrue or unfair
reports from the Soviet Union. The question of my getting a
visé was clinched, unless I am mistaken, by a story I wrote on
the 12th of August about the new N.E.P. decree, which was
published in the *Pravda* on August 9th and reached Riga two
or three days later. Markov not only translated the decree for
me but explained what it meant and why, and I had a big exclusive story on the subject which I remember began with the sensational (and, as events proved, incorrect) phrase, "Lenin has
thrown Communism overboard." If I had inserted the word

"temporarily" it would have been all right, but at that time all non-Communists in Russia, and for that matter a good many Communists too, paid little attention to Lenin's statement that N.E.P. was "a tactical retreat to prepare for a fresh advance later," and believed instead that it marked the turn of the tide back to Capitalist "normalcy." My story was regarded in Moscow as objective (a Soviet word of praise), fair, and more accurate than they had any right to expect from a *bourgeois* reporter, so that I was gratified to find myself one of a group of a dozen American correspondents who left Riga for Moscow two or three days after Litvinov and Brown had signed their treaty.

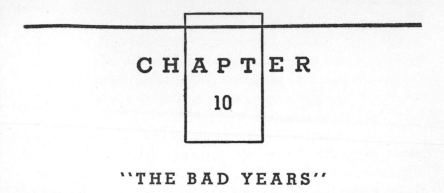

CHAPTER 10

"THE BAD YEARS"

So WE came to Moscow, five days in a hard car on a train which provided no light, food or bedding, with nearly a full day's wait on the frontier where unsmiling Red officials minutely examined our suit-cases and bed rolls and portable typewriters and boxes of canned food. They took nothing away and charged no duty, and if they had any thoughts on the subject they kept them to themselves. The Soviet Mission in Riga had said that we should be met at the terminus in Moscow, and we all believed that the Cheka would encompass us by day, and perhaps by night, with a host of spies in the guise of interpreters—feminine, alluring and dangerous. There was not even a porter at the station, so we piled our baggage out on the platform and sat on it like castaways on a desert island. This blank neglect was a douche to our illusions. Finally we decided that Mohammed would go to the mountain, and the sole colleague who spoke Russian plunged into the railroad Cheka office while the rest of us bunched round the door gaping at the first snappily dressed officer we had seen. He explained that no one met anyone in Moscow because they never knew when the trains would arrive. At the time I thought this was a sinister evasion but later found it was true enough. After a lot of conversation it appeared that the Foreign Office would send a motor truck for us. It came at last, and round-faced young Cheka soldiers helped us load the baggage, grinning ready acceptance of American cigarettes. We clambered aboard the truck which plunged ahead, rolling like a ship at sea amongst the holes and hummocks of the ill-paved streets.

The Foreign Office, or anyway its Press Department, was located at the corner of Theatre Square in the center of town behind the Metropole Hotel, and it was a seedy spot. We parked the truck in front of the broken porch, and someone asked whether our baggage would be all right there. A fat youth from the Press Department who had come with a truck and spoke some English, fired a burst of Russian at the driver, who pulled out a big revolver and waved it carelessly around. We wandered through a lot of dirty corridors to the room of the Press chief, which was bare but cleaner. He seemed affable, although his eyes did not match, and he spoke fluent East-side New Yorkese. He read out our names and when he came to mine he said, "Oh, yes, Mr. Duranty, I know you; they nearly put me in jail in New York two years ago on account of the cables you sent from Riga." In relating this incident I claim that I replied coolly, "Well, now you will have a chance to turn the tables," and that he said, "In Soviet Russia we do not put innocent men in prison," with the accent on "innocent." But I won't swear that's true. I do know, however, that one of my colleagues felt the official's eye upon him and cried hastily, "I'm not Duranty," to which the official retorted with more firmness than exactitude, "I know Mr. Duranty, I'm looking at him," and pointed to me.

We talked about going to the Volga to see the Famine, and the Press chief said vaguely that he thought it could be arranged "in a few days." Then someone asked where were we to stay and how should we get interpreters and, more urgently, what about lunch? It was then 3 P.M. and we had eaten nothing since breakfast. The Press chief was vaguer still. We were free to go where we pleased and get what interpreters we pleased and eat what we pleased. We might not know it, he said, but Soviet Russia was a free country despite lies in the Capitalist Press. Again he squinted furiously at me, and the colleague on my left jumped as if he'd sat on a pin. Finally there was a lot more telephoning and we learnt that we could have rooms in the Savoy Hotel.

Well, there *were* rooms and some of them had bedsteads, without bedding or mattresses, and a rickety table and chair or two. The electric light worked in most of them; so, surprisingly, did the telephone, but there was no running water anywhere. The only water in the hotel was for making tea in the morning, a kettleful per person, from a boiler in the kitchen, and they served no food. The rooms, though bare, were far from empty, rats and mice galore and outrageous swarms of every kind of vermin. All this, as the Press chief said, was free, gratis and without charge. Long polyglot inquiries elicited the fact that there was "a" private restaurant open, somewhere in the Arbat, wherever that might be, a long way off, the speaker waved his arm. He said it was the only private restaurant in Moscow, but we got there at last. footsore and weary, and had a good dinner. The proprietor spoke French and English and had two or three nieces or cousins or what not as waitresses, who eagerly volunteered to serve us as interpreters.

The city was incredibly broken and dilapidated. Physically and morally it reminded me of Lille when the French troops entered it in October, 1918, after four years of German occupation. There was the same air of exhaustion, bedragglement, misery—and hope. Looking back to-day it is not easy to realize that the first four years of Bolshevism were not much less repugnant to Moscow than the German occupation to Lille. Moscow was essentially a business city, and the period of Militant Communism had reduced business to nothing. One forgets, too, that in the early years of the Revolution the Bolsheviks were a small minority enforcing a new and unwelcome system.

It is hard for Westerners to understand how much "upkeep" our modern cities require. You can take a medieval European castle and besiege it for fifty years, and unless you smash it with high explosives there will be little outward change in its heavy walls and casement windows, but the structure of a modern city is more delicate. Light, heating, water-mains and drainage, the clearing away of refuse and the maintenance of public services all are part of an elaborate complex.

Moscow in 1921 was a strange hybrid between a modern city and a village. There were fine buildings, street-cars, electric lights, telephones, gas- and water-mains, drainage and public services of all kinds, side by side with wooden cottages of the seventeenth century, and the latter had suffered least. The contrast alone was startling but it was nothing to what we felt when our motor truck lurched out of the station yard into what had been a wide *boulevard* with its central trolley track and handsome houses on either side. The street was full of holes where water-mains had burst or where there had been digging in the attempt to clear choked drains. For two and a half years at least there was no running water in Moscow. Can you imagine what that means, you New Yorkers? And no steam heat, in a climate where thirty below zero occurs almost every winter. Somehow they kept the street-cars running and I don't think there was anything I saw which affected me so horribly. They were free of course; everything was free in Moscow in those days—if you could get it—and they looked like long, dingy boxes on both ends of which bees had swarmed; but the bees were human beings hanging on to each other. At one point where we stopped I saw a street-car start with a jerk and three or four of the human swarm rolled headlong in the dust. No one paid attention or even laughed. Further on at a corner the tail of a truck just flicked the edge of a similar swarm and knocked them off like insects. Some got up limping and one, a woman, lay where she had fallen. And no one seemed to care.

Little less horrible was the aspect of the houses. A big six-story building, each of whose sixty windows was defaced by a tin stove-pipe with an ugly black flare of smoke on the stone-work above—that's what Moscow had come to when its central-heating broke down and there was no more wood for the big Dutch tiled stoves, which had warmed Russian homes before central-heating was introduced. People built themselves little stoves of brick in each room, or three or four to a room if it was a big one, and burnt what they could, beams and framework from broken houses, green wood from the parks and woods around the city, their own furniture, and last, their floors and doors. I heard of a buhl cabinet whose owner had been a famous collector and loved it and kept it, and knew its value, which ran into thousands of dollars, but it went up in smoke at last, and after it the flooring of his room, which followed soon. Then the poor citizen died of pneumonia from sleeping on the damp earth and they only found him by accident weeks later, frozen stiff. When the Muscovites called 1919 and 1920 the hard years they knew what hardship meant. I myself saw a Persian prayer-rug, which Fifth Avenue would sell for $500 any time, depression or not, cut into a sort of kilt for a little girl with its fringes hanging down in front and behind.

When a window got broken they nailed a board across because there was no more glass. Later they took the board for fuel and sealed up the window with clay and bricks. There were plenty of bricks in Moscow for anyone to take from the houses that were smashed in the revolutionary fighting, and from the larger number that were gutted by fire when there was no water to quench the flames, and from others which had fallen down through age and lack of repair. Two weeks after I got there a row of houses at the other side of Theatre Square opposite the Foreign Office collapsed suddenly one night, just fell to pieces, burying two score people in the ruins. The *Pravda* gave this item three lines and said something ought to be done about it.

Life in Lille was hard enough under the German occupation, but I cannot believe that the inhabitants of any great city in modern times suffered so much as those of Moscow. The struggle for sheer existence was so grim that people became callous and indifferent. There was one Englishman in our party, rather serious-minded and full of moral values, who hadn't seen the War and still believed what they had taught him at school. One day he went out walking in Moscow and met an intelligent little boy about ten years old. The brat talked English and said that he had been the main support of his family during the "bad years." My colleague asked how, and the child said brightly, "By stealing things, mostly potatoes and cabbage, it was no good stealing anything but food. Once I stole a silver teapot but all I could get for it at the market was two carrots. And once I stole a horse's head, and oh, Mister, it made good soup." My colleague was horrified, but he did not wish to hurt his little friend, so he said kindly, "Don't you know, my boy, that stealing's wrong?" To which the kid replied with a look of infinite contempt, "All the boys in my street steal, but I steal better than any of them." This is a true story and my colleague got all sad and wrought up about it, and pointed a whole row of morals, but I thought then, and think now, that he was a silly ass, and told him so, although he didn't believe me, and seemed ready to shed tears about this corruption and perversion of youth; as if the law of survival was unnatural or perverted.

I've talked a great deal to people in Moscow about the "bad years," and all of them say that the worst thing was not hunger or cold, though both were bad enough, but the breakdown of the water supply and sanitation. This was where the people who lived in the little one-story houses and wooden shacks were luckiest. They still had the primitive sanitation of the village and got their water from a well at the end of the yard, but in a big modern building the effects of this breakdown must have been appalling.

Of all that I saw that first day in Moscow I think what struck me most was the fact that no shops were open. Remember that this was a city of traders with shops everywhere, even in the residential quarters. Some of them were boarded up, but in most cases the boards had been torn away for fuel and you saw empty windows or no windows at all, just holes, like missing teeth. I drove and walked that first day through six or seven miles of Moscow streets, and along the whole route only three kinds of shops were open, and mighty few of them: barber shops or had-been beauty parlors with grinning wax dummies in the windows; stores that sold scientific paraphernalia like sextants and microscopes and theodolites and surveying instruments and geographic globes and T-squares and boxes of compasses and measuring tools, which apparently the State had not cared to requisition; thirdly, little dingy stores with cabbages and potatoes and wizened pears and apples.

The people looked less hungry than I had expected, but their clothes were amazing. Of course, being summer, most of them wore cotton or canvas, or similar light materials, all of which were dirty because there was no soap to wash them. But one saw plenty of peasant sheepskins with the tanned hide outwards and hundreds of home-made garments which had obviously been sewn together from blankets and curtains or even carpets, like the little girl with her Persian prayer-rug. The clothes were dirty and the people were dirty, but they did not look aimless or disheartened. On the contrary, they were all bustling about like ants, most of them with a bundle or some other object in their hands or on their shoulders, and there was a light of hope and eagerness in the majority of faces, because, as I found later, the long winter of Militant Communism had ended, the icy bonds that had frozen the life and activities of the nation were broken and the warm sun of N.E.P. was stimulating it to new effort and activity.

.   .   .   .

N.E.P. (New Economic Policy) was introduced by Lenin in the summer of 1921. The formal decree inaugurating the new policy was not published until August 9th, but its most important feature, that of "free" or unrestricted trade, had been tacitly admitted since the spring. Both in Russia and abroad N.E.P. was regarded as a reversal of policy, which indeed it was, but it was also a reversion to policy. It reversed the policy of Militant Communism which had been enforced since the early part of 1918, but it also reverted to the original principles by which Lenin was guided when the Bolsheviks seized power in November, 1917. This sounds paradoxical, but it can be explained by a brief historical retrospect.

In point of fact, the very phrase "when the Bolsheviks seized power" is misleading. It would be more correct to say "when the Bolsheviks picked up from the ash-heap the neglected scepter which had fallen there," so complete was the anarchy which had followed the downfall of the Tsar. The period from the Tsar's abdication in March to Lenin's advent in November was hailed abroad as the dawn of liberty and democracy in Russia. In reality it was a time of growing chaos. When the Tsarist Empire broke under the strain of the War and by its own incompetence and the corruption of its core, there was nothing left to take the place of its highly centralized authority. The efforts of would-be Liberals like Prince Lvov and Professor Miliukov to create a democratic régime overnight were no more successful than those of their more revolutionary successors, Cheidze and Kerensky. The truth of the matter is that Russia was unfitted, or at least

unready, for a democratic system, as Kerensky sourly acknowl-
edged on the eve of his flight from the country he had tried to
rule. "No self-government is possible," he said, "for a nation
of newly liberated slaves."

There was, however, a curious anomaly in the Tsarist Empire
in that, although highly centralized politically, it had little economic centralization. An undeveloped, industrially backward
and mainly agricultural country, Russia was subject to foreign
influence in finance and mechanized industry. The War threw
both into confusion, especially after the German advance cut
off from the Empire the industrial centers of Poland and the
Baltic States. It is not generally realized abroad how intensely
local were production and commerce under the Tsars, but it is
safe to say that more than two-thirds of the food and goods produced and consumed by the Tsarist population were of local
origin. More than ninety per cent of the population lived in
villages and small towns. The food they ate was produced on
tiny peasant holdings which would not be dignified by the name
of farms in the United States, and the goods they consumed were
mainly the product of homecraft, of individual artisans or small
coöperative groups. The result was that the political paralysis
which followed the downfall of Tsarism did not have its economic counterpart, at least not with the same degree of rapidity
and acuteness. To a greater extent than in any other European
country the villages and towns of Russia were self-supporting
economic units.

No soil could have been less propitious for an experiment in
Marxian Socialism, which its founder had predicted upon a
highly developed industrial system with its corresponding centralization of finance and commerce. There is no reason to doubt
that Lenin was well aware of this in November, 1917, whatever
may have been the dreams of his more fanatic followers. Far
from attempting immediately to introduce wholesale Socialism,

his initial policies aimed at coöperation, not only with finance, industry and commerce, but with the various departments of the Provisional Government. Arthur Ransome, one of the few foreign newspaper men in Russia who knew what was going on in the autumn of 1917, once told me of Trotzky's first contact with the officials of the Foreign Office in Petrograd after his appointment as Commissar of Foreign Affairs. Trotzky summoned the whole staff to a large central hall and after announcing briefly that the new Government would take immediate steps towards peace, not only for Russia but for all the warring nations, he said, "We propose also to begin the work of national reconstruction, in which I call upon you to help me. We shall not tolerate incompetence or disloyalty but any of you who are willing to work with us will be allowed to do so." He left them to consider the matter and within an hour they all informed him that they would not dream of coöperating with the revolutionary Government of workers, peasants and soldiers. The same thing occurred in other departments, although the Ministry of Justice was for a time an exception. In consequence the Bolsheviks were compelled to improvise a new governmental system. They had no more success with the banks and large factories; at best they were met with sullen acquiescence and passive resistance, at worst by sabotage and active hostility. Here again they replied with confiscation and the replacement of recalcitrants by their own inexperienced staffs.

The Bolsheviks understood that their first and most important task was to reëstablish a strongly centralized authority, so that, apart from other considerations, they would have naturally preferred economic coöperation with the representatives of finance and industry, at least until the executive control of the country was assured. But they had no choice in the matter. As latent opposition hardened they were driven even further and faster forward along the path of "nationalization" of private enterprise.

In this respect, too, it is probable that the zeal of the rank and file of the party and of its supporters among the working-class population outran the wishes of the leaders. The campaign of assassination launched by the Terrorist group of the Socialist Revolutionaries in the summer of 1918, to which Lenin so nearly fell a victim, and the outbreak of the Civil War, made all further compromise impossible. Henceforth the Bolsheviks were committed to a policy of nationalization *à outrance*.

There thus began the period of "Militant Communism," as it was termed abroad, although the Russians themselves are more correct in describing it by the less aggressive word "Military," that is, pertaining to and made necessary by war. The confusion caused by the nationalization process and the failure of untrained workers to manage the banks and factories, not to mention the railroads and other forms of transportation, rapidly produced an economic crisis in the cities and larger towns. In an attempt to prevent the prices of food and other essential commodities from sky-rocketing, the Bolsheviks introduced laws of increasing severity against "speculation," whose final effect was almost completely to abolish private trade. Meanwhile the exigencies of war necessitated requisitions of food and other supplies from the peasants. At first, it is true, the peasants were "paid" with salt, kerosene, and manufactured goods; then, as supplies became exhausted, with paper promises of goods. Finally the requisitions became arbitrary and often brutal, which roused widespread resentment in the villages. The peasants for the most part had believed that the Revolution would assure them outright possession of the land, and were exasperated to find that the Soviet State had taken the place of the old régime or of private proprietors. The laws restricting speculation were soon extended to the smaller towns and villages, and the local production of goods and foodstuffs dwindled accordingly.

The development of Militant or Military Communism was

hurried by two mutually stimulating factors—one material, the other psychological. On one hand circumstances, sabotage, opposition, speculation, military necessity, and the attempt to create a strong centralized authority drove Lenin and the Bolshevik leaders towards the Communistic system; on the other the rank and file of the Bolshevik Party, less far-sighted but more enthusiastic, rushed the process of nationalization, the suppression of private trade and the requisitions from the peasants, in the ardent belief that they were thus hastening the Communist millennium.

The ravages of Civil War increased economic distress and disintegration. There was not much heavy fighting, but a vast amount of looting and raiding and often wanton destruction, not only of food and goods, but of the means of producing either. By the spring of 1920, after two years and a half of Soviet rule, the situation was almost the exact opposite of what it had been in November, 1917. Political anarchy had been replaced by order and a strong central authority had been restored; but economic self-sufficiency had vanished. The production of food had fallen to a minimum, commerce was utterly stagnant, and the wheels of industry had ceased to turn.

The Polish War might well have been the last straw to break the back of the overburdened Russian camel, but the Bolsheviks, as they showed repeatedly during those cruel years, were never so active and determined as when their cause seemed desperate. The spirit of national patriotism aroused by the Polish invasion enabled them to rally the country's flagging energies. Despite its defeat before Warsaw, the Red Army had enough vigor left in the winter of 1920 to turn savagely against Wrangel, the last of the White generals on Soviet soil, and fling him out of the Crimea into the sea.

The Bolsheviks had triumphed; their authority and their Communist system (Military or Militant) was everywhere established, but the cost had been terrific. Not only Moscow and the urban centers, but the whole country had been reduced to destitution, misery and semi-starvation, with the added scourge of pestilence to work greater havoc than the sword of war. There exists documentary evidence to show that Lenin had sweeping reforms in mind at the beginning of 1921, but before they could be formulated popular discontent with intolerable conditions flared out in a revolt of the Red fleet at Kronstadt. The revolt was suppressed by force, and the Bolsheviks ascribed it to the wiles of counter-revolutionary agitators, but for Lenin it was the Writing on the Wall. The echoes of the shots which "liquidated" the Kronstadt mutiny had hardly died away before a fresh and more dangerous outbreak occurred in the Province of Tambov, where the peasants began forcibly to resist the food requisitions. This, too, was described as rebellion fomented by Social-Revolutionaries, but troops sent to suppress it made common cause with the rebels. Lenin acted without delay. He ordered the requisitions to be stopped, and rushed into the affected area supplies of kerosene, salt, tools, clothing and other commodities most urgently needed by the peasants, and had them sold in the village markets, which had almost ceased to exist during the period of Military Communism. By sheer force of personality Lenin forced the Communist Party Congress, then in session, to a tacit acceptance of the reopening of markets on a "free trade" basis elsewhere, and informed it that the unpopular requisitions would henceforth be replaced by a tax in kind, "the single food tax," which should average ten to fifteen per cent of the total annual crop. When the Congress ended, it was committed to a new economic program that would sweep away much of the artificial Communism of the past three years.

During the years of discussion that followed, Lenin held to his new line with unswerving resolution, and it is significant in the light of future events that Stalin followed him implicitly,

whereas Trotzky, Bukharin and other leaders who had hitherto
overshadowed Stalin in popular esteem, voiced theoretical, ideological, one might almost say theological, objections to Lenin's
logic of facts. "Facts are stubborn things," Lenin told them. "If
you do not agree with me, go out through the country and see
for yourselves. The cities and towns are starving and the peasants refuse to produce more food than they need. For the time
being the peasants have beaten us; we have no choice save retreat. One day we shall resume the advance, but now retreat is
not only wise but imperative. The time element is against us.
We cannot yet give the peasants what they want in our way, so
we must give it them in their way." Stalin echoed his words, as
five years later, in 1926, he echoed them again when he refused
to admit that the time was ripe for the expropriation of the
kulaks (richer peasants) advocated by Trotzky and the "ultra-
Lefts." Stalin had played an important rôle in the Civil War,
although Trotzky won greater glory at home and abroad, but his
support of Lenin in the N.E.P. controversy marked him out as
a coming man and did much to secure for him the appointment
as General Secretary of the Communist Party, which was the
foundation of his subsequent success.

The essential feature of N.E.P. was that it allowed the free
buying and selling of goods by any individual, that is to say,
private trade, which had been almost wholly suppressed during
the Communist period. In consequence it offered a great stimulus to production. It brought other important changes such as the
introduction of piece-work, a sealed system of wages, income
and other taxes, and of course payment for public services like
street-cars, trains, theaters, and so forth, which had been nominally free before. Finally it allowed a limited traffic in money
by individual groups, and unlimited individual production of
goods, even small-scale factory production. N.E.P. was thus definitely a reversion to Capitalism, at least to the outward forms

of Capitalism. Nevertheless, Lenin from the outset intended it to be only a temporary reversion and, what is more, it was only a partial reversion, inasmuch as control of the main sources of production and means of production, transportation, big finance and big industry, and of mines and other natural resources was retained in the hands of the State.

In short, N.E.P. was an expedient to stimulate paralyzed initiative and revive moribund commerce, to renew the confidence and loyalty of the peasants, and to set turning again the motionless wheels of industry. It had also important social effects in restoring the influence and power of Money for the benefit of private managers, traders, middle-men and producers to the detriment of Communist officials, soldiers, policemen and the working masses.

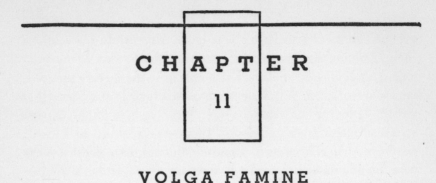

CHAPTER
11

VOLGA FAMINE

THE discomforts and difficulties of that first week in Moscow were envenomed for me and my colleagues by a purely professional matter. The Volga Famine was the biggest story of the year, but we sat there in Moscow fighting vermin and Soviet inertia, whilst Floyd Gibbons of the *Chicago Tribune* was cabling thousands of words a day from the Volga cities, beating our heads off and scoring one of the biggest newspaper triumphs in post-War history. Every day we received anguished and peremptory cables from our home offices about the Gibbons exploits, and all we could do was to run bleating with them to the Press Department and be told, "We are making arrangements; there will doubtless be a train for you to-morrow." It was an agonizing experience, but there was nothing we could do about it but gnash our teeth and wait.

Floyd fully deserved his success because he had accomplished the feat of bluffing the redoubtable Litvinov stone-cold. It was a noble piece of work. As the Brown-Litvinov negotiations in Riga were drawing to a close, Floyd Gibbons arrived like a Herald Angel on a big private plane he had chartered in Berlin from a German pilot-owner, and made loud inquiries at the Lettish air headquarters for extra supplies of oil and fuel, concentrated foodstuffs and maps of Soviet Russia. Then he "went to

ground" in a suite in Riga's best hotel. Meanwhile his minions
—the *Tribune* had two or three men in Riga—went about muttering mysteriously of daring plans. Within three days the trick
began to work, and Litvinov summoned Floyd to the Soviet Legation. "I learn," he said severely, "that you are contemplating
an act of deplorable rashness." There was a gleam in Floyd's
good eye, then it became as expressionless as the patch he wears
over the other's empty socket, a souvenir of a German machine-
gun bullet.

"I don't know what you're talking about," he said coldly.

Litvinov put a deprecating finger to his nose. "This is a small
town," he said, "and we have ways of hearing things. Your
secret has leaked out, Mr. Gibbons, and I know that you intend
to fly to Moscow and try to land on the Red Square."

Floyd simulated confusion, but said nothing.

"Do you realize," continued Litvinov, pursuing his advantage,
"that you will probably be met by a hail of bullets, and that if
you should succeed in landing you will be immediately imprisoned?"

Floyd muttered something about a white flag and a friendly
spirit.

"Nonsense," said Litvinov brusquely. "You cannot risk your
life like this, and besides, it might create an unfortunate incident at this stage of the negotiations."

"Then I knew I had him," says Floyd, "and shot the works."

He spoke bitterly of secret agents tracking reporters and of
his duty to the *Tribune* to be first with the news, of his contempt
for personal danger and his determination to let no thought of
risk interfere with his appointed mission. He was eloquent; and
Litvinov was convinced. He believed that Floyd really meant to
fly at once to Moscow. As it happened, he had just granted visés
to two American correspondents of distinctly "pink" sympathies who were to leave the following day, without waiting, like

the rest of the *bourgeois* reporters, for negotiations to end. He told this to Gibbons and added, "Suppose you went with them and abandoned your dangerous enterprise."

Floyd stuck it out. He would require the plane, he said, for visiting the Volga. In the *Tribune's* code, speed came first of all. Litvinov spoke hopefully of special trains, and Gibbons yielded with reluctance.

He reached Moscow a full week and the Volga ten days before the rest of us, and his exclusive stories of the Famine were reproduced in thirty-five countries of the world. Neither of his "pink" colleagues thought of sending back stuff by train and messenger from the places they visited or even from some of the larger cities by telegraph, as Gibbons did, to be retransmitted by cable from Moscow, and the frantic messages their offices sent them when Floyd's stuff was burning up the cables followed them two or three days late all along their journey.

"But would you have taken a chance on flying?" I asked Floyd afterwards.

"*I* would," he said cheerfully, "but when I hired that German plane in Berlin the pilot made an absolute stipulation that on no account would he fly over Soviet territory, not even across the edge. As it was I had to put up a bond of $5,000 before he would fly to Riga."

.   .   .   .

Yet those painful days in Moscow were not wholly wasted, because I read an article in *Pravda* which gave me a key, not only to the Famine situation, but to an understanding of the Russian character. The article was written by a rather naïve Soviet correspondent who, I think, was on the same special Volga inspection train as Floyd Gibbons and his two mute colleagues and Kalinin, President of the Soviet Republic. The *Pravda* correspondent expressed surprise that there were no acute evidences of famine in the towns and villages they visited, but in each one they were told that conditions in the next village were appalling, that men, women and children were dying like flies, and that the most horrible cases of cannibalism had already occurred. "When, however," he said, "we came to this next village, things were no worse than what we had already seen, but they in turn told us that the most horrible sights and scenes were to be found somewhere else, and there is no doubt," he concluded, "that the drought has caused a complete and disastrous failure of all crops, that the death toll this winter, unless relief on the widest scale is forthcoming, may total tens of millions, but none of the appalling stories which have reached Moscow and which are current here, have yet been substantiated by facts within my knowledge and observation."

Reading between the lines of this story, I came to a conclusion which I have never had occasion to modify, to wit that the Russians are a romantic folk whose innate sense of drama is stronger than their regard for truth. The average Russian would sooner tell you what you want to hear, especially if he suspects that you want to hear something lurid, than any plain, unvarnished fact. He is not consciously lying or trying deliberately to deceive—is, indeed, indignant if accused of such— but the division in his mind between romance and reality is more nebulous than with Western nations. Or perhaps it is that the Russian is polite and strives to please. Whatever be the reason, the fact remains that if foreign visitors ask Russians for tales of horror, misery, and woe, they will hear them in full measure, pressed down and running over. If, however, the foreigner seeks evidence that the Five-Year Plan is succeeding and that all is for the best in the best of all Bolshevik worlds, the native will provide that too, a little more reluctantly, perhaps, because the Russian soul is ever prone to gloom, but with enough chapter and verse to be convincing. Few foreigners understand this quirk of the Russian character, which perhaps accounts for the fact that so many of them talk and write such preposterous nonsense about Russia. And that most of them take home from Russia the proofs of what they went to find there, whether it is paradise for the peasant and worker, or hell on earth for all.

The most illuminating story about Russia, which every foreign visitor should learn by heart before arrival, is that of the Potemkin villages. Catherine the Great's generals had conquered the Crimea and flung the Moslem power back towards Constantinople. But the cost in lives and money had been great and her Imperial Majesty was fretful. She had reached, moreover, an age when she began to wonder whether her august position did not bulk larger in the eyes of her lovers than her own maturing charms. Even Empresses are human, and her shrewd Chamberlain, Potemkin, who knew his royal mistress more intimately than any of her courtiers since Orlov's downfall, decided that she needed diversion. He proposed a triumphant excursion to the Crimea, and Catherine eagerly accepted.

Then Potemkin summoned the directors of the Imperial Theatre and the scene-shifters and the stage carpenters. Her Imperial Majesty, he said, would travel slowly in royal dignity and comfort, but they must move fast and hustle. At two-day intervals along the chosen route, say fifty miles apart, they must construct villages where a gay and happy peasantry would meet their gracious Queen with dance and song. Money, Potemkin added, was no object, and supplies and transport would be forthcoming. But if the dance and song rang false and Her Majesty was not pleased with the homage of her subjects, well, there would be a lot of vacancies in the theatrical business in the near future. History relates that Catherine was delighted by her journey and returned home enlivened by the knowledge of her subjects' happiness and love for her, their Empress.

This story should be a "must" for all students of Russian affairs, past, present or future; and there is another, more legend-

ary, but no less apt, to sharpen and complete its lesson. As
Hans Christian Andersen tells it, to the court of a great king
there came two craftsmen who set up a loom and went through
the motions of weaving cloth. The timbers of the loom were visible, but there was no sign of warp or woof or any thread. They
were weaving, they declared, a magic cloth of gold and jewels,
but only those could see it whose loyalty to their lord the King
was entire and perfect. So everyone said they saw it and vied
with each other in admiration for its beauty. Even the King
came and said he saw it too, and vouchsafed his royal praise to
the busy craftsmen. Then they went through the motions of cutting the wondrous cloth and sewing it into robes and presented
it to His Majesty for a great procession through his city. The
King and his courtiers rode forth in solemn state to the blare of
silver trumpets and the roll of drums, and all the population
bowed in wonder before their monarch and his nobles in their
shining robes. Save one small child, who cried shrilly on his
mother's arm, "But, Mummy, they are naked. Take me home."

I have been fifteen years in Russia and I wish to cast no
stones, but I still think that this tale and that of Potemkin's villages are useful baggage for the Soviet's foreign guests.

. . . .

The first Volga town I visited was Samara, and at once I
began to learn things, although I did not understand their full
significance until later. Samara was a familiar name to me
because I had met in Riga some Lettish refugees newly come
from that once rich metropolis of Volga trade. They told me
that conditions were appalling, that hordes of hungry peasants
had descended upon the city like a swarm of locusts, and they
described with graphic ghastliness how the starving mob had torn
cab horses limb from limb in the city streets and devoured the
raw and quivering flesh. I wrote this story from Riga in all good

faith, and it was printed on the front page of *The New York Times,* God help me!

When I came to Samara the first thing I saw, and smelt, was a refugee camp of about 15,000 peasants in a big open space outside the railroad station. Sure enough, these poor wretches had flocked in from surrounding villages when they knew beyond doubt that the crop had failed, when their own meager stocks of food were exhausted and they knew that to stay where they were meant swift and certain death. The adults were wan and haggard but far less dreadful than the children, who looked like spiders with fat, bloated bellies and thin, shriveled limbs. That came from eating clay and bark and refuse, which they were unable to digest.

But this was no ravening swarm of locusts rushing to devour raw flesh. Like cattle in a drought they waited apathetic for death, and like cattle there went up from their multitude a moaning of despair, wordless but incredibly mournful. They sat there in their dust and squalor, waiting for death, without food or shelter, and the only movement among them was the steady train of stretcher-bearers carrying off the dead to burial. Few, save the children, died of actual hunger, but typhus, cholera, dysentery, typhoid, and scurvy, the diseases of malnutrition, took their plenteous toll. Right across from this herd of moribund humanity there was a food market, separated from their encampment by a narrow dirt track where there lounged one policeman with a rifle. It was only a little market, the firstfruits of N.E.P.'s new private enterprise, but there was fish for sale for those who had money to buy it, and vegetables and flour and griddle-cakes fried in fat, and even roasted meat, whose savory smell was carried by the breeze across the narrow road to the camp of starving peasants, who neither moved nor seemed to care. Tear horses in pieces, these poor sheep? They lacked strength or energy to cross that narrow road or face the sentry's rifle and seize what might have been half a meal for half of them from the market's meager stocks. The local authorities gave them such rations as they could, black bread, two ounces daily, and hot water in which bones and shins of animals had boiled—you could not call it soup. No medical attendance or medicine or care, save stretcher-bearers to remove the dead, and for each one that died there came five more, trudging slowly afoot from the country-side, with the same gray dust on their clothes and beards, the same haggard eyes of disease and hunger, and the same faint languid movements of despair.

That's what happens in Russian famines, and Chinese famines too, as Pearl Buck tells in that book of hers, the good book she wrote first. When they see that the crops have failed, they drift away from their villages, not ravenous like locusts, but helpless like sheep, without goal or purpose, knowing only that it is death to remain, and perhaps a hope, however slim, of life if they move away. All along the Volga they were moving through the dust under the blank blue sky by tens and hundreds of thousands, and across the steppes of the North Caucasus and the rich black earth of the Ukraine. It is said that 5,000,000 souls took part in that dreadful exodus, moved less by hunger itself than by their knowledge of hunger to come, and that disease killed ten of them for every one who died of hunger, and killed others too, by thousands in the towns and cities to which they came with their load of pestilence and woe. The Soviet authorities reckoned, and their figures were checked by the A.R.A. and Nansen's Red Cross Relief, that upwards of 30,000,000 people were made destitute by the Great Famine of 1921, that is to say, that all this vast number would have died without relief. The Soviet claimed it fed 13,000,000 souls at the peak of its relief work, and the A.R.A. peak was 11,500,000. Nansen and the Quakers and the other aids fed 2,500,000 more, a total of 27,000,000. When I say "fed" I mean gave them a daily ration sufficient to keep them alive, if their weakened forces could resist disease. Perhaps 1,000,000 souls, most of them children, died of actual starvation—I think that figure is too high—but 5,000,000 or 6,000,000 more fell victim to epidemics.

It is easy to see how completely the Soviet authorities of the Volga towns were overwhelmed by this invasion, which might well have taxed the resources of a prosperous and efficient administration. The Soviets on the Volga were far from that, and the towns and cities of the North Caucasus and the Ukraine were in no better plight. As I have said, the most striking characteristic of all Russia at that period was exhaustion. The whole country was on the verge of succumbing to the triple strain of Civil War, Military Communism, and the attempt at management by people who lacked the necessary training, ability and experience. The spur of war and the fanatic belief in the rightness of the Communist Cause had kept them going before, although hundreds were broken by excessive effort; but once the pressure was relaxed it seemed as if the whole country was paralyzed by nervous reaction. It must not be forgotten, too, that N.E.P. was bewildering and repugnant to the best and bravest Communists, especially in the provinces, where their intellectual level was often not high enough for them to understand the necessity for the New Policy and Lenin's motives in introducing it. They felt, as one of them told me, like officers of a vessel whose compass had ceased to function. "Has all this bitter struggle been in vain?" he asked me sadly, "that now when the victory seems won we are ordered to retreat and abandon what we fought for?" He did not know, as Lenin knew, what price the "victory" had cost. In the words of Tacitus, the Bolsheviks and their Military Communism had made (of Russia) a wilderness, and called it peace.

It was therefore unfair of me to be shocked, as I was shocked, by the apathy and hopelessness of the local authorities at Samara and the other Volga cities I visited, in face of the famine-refugee problem. In Samara, for instance, I went to a so-called "children's home," which was more like a "pound" for home-less dogs. They picked up the wretched children, lost or aban-doned by their parents, by hundreds off the streets, and parked them in these "homes." At the place I visited an attempt had been made to segregate those who were obviously sick or dying from their "healthier" fellows. The latter sat listlessly, 300 or 400 of them in a dusty court-yard, too weak and lost and sad to move or care. Most of them were past hunger; one child of seven with fingers no thicker than matches refused the chocolate and biscuits I offered him and just turned his head away without a sound. The inside of the house was dreadful, children in all stages of a dozen different diseases huddled together anyhow in the most noxious atmosphere I have ever known. A matron and three girls were "in charge" of this pest-house. There was noth-ing they could do, they said wearily; they had no food or money or soap or medicine. There were 400 children or thereabouts, they didn't know exactly, in the home already, and a hun-dred or more brought in daily and about the same number died; there was nothing they could do.

"At least you could make fires and heat some water and attempt to wash them, even without soap," I said indignantly, "and surely you can get some rations from the city Soviet to make soup or porridge for some of them."

The matron shrugged her shoulders, "What is the use?" she said. "They would die anyway."

At first she had tried to do something, she said, and the city had tried, but now there were too many. She suddenly stiffened into protest. "God has hid his face from Russia," she cried. "We are being punished for our sins. In one month there will not be a soul alive along the Volga. I tell you and I know." She slumped into a chair and buried her face in her hands.

I went away feeling sick, and hating myself for being healthy and well fed. There was nothing I could do either, except write the story in its naked ugliness and hope that it would move people in America and hurry their promised aid.

Everywhere we went through the stricken villages there was the same urgent cry for haste, "Enough food for a week or two weeks or a month, and after that we die. If you wish to help us, help us quickly." That was the message they gave us and we sent it; and America responded. The A.R.A. bought foodstuffs in Europe and rushed them to the ports of the Baltic and the Black Seas, and before the cargoes were unloaded its men were hurrying across Russia to take charge of distribution.

The A.R.A. followed the same system of operation in Russia as had been developed in Belgium and post-War Europe. They selected a given town in each district as the center of their work and immediately secured three sets of premises; first, living quarters and offices for their personnel; second, a depot or warehouse to store their food; third, a large hall or public building where the children were fed. I say children, because the Hoover Relief up to the spring of 1922 in Russia was given only to children, and it was not until the utter destitution of the villages in the famine-stricken area was realized in America that the A.R.A. perforce broke the child-feeding rule and began to give aid to adults also. There was no choice in the matter; it was impossible to keep children alive and let their parents die.

Nevertheless, in Moscow, Petrograd (as it was then called), and the larger towns of the famine area, the A.R.A. maintained its principle of giving meals to be consumed on the spot in the aforesaid hall or theater or what not, where it could control the ration for every recipient rather than distribute food to be taken home and cooked there. As I have said, they had to follow the latter course in the villages, but even then their system of checks and control was so thorough that all save an infinitesimal quantity of food went direct to the sufferers for whom it was intended.

In each provincial center there was formed a committee, of which the local A.R.A. chief was president, composed of representatives of the local Soviet—plus doctors and social workers irrespective of their standing with the Government or their previous positions. The Litvinov-Brown agreement enjoined that the choice of this committee should be left to the A.R.A. district chief with the proviso that he would do his utmost to coöperate first of all with the local authorities. It was further stipulated that no member of this committee might be arrested without the district A.R.A. chief being informed of the arrest and the reasons for which it was made. The agreement extended similar rights to all Russian employees of the A.R.A., whose number at the peak of the Famine was over 100,000. By employees of the A.R.A., I do not mean men and women on a salary basis, but persons engaged in the food distribution from depot clerks to sleigh-drivers, whose status was really that of volunteer workers receiving a small food allowance in return for their services.

To the credit of the Soviet authorities it is worth recording that there were hardly any infractions of the agreement about arrests, although it is true that after the A.R.A.'s withdrawal in the summer of 1923 a considerable number of men and women who had worked on their committees or served them in other capacities were arrested by the G.P.U. The Moscow Foreign Office gave a somewhat naïve explanation of these arrests. They said that the G.P.U. had had its eye on the people concerned for some time for one reason or another, but that it had refrained from arresting them in order to avoid friction with the Americans and to keep faith with the letter of the Litvinov-Brown agreement. Once, however, the A.R.A. had finished its work and withdrawn from Russian soil there was no reason why these "miscreants" and "counter-revolutionary elements" should enjoy further immunity. Mr. Hoover and all the A.R.A. headquarters in the United States waxed most indignant over these arrests, which increased Mr. Hoover's already strong prejudice against the Soviet Union, and reënforced in no small degree his unwillingness to recognize the Soviet after he became President. At the time I shared his indignation, but I am inclined to think that the Foreign Office statement, naïve as it sounded, was sincere enough. There were probably quite a number of the 100,000 Russians employed by the A.R.A. who had abused their position somehow or other, or anyway, had done enough to warrant action by the G.P.U.

Which does not mean, however, that the A.R.A. did not select its committees with the utmost care, or failed to have them approved as far as possible by the local Soviet. I was in Kazan, the capital of the Tartar Republic on the Volga, when the A.R.A. first came there, and I attended the preliminary meetings between the A.R.A. chief and the President of the Soviet at which the committee was selected. The Americans naturally wanted some people on the committee who spoke French, German or English, and these no less naturally belonged to the old régime, that is to say, to the more cultured classes rather than the proletariat. But the only point of friction which arose was with regard to a priest of the Orthodox Church. The A.R.A. district chief, who had done relief work in Belgium and Poland, declared that he made it a rule of always having a priest on his committees, not for any religious reason, but because the priest was well acquainted with the living conditions of his community. The President of the Kazan Soviet was a hard-boiled Bolshevik atheist, and a Tartar to boot, that is to say, he had been brought up in the Mohammedan faith. He would have no priest at any price. The American offered to compromise on a mullah. "No," said the Tartar, "mullahs are worse than priests." Ultimately they found an Old Believer, one of the many heretic "sects" by which the Greek Orthodox Church was surrounded. The Old Believers had been mercilessly and continuously persecuted under Tsarism, which perhaps made a difference to the Soviet President. So the Old Believer "pope" got a place on the committee, although his flock was not more than one-tenth of one per cent of the city's population.

I went with the A.R.A. district chief to look over the large modern house in the center of town which was offered him as living quarters and central office. There was some difficulty about interpreters, but we found a bedraggled old gentleman wandering aimlessly about the yard who talked French and showed us over the house. "All right," said the A.R.A. chief in English to me, "tell him to tell them that we'll take it. I and my two assistants will move in to-night and the rest of our personnel will be along in a few days; we shall provide our own food and bedding and we can see about furniture later, and about having the place cleaned up. What matters most is to get action right away." The Americans lost no time; they knew that every hour meant human lives.

As we were going away the old man caught me timidly by the arm. "Might I ask a small favor?" he said. "I have a room here; I live in the cellar with my wife and two daughters. My wife isn't strong and one of my daughters has symptoms of tuberculosis. Would it be too much to ask that we might stay here when the Americans move in? Perhaps I could be of use in some way and my second daughter speaks English. And you see," he added, "I have nowhere else to go, and am rather attached to this house, because I used to own it."

This man had been one of the chief engineers on the Moscow-Kazan Railroad. Starting life without fortune, he had worked his way up to a position of comfort and responsibility, and at the age of fifty-five had retired in prosperous circumstances and built himself this large house in the best residential part of

Kazan. Three years later the Revolution reduced him to penury through no fault of his own. I don't know what became of him later, but the A.R.A. moved him and his family from the cellar to the top floor and gave him and his daughter rations and employment, as well as medical treatment for his wife and the other girl.

A neat little parallel to this story was written by a Russian in New York, Olgin I think it was, and published in the *New Republic*. In the old days, he said, there lived in St. Petersburg a distinguished Russian General whose house had a porter's lodge at the outer gates. Every morning as the General, who was also a Baltic Baron, drove forth to his duties at the War Office the porter saluted, "Good morning, Lord Baron General." And the Baron affably waved his hand. He was a kindly man, the Baron General, and used his influence in favor of the porter's son, a likely lad of sixteen. Then came the Revolution, and the wheel of Russian society turned with it until the bottom was on top and the top became the bottom. The "likely lad" had joined the Bolshevik Party and won swift promotion, so that one day he attained the rank of General, with duties in the War Office, and was allotted quarters in the house where the General Baron had formerly resided.

The new Red General was mindful of past favors and secured for the former owner permission to live in the porter's lodge.

"And so," Olgin concluded, "each morning when the automobile from the Commissariat of War comes to fetch the 'Comrade commanding a Division' (for they no longer use the title of General in the Red Army) the Red 'General' steps into the car and says to the chauffeur, 'Good morning, Comrade Chauffeur.' And the chauffeur replies, 'Good morning, Comrade Commander,' and they drive down to the gate by which stands the former Baron General. 'Good morning, Comrade Porter,' says the young Red officer, affably, but the porter clicks his heels and salutes. 'Good morning, my General,' he replies, because he at least knows the respect that is due to a General of the War Office."

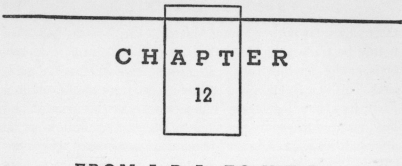

CHAPTER
12

FROM A.R.A. TO N.E.P.

Moscow had changed during my three weeks' absence on the Volga. Everywhere dilapidated and half-ruined buildings were being refurbished and restored, and the fronts of the houses cleaned and painted. Shops, cafés and restaurants were being opened in all directions. Scores of shabby one-horse victorias like the old French fiacres had appeared, and traffic on the streets had increased tenfold. The city was full of peasants selling fruit, vegetables and other produce, or transporting bricks, lumber and building materials in their clumsy, creaking carts. Suddenly goods began to appear from unexpected corners, hidden or hoarded, or perhaps if the truth were known, simply mislaid or lost in the fog of bureaucratic red tape.

For a month or six weeks after its inception N.E.P. must have seemed too good to be true to most of the people of Moscow. The population of the city had shrunk to little more than 1,250,-000 in the three "hard years." Of this number, not more than two per cent were Communists and only a comparatively few of the non-Communist working-class population received any material benefit from the new régime. It might please the working masses to be told that they were the sovereign proletariat and that every man Jack of them was better than his former Master, but these fine words did not put food in their bellies or clothes on

their backs. Of the remaining Muscovites nine-tenths had lived
before by trade, and one-tenth had been the leisured-class officials, nobles, landlords and rentiers with their servants and para-
sites. This last fraction had suffered most from the Revolution.
From its abounding luxury and power under the Tsars it had
been reduced to penury and danger. On the night following the
attempt to assassinate Lenin five hundred members of the former
ruling class in Moscow had been torn from such homes as were
left to them, attics or cellars in their former mansions, and shot
before dawn, not for any guilt of theirs but as a symbol of the
Red Terror.

For these former aristocrats and rentiers N.E.P. was a respite
from pressure, to restore perhaps a semblance of the respect
and position they had lost, and if the fates were kind, a chance
to escape abroad. To the Communists and to the small group of
proletarian leaders who had benefited by the Military Communist period N.E.P. was doubtless repugnant, but to the mass of
the workers it brought jobs that would henceforth be paid in
money instead of valueless paper or moldy rations, and the certainty that with money they could buy the food and necessities
of life that had previously been lacking. To the traders N.E.P.
meant opportunity and the dawn of better days. Until August
9th it was technically a crime to possess goods of value, gold or
silver or jewels or foreign currency, and a crime to buy and sell
anything. It is true that many people continued to own valuables
and that buying and selling was practiced more or less overtly,
even in public markets, but the latter were continually raided
to "suppress speculation" and any owner of valuables might
find himself denounced, arrested, and his property confiscated.
The N.E.P. decree changed all that, and the people of Moscow,
after a pause of bewilderment, seemed to realize N.E.P.'s possi-
bilities simultaneously, and rushed at them like famished swine
to a feeding trough.

The most striking features of N.E.P. in this early stage were its rapid acceleration, its confusion, its opportunities for quick and easy profit, and the immense stimulus it gave to employment of all kinds. Not to mention its growing contempt for the rules and restrictions which had previously been enforced by the Bolsheviks. The first twelve months of N.E.P. were like the old Roman Saturnalia, when for three days each year slaves and underlings might usurp with impunity the pleasures and privileges of their masters. Its waves, thick with greed and eagerness to tear from life the joys which had been denied so long, swept over Moscow and the rest of Russia like a flood which the Bolsheviks were powerless to check. They stood aghast before this Frankenstein of their own creation, which was changing with startling velocity laws and values they had accepted as immutable. Their leaders watched the flood and let it roll, serenely conscious that it was bringing a new silt of energy and growth to Russia's frozen soil. Others, less far-sighted, strove to resist the current and were engulfed. Some plunged into it headlong and swam lustily to capture the spoils that floated on its surface.

Ill-informed foreigners like myself naturally saw first the superficial phases of N.E.P., its reckless gambling and easy money, its corruption and license; which were real enough, but were not all the truth, because the years of N.E.P.'s flourishing, the last quarter of 1921 until the end of 1923, were also years of national recovery and development. But the seamy side was uppermost, as I soon had proof. Amongst our flock of American wage-slaves there was one white crow in the person of Herbert Pulitzer, the principal owner of *The New York World*, in whose vineyard he then chose to labor as a mere reporter. The knowledge of his wealth must have reached Moscow, for one day a Russian came to his room at the Savoy, where I was sitting, and circumlocutively invited him to buy a carload of sugar. I think the price was $1,200, and the Russian, who had a note of recommendation from the restaurant in the Arbat where we always took our meals, declared that it could be sold immediately for $5,000. There would be some small commissions, he smiled knowingly, but we could count on a clear profit of at least 200 per cent. I was interested, but the rich Pulitzer asked crudely, "Who owns the sugar now, and where is it?" "Oh," said the Russian airily, "it is Government property stored in freight-cars at one of the Moscow depots. But they've forgotten all about it, and of course some of it would go to sweeten the only official who knows anything. I assure you there is not the slightest risk."

Apart from the fact that the death penalty for theft of Government property was still in force—incidentally, after being repealed for ten years, this law was restored again in 1932, which speaks volumes—the Russian may have been right, but we said primly that we didn't believe that our papers would like us to engage in such transactions. The Russian shrugged his shoulders and retired, but we met him again that evening at the restaurant. reinforced this time by some friends and some excellent French champagne. I may add that Prohibition of all spirits, wines and beer was still in force.

Thus fortified the Russian returned to the charge and ended by borrowing half the money from us, $500 from Pulitzer, and $100 from me as a strict loan with no strings to it, to be paid without accretion in four days. He and his friends were apparently able to raise the rest among themselves. I felt badly about this the next morning and kissed my $100 good-by, although that wine was nearly worth it, but sure enough three days later the proprietor of the restaurant led us aside at lunch-time and announced that the deal had gone through and that its happy perpetrator was giving a banquet that evening in an upper room, at which, he added, Citizen Pulitzer and myself would be honored guests.

It was a big jump from the starving children in Samara to this banquet of forty covers with a dozen courses, everything from fresh caviar to peaches and coffee, from vodka and vintage wines of France and Germany to benedictine, fifty-year-old cognac and real fragrant coffee. "I can't believe it's true," said the girl on my right, as she sipped her coffee. "Do you know that in the last four years, more than half the people here tonight have been in prison, that I haven't tasted wine or coffee for more than two years, that we'd forgotten what fresh caviar looks like, and salmon and chicken and burgundy; I can't believe it's true."

Pulitzer and I were the only foreigners present. The others were Russians, nearly all Muscovites, not nobles or people of former importance, but members of what would be called in England "the upper middle class," business and professional men, engineers, lawyers and former civil servants. Our host, who had successfully handled the sugar coup (before the party began he punctiliously repaid the $600 Pulitzer and I had advanced him), was a rising barrister when the Revolution occurred, who had been exempt from military service because the law firm for which he worked was engaged in 1914 in litigation on behalf of one of the Tsar's uncles, and he was needed to plead the case, which he duly won in 1916. "I got a bonus for that of 50,000 roubles," he told us, "but it didn't make me feel half so good as the $1,000 I made from this sugar business. After the way we have lived in the last four years, it is wonderful to have a real party again."

The proprietor of the restaurant told me afterwards that the dinner cost $500 and added proudly, "I mean that was what it cost, because of course I didn't make any profit on it; these people are all friends of mine. And you know it wasn't easy to get all that wine and the caviar and coffee and things on such short notice; I had to scour half Moscow. My God!"—he interrupted himself suddenly—"do you know that a year ago to-day I was arrested because someone told the Cheka that I had five ten-rouble gold pieces hidden in my mattress. I don't know who told them, but the bastards came and took it and put me in prison because they thought I had some more. I hadn't luckily, and I suppose they believed me, because they let me out at last."

"What did you do then?" I asked.

"Oh," he said, "I went down to the country and worked on a farm. One of the peasants in the village was the brother of my mother's old cook and he was vice-president of the village Soviet and let me live in his house. It was hard work but at least I had enough to eat. And as a matter of fact that's how I came to start this restaurant. This summer before N.E.P. began I had been selling chickens and eggs and things in the Moscow market and made a little money. When the decree came out I suggested to this old peasant that he would send stuff in fresh every two or three days, the village is only thirty miles away, and that I'd give him better prices for it in my restaurant than he could get at the market, which is true. I'm making money, hand over fist, and if your friend," he nodded towards Pulitzer, "would like to take a share in a larger place, I have an option on four rooms near Theatre Square; it wouldn't cost more than 10,000,000 roubles to fix it up and start us going. We'd get that back in the first week at the rate I'm doing business here." Ten million roubles was about $2,000 at that time, and the rate was fairly stable for several months, although later it dropped rapidly as the printing-presses went to work to deal with the new volume of business produced by N.E.P. As a matter of fact the Bolsheviks cut three or more zeros off their currency every year, so that when the rouble finally was stabilized in 1924 at the ratio of 500,000 to the dollar it really should have been 50,000,000-000,000 if all the zeros had been left untouched. At the beginning of each year it was announced that the new notes of say 1,000 roubles would have the same value as the old notes of 1,000,000 roubles and it was done, as easily as that.

Everybody at the banquet, men and women, talked excitedly about business and ways, mostly dishonest or anyway illegal, of making easy money. No one seemed to bother about the hardships of the past or have any anxiety for the future. They were Russians, you see, whose racial quality it is to live intensely in the present and dismiss doubts or fears or horrid memories with the easy insouciance of children. *"Nichevo"*—"what of it" or "no matter"—has been for centuries the Russian national watchword, and the general spirit of indifference to which it bears witness is an element both of strength and of weakness. I had further proof of that before the evening was over, for after dinner they began to play *chemin de fer*. Pulitzer had an amazing run of luck, and when at last we went home about five o'clock he had won over $1,000 and held I.O.U.'s from most of the company for at least twice as much more. Few of them were paid in cash, but for weeks after he received goods, furs or pieces of jade or porcelain, a jeweled dagger or a silver teapot, from his debtors. The host rapidly lost the whole of his sugar profits but showed no signs of distress. He made $1,000 in one day and all of it had gone, *nichevo,* there was more where that came from. In his case it proved true. I didn't see him again but I was told that he made $40,000 or $50,000 in the next few months by speculation in goods, then prudently retired with it to Paris. Passes to leave Russia were easier to get than in later years, and in any case the frontiers were loosely guarded. A great deal of smuggling went on between the Soviet and Finland, Esthonia, and Latvia, and some of the smugglers would convoy passengers at a regular rate of from $150 to $250.

The restaurant proprietor was a typical case of the earlier N.E.P.-man. He began to speculate in apartments and furniture and made a lot of quick money. At one time he had a fine eight-room apartment of his own, no less than three automobiles, two mistresses and a large amount of gold, foreign valuta and jewels. His niece told me that he reckoned himself worth $100,-000 and was gradually getting it into liquid form prior to flight abroad when he was arrested by the Gay-pay-oo, which made short work of him. All his property was confiscated and he was sentenced to ten years' imprisonment on the lonely isle of Solovetsky in the White Sea.

Without going so far as to say that the authorities approved or encouraged N.E.P.'s excesses, there is no doubt that for a time they deliberately "took the lid off" in many respects. Gambling hells and night clubs had no difficulty in getting licenses from the municipality on condition that part of the receipts was reserved for the State in the same way as in the Casinos in France. It was estimated that the receipts of the Moscow Soviet from this source were 4,000,000 gold roubles in the year 1922, which was used for much-needed repairs to the streets, sidewalks, drainage and lighting systems.

The biggest gambling establishment was a place called Praga at the corner of the Arbat Square. In the main outer room there were two roulette tables both with zero and double zero, two baccarat tables and a dozen games of *chemin de fer*. Banks at baccarat frequently ran as high as $5,000, a dozen different currencies were used, from bundles of Soviet million notes to hundred-dollar bills, English five- and ten-pound notes, and most surprising of all, no small quantity of gold, Tsarist ten-rouble pieces, English sovereigns, and French twenty-franc coins. As in France, there was an "inner *cercle privé*," where only baccarat was allowed and play was higher, with banks of $25,000 or $30,000.

It was a strange sight, this Praga, in the center of the world's first Proletarian Republic. Most of the men looked like what they were, the low-class jackals and hangers-on of any boom, with fat jowls and greedy vulpine features; but there were others of a better class, former nobles in faded broadcloth and Red Army soldiers in uniform, back from fighting Moslem rebels in Central Asia or from "liquidating" Makno's anarchist movement in the Ukraine, eager for Moscow's fleshpots and a flutter at the tables. A smattering, too, of foreigners, fixers, agents and the commercial vanguard of a dozen big firms attracted by Lenin's new policy of Concessions, hurrying to find if the report was true that Russia might again become a honey-pot for alien wasps. And women of all sorts, in an amazing variety of costumes, mostly daughters of joy whom N.E.P. had hatched in flocks, noisy and voracious as sparrows. Later in increasing numbers the wives and families of N.E.P.-men, the new profiteers, with jewels on their stumpy fingers and old lace and ermine round their thick red necks. And one night I saw a grand dame of the old régime, spare and prim in a high-necked silk frock that she had worn maybe at the Court of Queen Alexandra of England. I had made her acquaintance some weeks before at the open-air market where she was selling the last of her trinkets, as she told me in fluent French. But the high-born lady took readily to commerce and found, she said, genuine satisfaction in the whirl of exchange, intrigue, and petty *combinazione* that was N.E.P. This night at Praga she opened a bank at *chemin de fer* with two English ten-pound notes, "passed" seven times with impassive countenance, then left the game with the equivalent of £1,000. *"Plus amusant que le marché et moins froid,"* she whispered as she went past me to the door, *"mais le public laisse également à desirer."*

Then there was a restaurant called "Bar" not far from the Savoy Hotel. In the winter of 1921–22 it sold good, simple meals in one large dining-room where there was music in the evenings. The following summer "Bar" blossomed out with

small private dining-rooms in sheds in a back-yard. It simultaneously acquired upstairs premises by remodeling a derelict
hotel, and an era of naughtiness began. At first clients who took
a girl friend or two to one of the private dining-rooms would
receive a modest hint from the waiter that there were rooms upstairs if they were in no hurry to go home. Then "Bar" started
a cabaret and it was understood that the artists were ready to
solace the evening of a lonely N.E.P.-man, and would doubtless
not refuse to spend the night with him. By the fall of 1922,
"Bar" was doing a roaring trade as a snappy restaurant, night
club and brothel all in one. The sale of wine and beer became
legal that year, but at "Bar" there were vodka and liquors as
well. In the winter of 1922–23 they went further and cocaine
and heroin were to be had, for a price, by clients in the know.
A merry little hell it was in the spring of 1923, although the
American colony tended to boycott it because one of our number had been robbed there in a tough and flagrant way, which
indicated all too obviously police connivance and "protection."

In the end the game was spoilt, not by police interference,
but by a tax collector who somehow nosed out the fact that
"Bar's" profits were much greater than reported. An investigation was held and within a week all the "Bar" directors were in
jail, and there were a number of arrests among police officials
of the precinct in which the place was situated. The gang had
been paying taxes on a declared profit of $1,000 a week, but
the probe revealed that the weekly profits from all sources, including dope and girls and a most remunerative sideline in
blackmail, were upwards of $10,000. I do not think any of the
people concerned in this affair were shot, and at that they were
mighty lucky, but they all received long-term imprisonment.

No better than "Bar," if less flagrant and luxurious, less
"protected" and profitable, was the Red Light district, which
sprang up near the Trubny Square off one of the *boulevards*

which encircle the city of Moscow like green belts, with their grass and trees and a broad central alley where people can walk and children play without fear of traffic. In the Trubny district there were a dozen big tenement houses, regular rabbit warrens with deep communicating cellars, which for some reason became the haunt of an alien population—Chinese, Gypsies (the celebrated Russian Tziganes), and a host of so-called students of both sexes. There were corridors in these buildings where the rank, sweet smell of opium smoke hung, one might say unnoticed, day and night, and where beside the name and number of the small cell-like rooms was tacked a photograph of its fair occupant in the scantiest of costume. Worse still were the famous "Catacombs," as they were called, the cellars and two lower stories of an unfinished brick building right in the middle of town where now stands the central post and telegraphic office. The latter building now occupies a whole city block, but in the days of N.E.P. there were only rusty ruins in the middle of a muddy field. The "Catacombs" was a notorious haunt of thugs, robbers, and the lowest street-walkers, and ten murders a week was supposed to be its average. I myself saw a corpse there in the field one morning, naked, gashed and unheeded. For a year or more its denizens lived as they pleased, with little save occasional molestation by a police squad armed to the teeth, when some unusually atrocious crime had stirred authority to action.

Yet all these sooty manifestations of N.E.P. could not hide the fact that it was a period of genuine growth and expansion. I had proof of this under my own eyes. Pulitzer and I soon wearied of the Savoy and secured from the Moscow Soviet a small apartment which had been a ruined restaurant. We got it rent free for three years on condition that we mended the floor and windows, fixed the stoves and plumbing, and generally put it in good repair as dwelling quarters. It cost us the equivalent of $1,000 if I remember rightly, and when you think that our example was being followed all over Moscow, or rather that we were following the general example, it is easy to gauge the extent of the building "boom," which always means prosperity to any city.

One morning at the top of my street I saw a man sitting on the sidewalk selling flour, sugar, and rice on a little table formed by two boards across trestles. He explained in German that his stock was part of an A.R.A. food-packet which he had received from his Finnish relatives in Helsingfors. These food-packets contained ten dollars' worth of flour, sugar, cocoa, rice and tea at American wholesale prices, which the A.R.A. delivered in Russia on order and payment abroad. In 1921 they were worth from thirty to forty dollars in Russian values, sometimes far more than that in the famine areas, and they formed the foundation of many small businesses, especially amongst the Jewish population of the southwest, where many people had relatives in America.

The Finn's venture flourished, for at the end of a week his "table" had doubled in size and he was selling fresh eggs and vegetables. That was October, and by mid-November he had rented a tiny store across the street, handling milk, vegetables, chickens and the freshest eggs and apples in Moscow at prices below those of the markets. By the following May he had four salesmen in a fair-sized store, to which peasants brought their produce fresh each morning. As his own middle-man he paid them more than they could get at the market, which he continued to undersell. In July he opened a dry-goods section, then added hardware. In October, after a year's trading, he sold out to a coöperative and returned to Finland with enough money, he told me, to buy a farm and live independently for the rest of his life. I gathered that, starting from nothing, he had made $20,000 or $30,000 clear profit, but the point is that his enterprise stimulated scores of peasants to fatten chickens and little pigs, or plant vegetables, or fashion wooden bowls and platters and forks and spoons and produce clay pots and the rest of village handcraft. The same thing was being done all over Russia and the effects were amazing. In a single year the supply of food and goods jumped from starvation point to something nearly adequate, and prices fell accordingly. This was the rich silt in N.E.P.'s flood, whereas the gambling and debauchery were only froth and scum.

CHAPTER
13

LOVE AMONG THE RUINED

In the fall of 1922 I went down to the Volga on a rather gloomy mission. The A.R.A. had been extremely lucky—and careful—with its personnel, despite the risks of infection to which they were exposed and the fact that some of its "field-workers" were alone in bandit-ridden districts, with food supplies under their control worth hundreds of human lives. One boy had died of typhus at Orenburg in the winter of 1921–22 and another was driven temporarily insane by what he saw in a region where cannibalism was rife and piles of naked corpses were heaped up in the cemeteries that same winter, awaiting burial until the ground thawed, to be torn meanwhile by starving dogs and carrion crows.

Carrion crows are one of the first things to strike a visitor to Moscow. They wake him up in the morning by their cawing and at dusk they wheel in gigantic flights over the city prior to flying a few miles southwards to the woods where they spend the night. "Now I know that I'm in Asia," a Frenchman, who had spent most of his life in the Far East, once said to me. It was his first trip to Moscow—he was traveling by the Trans-Siberian— and in the interval between trains I had taken him to the river bank to see the Kremlin, above which the crows were wheeling in serried masses. "All the way across China to the Yellow Sea,

151

you'll see crows like that; carrion crows and bugs and lice are Asia's dearest friends."

Crows grew fat in the famine year on the Volga, but although the population was starving I did not find a single case, despite inquiries everywhere, of crows being killed and eaten as food. Allowing for natural repugnance, I could not understand how a population reduced by hunger to such desperate straits as cannibalism did not kill the crows and make them into soup. I heard once in Dijon—I believe that the incident is recorded in ecclesiastical history—that the edible qualities of Burgundy snails were first discovered in a famine in the fourteenth or fifteenth century. There was a poor landless widow with four young children, but when her neighbors were dying like flies she and her brood remained rosy and well-nourished. The news came to the ears of the Lord High Abbot before whom the woman was charged with witchcraft, as nothing, it was thought, save the Powers of Darkness could account for this exception to the general hunger. On trial the woman declared that she sent her children to collect snails from the vineyards and made them into soup. There was a movement of horror amongst those present, but the widow continued boldly, "So please your Lord Abbot's Grace, the snails I warrant are God's creatures and the Devil hath no part in them. Well stewed with herbs and a nubbin of garlic they make fair and savory meat." The Abbot was broader-minded than most of the churchmen of his day, or more interested in food. He sent immediately for a dozen snails and bade the woman prepare them with herbs and garlic as she had said. As cooking proceeded the Abbot wrinkled his nose at the fragrant odor and called for a flagon of burgundy. "No witchcraft this, meseems," he cried with a sniff of anticipation, "but unless my nose betrayeth me, a most notable discovery." When the dish was ready the Abbot blessed it solemnly and sipped a spoonful, then a second. "These are indeed God's creatures," he pronounced warmly. "The woman is acquitted." Yet I could find no trace of a Russian widow bold enough to save her babes by making soup from crow.

My friend, Freddy Lyon, who was in charge of the A.R.A. station at Ufa, told me a story about the worst phase of the Volga famine. Some A.R.A. "higher-ups" from New York were making a tour of inspection in Russia and duly came to Ufa. Among them was a worthy but sentimental citizen who gushed about the unhappy Russians and the poor little starving children and what a privilege it was for Mr. Lyon to be doing this noble work for humanity and so on and so forth until Lyon said he was ready to choke him. After lunch the visitors suggested they would like to visit the cemetery. It was, said Freddy, a horrid sight, nude dead bodies piled up ten high like fagots, because the population was so destitute that every stitch of clothing was needed for the living. The visitors were sickened by what they saw, and even the gushing one was silent as they walked back to the cemetery gate. Suddenly he caught Freddy by the arm. "Look there," he said. "Is not that something to restore our faith in the goodness of God in the midst of all these horrors?" He pointed to a big woolly dog, lying asleep on a grave with his head between his paws, and continued impressively, "Faithful unto death and beyond. I have often heard of a dog refusing to be comforted when his master died, lying desolate on his grave, but I never thought to see such a thing myself." That was too much for Freddy Lyon. "Yes," he said cruelly, "but look at the dog's paws and muzzle"—they were stiff with clotted blood—"he's not mourning his master, he's sleeping off a meal. At which point," Lyon concluded his story with gusto, "that talkative guy did the opposite of sleeping off his lunch in a very thorough manner, and there wasn't another peep out of him until we put him on the train."

It may seem to a squeamish reader that Lyon had made light

of a dreadful subject, and for that matter I, too, in writing it, but he had seen worse than that, and so have I. In my own case, I supped deep of horrors in my tender youth. When I was a child in England secular books were not considered suitable reading for the young on the Sabbath Day, and their place was taken by improving works, like *Pilgrim's Progress* or, as in my home, by Foxe's *Book of Martyrs*, profusely illustrated. There was one picture which always puzzled me. A nude saint (or martyr) was stretched upon the ground, his middle covered by a tin basin from which protruded the tail of a cat, all fluffed and bushy, as cats' tails are in moments of stress. Two hard-faced men were piling red-hot coals on the top of the basin, but what this meant I could not understand. As time passed and my knowledge grew, I worried out the letter-press and learned that the cat also had to worry out its way from the impromptu oven, through the poor martyr's living flesh. I cannot believe that such things are "good" for children, but those were the days of Empire and Kipling and the White Man's Burden. No child who had absorbed Foxe's *Book of Martyrs* with his morning porridge—and survived it—need blench at anything he saw in the jungles of darkest Africa.

African jungles are a long way from Simbirsk on the Volga, the town to which I went in November, 1922. One of the A.R.A. men there named Shields had disappeared four days before. He went out for a walk about five-thirty in the afternoon and was never seen again. He did not live at the central personnel house but in an apartment with another American near the A.R.A. supply depot, of which he had been recently put in charge, and when he did not come home in the evening his friend thought that he was staying at the central house. The men there naturally thought he was in his apartment, so that it was not until the next morning that he was known to be missing and a report was made to the police. Six hours later the police came in with

Shields's hat, which they said had been found floating near the Volga bank twenty miles upstream, from which they obligingly deduced that he had gone off on a trip somewhere. I still think that such promptitude on the part of a provincial Russian police force was more suspicious than auspicious, but that was the only clew to the mystery. After two days of fruitless inquiry and an urgent exchange of telegrams with Simbirsk, Colonel Haskell, the A.R.A. chief in Moscow, decided to investigate for himself, and I went with him. The Colonel said that he would stand Simbirsk on its head to find the missing boy, and he nearly did, but his efforts were unavailing. My theory was that Shields fell a victim to the Russian habit of putting two and two together and making ten of them, of which I shall later give an instance that happened to me. Some weeks earlier several tons of sugar, worth at that time on the Volga the equivalent of $3,000 or $4,000, had been stolen from the A.R.A. supply depot. Some of the thieves were arrested just at the time that Shields, who had previously worked on quite a different job, was put in charge of the depot, and there was every reason to believe that these thieves had accomplices amongst the local authorities, possibly even in the local police. It is probable that the more influential culprits believed that Shields had been trailing the theft from the beginning, that his promotion was a reward for what he had discovered already, and that he knew enough to make things hot for them, and therefore "knocked him off" lest worse befall. That sounded logical and fitted with the hat so quickly found upstream, which seemed far, far too good to be really true. On the other hand, Shields' personal secretary, a haggard dark girl in her early thirties, was convinced that it was a *crime passionnel* and hinted darkly of an affair between the lost boy and the blonde wife of the head of the Simbirsk Gay-pay-oo, a man of notoriously jealous habits. For this hypothesis there was no confirmation beyond the fact that

Shields and the lady in question had danced together at one of
the A.R.A. parties and that the husband had remarked audibly
that Communist women should be ashamed to dance *bourgeois*
foxtrots. I thought the girl was wrong, or perhaps she was jealous of Shields herself, which made her talk like that. But I was
not sure because I knew another story of something that had
happened not long before on the Volga in one of the A.R.A.
personnel houses, and the memory of it was still fresh enough
to hurt me and make me doubtful.

During my absence in Paris in the spring of 1922 I had let
my apartment to a friend in the A.R.A., whom I will call Joe
Parrott, which was not his name, but shortly before my return
he was transferred to the Crimea. I had not been back three
days when there came a ring at my door-bell and there was a
tall slim girl inquiring for "Mister Parrott." "He doesn't live
here any more," I told her, "he's gone away from Moscow."
"Yes," she said plaintively, "that's what they told me at the
A.R.A. headquarters when I asked there, but they wouldn't say
where he'd gone." She was a pretty girl, with a shock of light-
brown hair and dark-blue eyes, young and rather callow, I
thought, but there was something appealing in her precise English speech with its little touch of Scotch accent. "That must be
a mistake," I said readily. "Why don't you come in and I'll
telephone myself to the A.R.A. headquarters about Parrott.
Have you known him long?"

It seemed she had not, but she evidently liked him a lot,
which was regrettable to me. If there is one thing I have learned
in a not always well-spent life, it is that running after girls who
are crazy about someone else is a waste of time and, as Solomon wisely remarked, who had more experience in the matter
than I, "vexation of spirit." I gave Nina Nicolaievna some tea
and telephoned the A.R.A. to find that the missing Parrott had
been transferred, as I already knew, to the Crimea and could

be reached by a letter or cable at the address A.R.A., Yalta, Krim. She was a funny kid, this Nina, and I liked her very much. A bit crazy, of course, but one expects that from Russians, and always nice to have around. She used to drop in quite often to see me and sat curled up in a big chair eating candy and babbling about Mister Parrott, as she always called him, and how marvelous he was. I let her talk—I think that was why she liked me—but I did wish sometimes that he had been drowned at birth or that I had met Nina first. She had the combination of sweetness and dumbness and youth which appeals to men like me, who earn their bread with their brains and are glad of relaxation; or why read Edgar Wallace and the *Saturday Evening Post?* Then Parrott was transferred again to one of the Volga towns, where Nina had some relatives. I don't much like writing this story because I was fond of Nina and in a way I was responsible for what happened. Because I said, "Why don't you get a job with the A.R.A. down there; you talk English so well, and that's what they need most. Could you stay with your relatives there if I got you a job with the A.R.A.?" She jumped up and danced with joy. "Oh, that's wonderful," she said. "My uncle there is a doctor and he speaks French and German and would probably be working for the A.R.A. too. Oh, that's wonderful! Please telephone at once and get me a job."

She got her job all right and went off to the Volga the next week, and I had an ecstatic letter from her ten days later; everything was wonderful, and Joe—no longer Mr. Parrott —was most wonderful of all. She never wrote again, poor kid—although at that it wasn't Parrott's fault. Nina threw herself at his head and he took what the gods offered, as who wouldn't. He was not much older than she was and talked to his friends about marrying her and taking her back with him to America, but there was one thing, he said, which worried him about Nina. She was fantastically jealous in a morbid Russian way. Russians are like that; they are either what seems to us shockingly casual and promiscuous about sex or so intensely devoted to a single person as to be an infernal nuisance. All men like their girl friends to be faithful and devoted, and I suppose the same is true of women, but there is nothing sounder in human philosophy than the proverb about having too much of a good thing. That was the case with Parrott. Nina and he between them had wangled her into the post of his secretary, which looked like an ideal arrangement, two hearts that beat as one to share their daily toil. Unfortunately one day Nina noticed feminine writing on one of Joe's letters from the Crimea and opened it and read it—and threw fits. The signature "your darling Katya" settled any doubts that the rest of the letter might have left. When Joe came in she danced about the office like a fury and ended by tearing the letter to pieces and throwing it in his face.

As I have said, Joe was not much older than Nina, which perhaps excuses him for thinking he "could teach her sense." This is one of the more common fallacies that men entertain about women, although they generally grow out of it. Joe told Nina that she was a silly and naughty girl but he loved her just the same. That was all right as far as it went, and if he had only ended up by smacking her, everything would have been all right. Instead he told her, far too seriously, that if she was naughty again he would send her back to Moscow and tell Katya to come quick from the Crimea. The mistake Joe made was in thinking that because Nina was a jealous, loving woman she was therefore grown up. Perhaps she might have grown up later, or perhaps she was the type, which is common enough in Russia, that never outgrows the passionate single-mindedness of childhood. At all events a few weeks later she made a scene again one evening when Joe danced three or four times with an-

other girl at a party. Nina said this and said that and raised the
devil in all directions until Joe got mad and decided to teach
her a lesson, which was worse, because more concrete, than his
previous idea of teaching her sense. The next morning he typed
out a cable to the girl called Katya in the Crimea, saying, "Want
you to come here immediately stop have arranged for you to
get ticket and journey-money from our office in Yalta. Love—
Joe" and left the carbon copy on his desk for Nina to find. Of
course he did not send the original, never dreamt of sending it,
only thought, poor boy, that he would teach Nina a lesson. He
left the carbon on his desk about twelve o'clock, went out to
lunch with the Soviet Relief people and forgot all about it.
When he came back Nina was not there but the cable was gone.
Someone in the office told him that she had come in about
twelve-thirty, found it, and rushed away immediately. She
looked very sad, one of the girls said, and she held the paper
crumpled up in a ball against her heart. She did not say anything, but she looked strange, as if she was ill. I don't suppose
Joe liked this very much, but he probably thought that his lesson was bearing fruit. If he did think so he was right. Anyhow,
he went on with his work all afternoon, and if he was worried
because Nina did not appear he gave no outward sign, although
he stayed longer than usual in his office as if waiting for her to
come. Finally about six-thirty he went home to the A.R.A. personnel house. It was nearly seven and the night was falling. He
went upstairs to his room on the second floor. The electric light
was badly arranged; the switch was not near the door, but
across the room by the bed. He walked over towards the switch,
stumbled over something on the floor and fell, then rose with
sticky hands, a prey to gasping terror, and staggered to the bed
and turned the switch, and looked, and saw. His hands were red
with blood, Nina's blood, and her body lay there beside his bed,

Nina's body, with the back of its head blown off. Near it a re-volver, his revolver.

In the next room one of Parrott's friends was getting ready to go out to a party; he was shaving himself with an old-fashioned long-blade razor. He said afterwards, "By the devil's own luck I was wiping the blade on a piece of paper or I'd have cut my throat, for the scream I heard from the next room was the most dreadful thing I ever heard in my life. It was dreadful! I mean that's all I can say about it. It was dreadful! I made three jumps to Joe's room, and there I saw him sitting on his bed with his face in his hands, swaying to and fro. As I came in he took his hands down and my first thought was that he had killed himself; his face was all blood and there was blood all over his hands. He put out one hand, pointing at the floor, and made a funny kind of whining noise, and passed out cold. Then I saw the girl on the mat beside the bed. Her face was not touched— a pretty kid too, Nina something her name was—but she had made a thorough job of it, blew the back of her head right off; the floor was flooded with blood and mush of brains. She must have put the gun on the top of her head and pulled the trigger. I never saw such a mess. I rushed downstairs as I was with my face all covered with soap yelling fire and blue murder. Luck-ily none of the Russian servants were about and the station chief kept his head. Otherwise God knows what a scandal there might have been."

The station chief, as it happened, was a soldier who had fought under Colonel Haskell in France, and Haskell had got him a job with the A.R.A. in Russia because he thought he was a man he could rely upon in a pinch. He proved it that night. He went upstairs to the scene of the tragedy and looked it over, calmly; then he called his own American A.R.A. doctor and told him to give Parrott, who was still unconscious, a shot of something that would keep him quiet for twelve hours, and put him to bed in another room. "Wash his face and hands," he said, "then take his clothes off and put him to bed." Next he telephoned to Nina's uncle. "I want to see you here at once. I'm sending a car for you; will you be here in ten minutes?" When the uncle came he told him what had happened, or what he thought had happened, because they didn't know much at that time. One thing was certain, as the doctor found immediately; the girl had been dead many hours before Parrott came home; her body was cold and it was certain that he had not been in the house between breakfast and 6 P.M. To make it easier they found the copy of the cable which Parrott had not sent, crunched up in a little ball beside her body. At the time they thought he had sent it, but anyway there was the motive. Then the A.R.A. chief and the doctor sat down and took counsel together. On one thing they were agreed, scandal must be avoided at all costs. Which of the two suggested the heroic course they followed I do not know, but follow it they did. They took the dead girl and bathed her face and bandaged the back of her head—what was left of it—and put her hat on and wrapped her up in a cloak so that none of the bloodstains would show. They then carried her downstairs. The car which had brought the doctor was still waiting at the gate. They walked the girl between them across the little yard to the gate and put her into the car. To make it seem more natural the uncle said to the driver, who was a Russian, "Nina Nicolaievna isn't very well to-night; I'm taking her home." The driver grinned coarsely. "Not the first time," he said, "but none of these kids know when to stop nowadays." They drove to the doctor's house and repeated the ghastly pantomime, marching the corpse upstairs. They had brought with them the revolver and the bloodstained rug, and the little ball of paper. They took her to her bedroom and removed the bandages and bloodied her face again and laid her on the mat with the gun and the paper beside her. Then the

A.R.A. man went home and the doctor telephoned to the police. The facts of the case were clear enough. There was a formal inquiry and a verdict of suicide, but there was no scandal.

Parrott woke up raving the next morning. He had really loved Nina, I believe, and the shock was too much for him. He had a complete nervous breakdown and was sent home with a male nurse to watch him all the way back to America, but he was young and recovered, and for all I know is alive and living happily to-day. This was one of the stories I did not write for *The New York Times* from Russia, although I heard of it not long after it occurred. I don't know what its "moral" was unless you take the words of the Russian chauffeur, "None of these kids know when to stop."

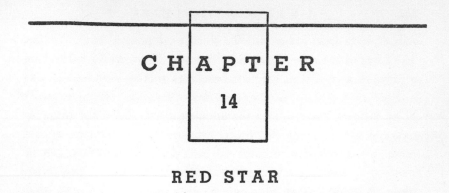

CHAPTER
14

RED STAR

I RETURNED to Paris at the end of January, 1922, after spending five months in the Soviet Union. By this time certain definite ideas about Russia had begun to form in my mind. When I first went there at the end of August, my only instructions from New York were to report the facts as I saw them, but to avoid quoting statements of Soviet spokesmen or newspapers, unless in the form of direct interviews given to foreign correspondents by Commissars or other leaders, "because we do not want to make *The New York Times* a vehicle for Bolshevik propaganda." So great was the fear of the Red Bogey in orthodox America, despite the belief it shared with the rest of the non-Soviet world that N.E.P. meant return to a modified form of Capitalism. During the first two or three months I had been too busy reporting the famine and the fantastic phenomena of Soviet life to pay much attention to politics, but I tried from the outset "to lean over backwards" in being fair to the Bolsheviks rather than allow my own prejudices or those of my paper and its readers to influence my work. The New York office was evidently satisfied because I received a raise in salary at the end of the year, without my asking for it, and the message, "Henceforth you may quote Soviet newspapers or spokesmen, but be

163

careful to make it clear that you are quoting, not expressing your own opinion."

This appeared simple, but I sometimes found that the copyreaders in New York had added the words, "it is thought here" in parenthesis to my dispatches, in order to dissociate me and by consequence *The New York Times* from responsibility for views expressed. With this minor exception my copy was never altered or cut in New York, which as every foreign correspondent knows is as rare a privilege as it is encouraging to the writer. I particularly appreciated this treatment from *The New York Times* because much of my copy contained facts and statements about Soviet progress that were both startling and unwelcome from a capitalist viewpoint. I soon found that the course of life in Russia was so remote from American habit and comprehension that a great deal of explanation was required, which led no less an authority than Heywood Broun to charge me with "writing editorials from Moscow disguised as news dispatches." I still believe that interpretation of news is quite different from editorial writing and that I had no alternative. It is better, no doubt, for a foreign correspondent to stick to the facts as far as he can and allow the interpretation to be provided editorially by his home office, but if the latter lacks sufficient information, as was the case about Russia in the early 1920's, it is, I think, the duty of the correspondent to fill the gap where he can.

I stayed in Paris until April to replace the regular correspondent of *The New York Times*, Edwin James, who was covering the Genoa Conference. It was now clear that I could have a permanent position in Moscow if I wanted it; I decided that I did, for three reasons. First, I wished to be independent and have a job of my own. Second, I could see that work in the Soviet Union would be highly specialized and that a careful study of Bolshevik mentality and methods would be as essential as a knowledge of the Russian language. There were many representatives of the *bourgeois* Press and diplomacy who could speak Russian, but few seemed anxious to discover the whys and wherefores of Bolshevik policy; indeed, most foreign observers, and business men also, were convinced that the Bolshevik experiment, as they called it, could not possibly last long and that N.E.P. was the beginning of its end. Third, I on the contrary, was confident that the Soviet Government had a great future. In almost the first dispatch of a political nature that I sent from Moscow I wrote that as far as could be seen nothing would upset the Soviet régime save a disastrous foreign war or a bitter struggle among the Bolsheviks themselves. From that day to this I have found no reason to change my opinion.

In the spring of 1922 the Soviet was invited to a conference at Genoa with the leading powers of Western Europe for the purpose of solving the vexed questions of Russia's foreign debt. Three categories of debts were discussed—loans by foreign Governments, loans by private business, and claims by foreign nationals for property seized or destroyed by the Soviet Government since the Revolution. The total was estimated at the colossal figure of 60,000,000,000 to 75,000,000,000 gold francs; in those days statesmen still believed, or professed to believe, that the payment of enormous debts by one nation to another was feasible. The Bolsheviks advanced a counter-claim of equally fantastic dimensions for damages alleged to have been inflicted by foreign intervention and aid to the White Armies on Russian soil. As might have been expected, the result was a complete deadlock and no way out of the impasse was found at a second conference held at The Hague later in the same year. The Bolsheviks, however, used the arduous negotiations of Genoa as a smoke-screen behind which to formulate and sign, at the neighboring village of Rapallo, a treaty with Germany, whereby the latter not only abrogated the onerous

terms of the Brest-Litovsk Peace, but renewed full diplomatic
recognition and agreed to leave the whole question of debts and
claims in abeyance on condition that if at a subsequent date the
Soviet should make any settlement of foreign claims public or
private, Germany would be entitled to reopen the subject and
use the said settlement as a basis of discussion. The secret of
Soviet-German conversations had been well kept and the announcement of the treaty came as a bombshell to the rest of the
world; it was an intimation that Soviet Russia henceforth intended to play a positive rôle in world politics and an unmistakable warning to the former enemies of Germany that the Soviet did not feel bound to subscribe to the Treaty of Versailles,
or other "force-imposed unilateral peace treaties," as Chicherin, Commissar of Foreign Affairs, once termed them, in
whose framing it had been denied a part. For the next ten years
hostility to the "unfair" peace treaties and close collaboration
with Germany and Turkey were the bases of Soviet foreign policy. The Treaty of Rapallo confirmed my impression that the
Red Star was destined to rise high and shine bright in the international heavens.

When my friend Knickerbocker read this line in my manuscript he commented quickly, "And then you decided to hitch
your wagon to that star." "Yes, in a sense," I replied. "Of
course I didn't go Bolshevik or think Bolshevism would work in
Western countries or be good for them. I don't believe I even
cared in those days whether it would be good for Russia, or
work there in practice. But I did think that the Bolsheviks
would win in their own country and that the Soviet Union
would become a great force in world affairs. If you want to
know, Stalin himself expressed my attitude rather neatly the
last time I saw him, on Christmas day, 1933. He said, 'You have
done a good job in your reporting of the U.S.S.R. although you
are not a Marxist, because you tried to tell the truth about our

country and to understand it and explain it to your readers. I
might say that you bet on our horse to win when others thought
it had no chance, and I am sure you have not lost by it.' "

"Did Stalin say that?" Knick asked in surprise. "Then there
must be more humanity than I thought in that steel skull of
his." "Of course he's human," I said, "but the trouble with you
and so many other people is that they won't admit that the Bolsheviks regard themselves as fighting a war in which it is their
duty to be just as ruthless and dispassionate in gaining their objectives as any leaders in any war. As far as I'm concerned, I
don't see that I have been any less accurate about Russia because I failed to stress casualties so hard as some of my colleagues, than I was in reporting battles on the French Front
when I said more about the importance of the victory than the
lives it cost. I saw too much useless slaughter in the World War
—for that matter I think the War itself was useless, unless you
believe that Hitler in the Kaiser's place is a benefit to humanity
—to allow my judgment of results to be biased by the losses or
suffering involved. I'm a reporter, not a humanitarian, and if a
reporter can't see the wood for trees he can't describe the wood.
You may call that special pleading or call me callous, and perhaps it is true, but you can't blame me for it; you must blame
the War, because that was where my mental skin got thickened."

. . . .

I went back to Moscow in April. I had secured a private
apartment, which had formerly been a small restaurant in a
side-street near the center of the city. The Foreign Office was at
first reluctant to allow foreign correspondents to leave the
Savoy Hotel, where it was easier to keep an eye on them, or as a
Foreign Office spokesman put it, where they would be more
comfortable and less exposed to danger of theft or even personal attack. Several weeks in the Savoy, however, had given
me so low an opinion of its comforts that any other quarters

seemed preferable. My large room, which had been the main dining-room of the restaurant, was dark and hard to heat even with three tiled stoves, but I installed an open English fire-place in one of the smaller rooms, which made a pleasant study, and had a bedroom and bathroom in addition, as well as a kitchen with a separate entrance.

I owed much to that fire-place during those early years in Moscow; it was almost the only one in the city and made a great appeal to foreign hearts irrespective of the political chords to which they thrilled. It attracted my colleagues and the A.R.A.-men and Englishmen from two opposite camps, the diplomatic Mission and Communists from the Lux Hotel, which was less than a quarter of a mile from my apartment. The members of the Mission were required to know Russian perfectly and had all been diplomats, soldiers or business men in Russia during or prior to the War. They were naturally hostile to the Bolsheviks on account of what had happened to them and their friends during the early days of the Revolution, which most of them had actively opposed. I soon found that although I was on good terms with the members of the British Mission as individuals I was forced to question the justice and acumen of their political views. There was a most level-headed Scotchman named Peters, far less violent in his prejudice than most of his colleagues, who marshaled facts and figures in the spring of 1922 to prove that the Soviet transportation system must soon collapse utterly, not only because the rails and rolling-stock were falling to pieces but because the sleepers were so rotten that nothing save the frozen water in which they were saturated held them together. Peters failed to take into account Djerzhinsky's energy and the terror of his name, although that is another story which will come later.

It is rather strange that two years before in Riga I had been associated with exactly the same type of English and other for-

eigner as was represented by the British Mission in Moscow
without ever feeling inclined to doubt their judgment or ask
whether there was not something to be said for the Bolshevik
side also. Perhaps it was that William Bolitho had taught me in
the interval to think for myself or merely that the facts of the
last two years spoke louder for the Bolsheviks than words. In
any event I gradually found that the glib prophecies of Soviet
downfall, which were made every day in foreign circles in Moscow, began to rouse my antagonism rather than acquiescence.
Moreover it was tiresome to be treated like a new boy at school
by these old Russian hands with their incessant "Well, of
course you don't know this country yet. A man can't understand the Russians until he speaks their language. When you've
been here a year or two and learnt some Russian you will think
quite differently." They were quite impervious to any of my
arguments, the only effect of which was to create the impression
that I was tinged with pink myself.

My Communist visitors were even more dogmatic and at
times no less irritating. It was easier to talk to American "Lux-
ites" like Bill Haywood and a group of former members of the
I.W.W who had been sentenced to long-term imprisonment
in America during the anti-Red drive of 1919–20 and had
"skipped" to Russia, as they termed it, when released on bail
pending an appeal against their conviction. They had little love
for the land they had left behind them, but their political con-
victions were for the most part more negative than positive. As
Big Bill once said to me, "The trouble with us old Wobblies is
that we all know how to sock scabs and mine-guards and policemen or make tough fighting speeches to a crowd of strikers but
we aren't so long on this *ideelogical* theory stuff as the Russians." I suggested that there might be another difficulty, that
the Wobblies had been trying to destroy, like the Bolsheviks
prior to October, 1917, whereas the latter were now trying to

build. Haywood replied shrewdly, "There's something in that but it goes far deeper. These Russians attach the hell of a lot to *ideelogical* theory, and mark my words, if they're not careful they'll come to blows about it one of these days. Don't you know yet that most of them would sooner talk than work, or even eat?"

Bill himself was out of place in Soviet Russia and his lion-hearted energy had begun to flag. He tried once to organize a group of American radicals for work in the Kusnetzk iron basin in Western Siberia, but the venture was a failure. He stayed in Russia until his death six or seven years later, but I believe that he would have returned to America if he had been given the assurance that he would not have to spend the rest of his life in prison.

Another American radical, Bill Shatoff, was more fortunate. He was several years younger than Haywood and had the advantage of having been born in Russia and knowing the language. Shatoff is a big burly fellow and a real man-driver. He played an important part in repelling the Yudenich attack on Petrograd, then became in rapid succession a banker at Rostov, director of an oil trust in the Caucasus, and head of a steel plant, all of course in the service of the State. After that he was put in charge of construction on the Turk-Sib Railroad which he rushed to rapid conclusion. He has now a similar but much more extensive job on the new main line that is being built to connect Moscow with the Donetz coal-fields.

The best of my radical friends was McManus, who worked in the Comintern headquarters as representative of the British Communist Party. Little Mac, as he was called, was a Scotch Irishman from Glasgow in his early thirties, who died a few years later from heart failure. He was one of the few sincere Communists who were willing to argue—all night if necessary—with someone who did not hold Communist views but wished to hear them. He was wholly self-taught but had a Scotchman's aptitude for dialectics plus a ready Irish wit. I asked him once why he became a Communist. He said, "Because they put me to work at the age of six, stoppering bottles in a soda-water factory, and kept me at it ten hours a day, for all the laws against child labor. When the inspector came round all of us nippers used to rush to a hidey-hole and stay there quiet as mice till he went away; an' they still do it, as I know; don't tell me there's no child labor in Glasgow. That's why I'm a Communist, if you want to know."

I learnt a great deal from Little Mac and have a warm regard for his memory. He generally defeated me in argument, but I think he was not trying to convert me but to make me understand what the Bolsheviks were aiming at, and why. I remember he said once, "When you come to know more you will understand the superiority of Marxism in two respects of immediate practicability. They know what they want and why they want it and are determined to get it by fair means or foul. They're a hard lot, these Bolsheviks, but when you know what they've suffered from the devils who held power in Russia in the old days, the Tsars and officers, landlords and gendarmes, you won't blame the Bolsheviks for anything they have done. And mind you, man, they're set in their ways, are the Bolsheviks; you may think that this N.E.P. will last forever with all its hoorin' and gamblin' and dirty work at the cross-roads, but Lenin doesn't think so. Did you hear of the speech he made awhile back (this was in the autumn of 1921) with his talk, 'Kto Kavo' they call it, which is Russian for 'Who beats Whom.' They must learn to trade, he told them, and beat the N.E.P.-men at their own game. When they'd learnt that and got their trading organized they could begin an attack on the N.E.P.-men and put them back where they belonged. Then later, said Lenin, they must organize industry and distribution and production

When they can put tractors and combines and farm machinery in the fields, then they can begin again to try and socialize the villages. The truth of it is, Lenin didn't want to go so fast with the peasants and harry them with requisitions and stop their private trade, but it was forced on him by the hard logic of civil war. He wrote himself, 'We committed the error of trying to carry out a direct transition to Communist production and distribution. We decided that the peasants would give us enough through the grain quotas but we were wrong.' But he never meant to give up Communism and lead the people back to Capitalism. It is only a temporary retreat, I tell you, two steps backward after three steps forward, as Lenin said." I dissented violently, but Mac went on. "You mayn't believe me, but I know what I'm tellin' you and you'll live to admit that I'm right."

A few months later Lenin told the Eleventh Party Congress, "The coming decisive struggle is not against foreign capitalists but against our own (N.E.P.-men). It is our task to link up with the peasant masses and move forward infinitely more slowly than we had intended but in such a way that the whole mass shall move with us. Then our joint movement will begin to accelerate at such a rate as we cannot dream at present." In the same spring Djerzhinsky, the first chief of the dreaded Cheka, who had recently been appointed Commissar of Railroads, gave proof of the Bolshevik hardness to which Little Mac referred. As Peters had predicted, transportation collapsed badly, and although it did not quite fall to pieces, failed in the task of conveying the Siberian grain crop, which had been fairly plentiful, to the starving Volga. Millions of lives were at stake but the grain did not come through the Ural Mountains despite the most peremptory orders. Djerzhinsky decided to look into the matter for himself. He traveled to Omsk, the capital of Western Siberia, and made a careful investigation of the railroad organization. Everything seemed in order, but one thing was certain, the grain was not being moved. Djerzhinsky hitched his private car to an eastbound train until it reached a small local junction two hundred miles from Omsk. "When the station Commandant heard the name of his visitor," my informant told me, "he crossed himself, although he was listed as a Communist. Djerzhinsky paid no attention. 'Send a cable,' he said curtly, 'to the railroad headquarters in Omsk stating that a freight-car full of grain is stuck here. Send it *molnia*' (literally lightning, which is Russian for triple urgent). Djerzhinsky spent most of the night in his car on the siding studying reports. The next morning he sent to ask why the station Commandant had not brought him a reply from Omsk. 'There is no reply,' said the Commandant. 'Send another *molnia* message stating that a high Soviet official is stranded here and demands immediate transportation.' At eight that evening, there still was no reply. Djerzhinsky's eyes hardened. 'Send a message that I, Djerzhinsky, am stuck here and that unless I receive immediate transportation and a satisfactory explanation of the failure to reply to my two previous messages—say that they were sent by me—I shall take appropriate measures.' "

My informant paused. "There was no reply to that one either," he continued impressively. "You can guess how Djerzhinsky felt. He worked all that night too, driving his secretaries like horses in a race. In the morning a westbound train came through to which he attached his private car. It was late at night when the train reached Omsk, but Djerzhinsky called an immediate meeting of all the employees of the central railroad administration, from the head director to the office boys, and told them what had happened. After his last words 'I demand to know what became of those telegrams,' there was dead silence for nearly a minute. At last some small clerk squeaked out that he had received them.

" 'Yes,' said Djerzhinsky quietly, 'and what did you do then?'

" 'I filed them for reference.'

" 'Was that all?' asked Djerzhinsky no louder than before.

"The man nodded, then muttered something about that being the rule of the office.

" 'Very good,' said Djerzhinsky. 'I shall now take steps to prove your rule is broken forever. Henceforth all telegrams must receive a reply within an hour, and I shall hold the heads of departments responsible, as I now hold you and you,' pointing to the chief official present and his immediate subordinate. 'You are under arrest,' he said. Then he summoned a guard detail that was waiting in the court-yard and said, 'Take them out and lose no time.' Within a minute all heard the volley of the firing squad."

That was Djerzhinsky's way, but the grain came through after that from Siberia to feed the starving Volga.

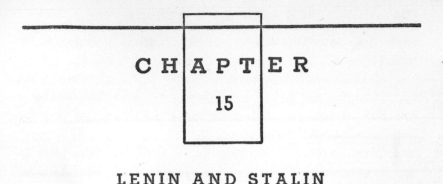

CHAPTER
15

LENIN AND STALIN

IF THE Treaty of Rapallo marked a turning-point in the relations of Soviet Russia with the outer world, there occurred almost simultaneously an event of far greater importance to the country's future. I refer to the illness of Lenin, which proved fatal within two years, during the latter part of which he was unable to take any active share in the direction of affairs. At the time it was almost impossible for me to report the truth about the case, not only because the facts were veiled in secrecy but because Lenin's physicians were themselves uncertain of the nature of his malady.

In the autumn of 1921 the American correspondents had repeatedly petitioned the Foreign Office to obtain an interview with Lenin, and one or two of our number had pulled the most powerful strings through personal friends or relationships. We had been received by Trotzky, Kamenev, then a member of the Politburo and President of the Moscow Soviet, the Foreign Commissar, Chicherin, and Krassin, the Commissar for Foreign Trade. We knew that in the past Lenin had welcomed contact with foreigners, but all efforts, whether collective or individual, were unavailing. Somewhat reluctantly it was admitted by the Foreign Office that Lenin was suffering from headaches and insomnia, due, it was stated, to overwork in connection with the

sweeping economic changes which followed the introduction of
N.E.P. I saw him for the first time at the All-Russian Soviet
Congress a few days before Christmas, when he spoke for more
than an hour and showed no signs of weakness or ill-health.
Moreover, there were none of the rumors flying about Moscow
which always accompany any circumstances which cause anxiety or nervousness to the "higher-ups." Nevertheless Lenin's
headaches grew worse and in the middle of April, 1922, a con-
sultation of doctors decided that the trouble was probably
caused by the pressure of a bullet on an important nerve at the
back of his neck near the spine.

Three and a half years before, on the night of August 31,
1918, Lenin had been shot by a Social Revolutionary girl
named Fanny Kaplan as he was walking to his automobile
across the court-yard of the former Michelson factory in Moscow, where he had been addressing a workers' meeting. For a
time his life was in danger, but he rallied and it was thought he
had completely recovered, so that it was not judged necessary to
remove one of the bullets—he was shot three times—which had
lodged in the muscles at the back of his neck. On April 23,
1922, the bullet was removed. It had caused an abscess, which
naturally confirmed the doctors' opinion that their diagnosis
was correct. In the official *communiqué* issued on the following
day it was stated that the patient had borne the operation well,
but within a week he suffered a slight but unmistakable attack
of hemiplegia, in less technical language, a paralytic stroke,
which implies the bursting of a minute blood-vessel in the
brain. As a rule this malady occurs in later life, whereas Lenin
was in his early fifties, but it may result from high-blood pressure due to excessive mental strain. Lenin had been fond of
cycling during his years of exile, but from early 1917 onwards
he took no exercise, paid no attention to his diet, and worked on
an average eighteen hours a day. What is more, his sister once

told a friend of mine that their father had died from the same complaint when comparatively young, I think aged fifty-seven or fifty-eight.

To the best of my knowledge Lenin's condition was never dangerous in 1922, or if so not for more than a few days at the outside; nevertheless his closest associates must have realized that the hand of death had touched his forehead. A peasant or manual worker can have a paralytic stroke far more severe than Lenin's first and yet live on for years; there is hardly a village in Russia without its paralyzed elders who lie quietly in a warm corner and often outlive their sons and daughters. Lenin's first stroke was slight enough, nothing more than a temporary paralysis of the left hand and side, with a slight impediment in speech. The blood clot which produced these symptoms was quickly absorbed and in September, 1922, he was able to make a trip to the South of Russia to complete his convalescence. In October of that year he returned to work in Moscow and felt sufficiently well to receive Oscar Cesare the newspaper cartoonist of *The New York Times*. Cesare told me afterwards that he had spent an hour in Lenin's study in the Kremlin and that he could see no sign of illness in Lenin's appearance or demeanor.

On November 15th I heard Lenin speak at the opening of the Communist International Congress in the former Kremlin throne-room, which is now the Congress Hall of the U.S.S.R. He spoke in German and any slight pause or hesitation might be attributed to the use of a language which, although thoroughly familiar, was not his native tongue. I did, however, detect—and reported in my dispatch—signs of anxiety among his closest friends towards the end of his speech. A week later he spoke in Russian at a special session of the Moscow Soviet to open the electoral campaign for the coming All-Russian Soviet Congress. The session was held in the Grand Opera House and I

was sitting in the orchestra pit at the speaker's feet. Now beyond any doubt there was a slight thickness of speech and slur-
ring of diction, as if Lenin's tongue was too large for his mouth.
For the first time—so closely and well had the secret been
guarded, so many and bewildering the rumors—I was sure of
the truth; there is no disguising the accents of a paralytic from
anyone who knows. I said as much that evening to the Soviet
censor, but he would not let me write it. The most I could say
was, "The speaker's voice was full and strong but it seemed
rather thicker and less clear than last year, although not enough
so for anyone to miss his words." The lay reader might not
grasp my meaning, but I hoped that it would be clear to anyone
with medical training. Unfortunately, as things happened, I
was all too accurate. Some five months later, in April, 1923, on
the eve of the Twelfth Congress of the Communist Party, Lenin
suffered a second paralytic stroke of far greater severity than
the first. Although his mental faculties were not impaired, his
left side was paralyzed and he lost the power of speech.

Another decisive event occurred in the spring of 1922, almost unnoticed by foreign diplomatic or newspaper observers;
Joseph Vissarionovich Djugashvili, a veteran Georgian Communist who had had a score of aliases of which one was Stalin,
was elected General Secretary of the Central Committee of the
Party immediately after the Eleventh Congress in March, almost exactly a month before the operation to remove the bullet
from Lenin's neck.

Stalin at that time was hardly known outside Soviet Russia,
although he had been a member of the Politburo of the Central
Committee of the Communist Party since 1917 and had played
a far more important part in the Civil War than was realized
abroad. At the key-point of Tsaritsyn on the Volga, in the autumn of 1918, he rallied the weakened Bolshevik resistance to
the White General, Krasnov, and thus prevented a junction be-

tween the Southern and Eastern groups of the anti-Soviet forces.
Tsaritsyn was later named Stalingrad in honor of this exploit.
A year later Stalin, who was a member of the Supreme War
Council, opposed Trotzky's project to attack Denikin through
the Don Cossack region, which was unfriendly to the Soviet
cause, and suggested an alternative flank attack through the
southeastern Ukraine, which later was adopted with success.
These episodes were unknown to the Western World, which believed that Trotzky was the sole war-lord of the Red Army, and
did not realize until long afterwards that there was any war-
time rivalry between Trotzky and Stalin. Nevertheless, the
Tsaritsyn affair, more than five years before Lenin died, gave
evidence of conflict between the two men—to which it may be
added the records of the Communist Party bear ample witness
—as was revealed by the present Commissar of War, Voroshilov, a few years ago. Voroshilov declared that Stalin's characteristic efforts to "reëstablish the situation" in Tsaritsyn, which
meant the shooting of White adherents and the dismissal of
some doubtful Reds, met with Trotzky's disapproval. Trotzky,
as Commissar of War, sent Stalin a cable ordering him to re-
instate some of the Red officers he had dismissed. "That cable,"
said Voroshilov, "is still preserved in the archives of the Commissariat of War. Across it is scrawled in Stalin's writing the
words, 'Pay no attention.' "

Stalin and Trotzky were antagonists by character and circumstances. Trotzky was brilliant, proud, and independent. He
did not join the Communist Party until 1917, whereas Stalin
had nailed his flag to Lenin's mast as early as 1902, and had
never wavered in allegiance. After my first interview with him
in the fall of 1929 I wrote that he was "the inheritor of Lenin's
mantle." He changed the phrase to "Lenin's faithful disciple
and the prolonger of his work." There is a parallel which suggests itself. I mean the story in the New Testament about the la-

borers in the vineyard when some of them were hired in the early morning to work all day for a penny. At noon others were hired, for the same wage, and late in the evening a group was brought in to rush the work to completion, who still received the full penny, although they were only working for an hour or so in the cool of twilight. I have forgotten the moral of this parable, but quite naturally the morning-hired workers objected bitterly to the fact that the latest comers received the same pay as they who had sweated and labored throughout the heat of the day. That was Stalin's position with regard to Trotzky. When most of the Bolshevik leaders fled abroad after the abortive revolution of 1905–06, Stalin stuck it out in Russia to continue the seemingly hopeless task of organizing the remnants of the Bolshevik cause under one of the most bloody and pitiless repressions in history. More than any other he "sweated in the heat of the day," tireless and persistent, always being arrested yet always escaping somehow, until at last they caught him in 1914, and exiled him to the far north of the Ural Mountains within the Arctic Circle, whence escape was impossible. Even there he never lost heart. He made friends with his guards and went hunting with them and outshot them. While other exiles sat and moped or died of cold and hunger Stalin shot bears and wolves and ptarmigan, caught fish through ice, ate well and kept himself fit and strong and warm with thick skins and fur. Because there was an indomitable purpose in his heart. He was not brilliant like Trotzky or clever in the use of words; nor had he the humanity of Lenin, who ordered a Christmas-tree for the children on the country estate where he was living in the year before he died. Stalin would never have done that.

It is not too much to say that Stalin held together the Bolshevik Party in Russia during the bitter years which followed 1906. In those years a Bolshevik who did not weaken was a real man, and it was Stalin who picked these men, who saw them stand up or break under pressure and judged them by results. Intellectually Stalin is more limited than Trotzky, but one of the dangers of intellectual unlimitedness is that its possessor cannot believe wholeheartedly in anything except himself. Thus Trotzky believed in Trotzky, but Stalin believed in Lenin and in the Bolshevik cause and thought of himself as no more than an instrument or "chosen vessel." In this last phrase is implied all the resistless power of fanaticism when its exponent is, like Stalin, a man of inflexible will and great political adroitness. It is probable that Trotzky and Stalin are equally ambitious, but whereas Trotzky's ambition was personal, Stalin had sublimated his ambition to the service of Lenin and the Bolshevik Party, which gave him added strength.

Unlike most of the Bolshevik leaders, Stalin never raised his voice in opposition to Lenin on any point at any time. It was impossible, therefore, for him to forgive Trotzky's continuous criticism, which was further damned by his natural exasperation against this laborer who had been hired at the eleventh hour. He possessed, moreover, a strong weapon against Trotzky's brilliance—his Oriental patience and vindictive willingness to bide his time. Raymond Robbins once told me that he knew Stalin in the first winter of 1917–18. "He sat outside the door of Lenin's office like a sentry," said Robbins, "watching everyone who went in and out, no less faithful than a sentry and, as far as we then knew, not much more important." In March, 1922, Stalin received the reward of his faithful watching. He was made General Secretary of the Central Committee of the Communist Party, which gave him, as he well knew, control of the Party machine. One month later Lenin was stricken, and Stalin and the other insiders must have guessed what we foreigners only learned later, that Lenin's sickness was mortal. While Lenin lived and had his strength, the Party Secretariat was no more than an important cog in the machine that Lenin had created

and controlled, but with Lenin weakened and dying the cog became the keystone of the Soviet arch.

. . . .

Soviet historians claim that the Eleventh Congress of the
Communist Party in March, 1922, marked the end of the N.E.P.
retreat. From a strictly logical viewpoint there is some justification for their claim, in that Lenin made a vigorous speech to the
Congress attacking "panic-mongers" who believed, or professed
to believe, that N.E.P. meant a wholesale surrender to Capitalism and the abandonment of the principles of the Revolution.
Such talk, he said bluntly, was nonsense and defeatism; N.E.P.
had become necessary by force of circumstances and by their
own errors, but it was a tactical maneuver rather than a defeat,
and there was no reason for them to retire, or talk of retiring,
any further. Meanwhile, despite concessions to private enterprise, the control of means of production still remained in the
hands of the Government. There was some casuistry in this argument because the production of food, which at that time was
vital, had indeed passed back to the individual farmers, and
there were no ostensible signs in 1922, or for that matter during
most of 1923, that petty private production and distribution, that
is to say trade, would not be allowed to exist indefinitely.

Whatever the Bolsheviks may have hoped at the time, or written later, there was no doubt in the minds of foreign observers
in Moscow in 1922 that N.E.P. had come to stay and that it
was reviving the exhausted forces of the country with amazing
speed. Freed from the nightmare of food requisitions, the peasants planted a crop whose acreage compared favorably with
pre-War years. As spring passed into summer, the mortality
from typhus, which had been terrific during the past three years,
dwindled almost to nothing, and other diseases of malnutrition
rapidly decreased. In the regions afflicted by famine some 25,-
000,000 souls were being fed daily by the combined efforts of

the A.R.A., the Nansen and Quaker relief organizations, and the Soviet Government itself. In addition they were given an ample supply of seed grain with animals to work the land. On the Volga, which had suffered most from the famine, river traffic, which had been enormously reduced during the Civil War and Militant Communism period, began suddenly to flourish. Rafts, scows, and vessels of every variety, from coracles like those of the ancient Britons to patched-up river steamers, appeared like mushrooms overnight. The famous barter fair at Nijni-Novgorod was revived, much shorn, it is true, of its former glories, but indicative of the new spirit and interesting by the bird's-eye view that it gave of the competition between State or coöperative business and private enterprises, which was one of Lenin's slogans for N.E.P.

As far as I could see when I visited the fair, private trade was winning hands down, with the coöperatives a bad second and State business tailing away in the rear. The small private traders were eager to sell and to please their clients; their stocks, whether goods or food, were new and fresh and although the individual turnover was small, it was rapid as well as profitable. The coöperatives had a wider range of merchandise, but their foodstuffs mostly had a wilted appearance and there was a lot of delay in getting served, which did not compensate for slightly lower prices. I soon found too that many of the goods in their stores were samples, that is to say, for show only, and that it was hoped to do business on the unsatisfactory basis of "place your order now and pay the money and we shall order the goods from Moscow and you will receive them later." The State stores, which were the best-fitted and appeared to have the largest assortment of all, worked almost entirely on this sample-and-order principle, which was utterly out of place with the Volga peasants. They did, however, place some large orders with local coöperatives and State Trusts, which enabled them to make a good showing, at least on paper.

There was, too, a big salt deal—I think it was nearly $500,-000—concluded between the State Salt Trust and the government of the Nijni Province, and another running well over $50,000 with a group of Persian merchants.

As it happened, I shared a coupé in the international sleeping-car with the head of the Soviet Salt Trust, both on my way from Moscow to Nijni and on the return journey three nights later. He was particularly pleased with the Persian contract because it was not only a step to the revival of foreign trade, but indicated the possibility of doing business on Soviet lines. Like the State Trusts, the Persians had brought little more than samples to the Fair, dried fruits, wool, "astrakhan" furs, hides and other commodities. It was true, my traveling companion admitted, that the Persians intended to sell all their wares retail in the final days of the Fair, but in the meantime they had received orders from the State Trusts and coöperatives for a large amount, a little greater, if I remember rightly, than the salt and kerosene they had ordered.

He was an amiable, middle-aged citizen with a bald head, neatly dressed in a light-gray business suit. He talked German, which I knew poorly, but had some French to piece it out, so that we got along all right. On the journey down he told me that he had recently been appointed head of the Salt Trust and gave a most interesting and convincing explanation of how the Soviet intended its State business enterprises to work. I objected that there was a terrible lot of graft in State business. "Yes," he said, "you are right, but this is a period of beginning-growth. When a plant begins to grow you must let it alone and not dig up its roots to see if worms are eating them. Now we let our plant alone, but later"—he paused and frowned—"later, we shall tear these grafters like weeds from our ground and throw them into the fire."

When my train pulled out of the station about nine o'clock two evenings later, I was pleased to recognize the Salt Trust chief's bag in my coupé again, although there was no sign of him. I thought, quite rightly as the event proved, that I could get a story about the business his Trust had done at the Fair. In the meantime I sat in the corridor chatting with one of the secretaries of the Commissar of Internal Trade, Eliava, who had come down from Moscow to open the Fair, and whose private car was now attached to the train. The secretary talked French fluently and had a lot of useful information to impart. It was a hot night and I bemoaned the fact that I had exhausted the precious stock of Marcobrunner with which I left Moscow. About a month earlier the Councilor of the German Embassy, who was a friend of mine, had told me that the newly formed Soviet Wine Trust was "releasing" a large quantity of the most marvelous Rhine wines, Marcobrunner and Rüdesheimer, it had ever been his lot to taste. He was a connoisseur, so I rushed to the nearest wine store and bought ten dozen Marcobrunner at a price of about fifty cents a bottle. My German friend was right, it was nectar, veritable liquid gold; I don't think I have ever tasted such wine before or since, save once during the "inflation" days in Germany when I gave a little party at Pelser's in the Wilhelmstrasse in Berlin, which cost me the equivalent of two dollars, wine, coffee and liqueurs included, for six persons. We drank a Dedesheimer, if that is how you spell it, which had the same rich golden flavor as my Moscow Marcobrunner. The next morning one of the party trotted round to Pelser's and suggested that he would like to buy a few dozen bottles of this Dedesheimer; they must have cost five or six cents apiece at inflation rates, but the amiable Herr Pelser was not to be caught again. "I am sorry," he said, "there is no more of that wine left." "Are you sure?" asked my friend. "Can't you find a few bottles somewhere in your cellar?" "I am sure," said Pelser firmly, "but perhaps one day, if and when the value of the mark is restored, I might be able to get you some—at a reasonable price."

I had left Moscow with six bottles of my noble wine, but all the talk of salt on the journey down made us thirsty and I hadn't a drop to drink on the journey back after two hot days in Nijni, so I suggested to Eliava's secretary that there might be some liquor in his chief's car, and that he surely ranked a bottle or two. He thought he did not and we went on talking. A few minutes later my traveling companion came down the corridor from the rear of the train. He greeted me pleasantly and explained that he had been talking with Eliava and was going back there for supper. "I shan't be long," he said as he took some papers from his bag, "but I hope you won't be asleep when I get back because I have a lot to tell you about the business I have done here." I said, "That's fine," and moved aside from the door of the coupé to let him pass. He had only walked a few steps down the corridor when a bright idea struck me. "Excuse me, comrade," I said, "is there any wine down there in Eliava's car?" He turned and nodded smiling. "Yes," he said, "plenty, and what's more there is some of that splendid Rhine wine you gave me the other night. It's all right, I won't forget, I'll bring back a couple of bottles," and he went on with a wave of the hand.

I was startled by a strange gasping sound from my friend the secretary, who was sitting on one of the little hinged seats by the window that are found in Continental corridor-trains. His face was actually white and for a moment he was unable to speak. "Oh, my God," he whispered, "you talk to him like that, telling him to bring you wine? Don't you know?" He stopped with his mouth open. "Know what?" I asked. "I don't even know his name, but he traveled down with me the other day and seems a very nice fellow. He drank my wine then, so why shouldn't I—" "But that's Latsis," the secretary interrupted, "Latsis. Surely you've heard of him." "Never in my life," I said. "All I know is that he claimed he was head of the Salt Trust." "He is, but before that he was one of the top men of the Cheka. Djerzhinsky, Peters, Latsis and Menjinsky, and Latsis was the most terrible of them all. He wrote a pamphlet on Terror and what it meant and why." I said, "What of it, provided he brings back that wine?" Which Latsis duly did, and talked most interestingly and gave me a lot of dope about the fair, but much as I was tempted I did not ask him about his Cheka activities because the secretary had implored me not to for fear it might get him into trouble. The fear of the Cheka was so great those early days in Moscow that people made a detour rather than step on the sidewalk in front of its main building on Lubyanka Square.

With some difficulty I secured a copy of the pamphlet in question, which I think was written in the latter part of 1918 or early 1919. It explained in simple, lucid terms the principles by which the Red Terror was directed. The chief purpose, the writer said, was to strike terror into the hearts of the enemies of the Revolution; therefore action must be ruthless and, above all, swift. The destruction of enemies without delay might often, by paralyzing opposition, save many more lives later. Secrecy was also stressed, because that, too, was an element of terror. For this reason Cheka arrests almost always were made in the dead of night and the relatives and friends of arrested persons generally heard no more of them for weeks. Perhaps they would then be released; more commonly there would be a notification that clothing or food might be provided on a given date for Citizen So-and-so, who had been sentenced to a term of exile; sometimes a curt notice of execution.

The Terror, as such, no longer existed when I went to Moscow, although people still spoke in whispers of the night of the attempt on Lenin's life when five hundred people were executed without trial in Moscow, not because they were guilty of complicity, but because they were former nobles, landlords, bankers or generals, and as such were "class enemies" whose "execution" was carried out as an example and warning. In the official history of the Russian Communist Party, written by Popov in 1931, the facts are bluntly stated. "The system of mass Red Terror proved a weapon of tremendous importance. It came down with all its severity upon the heads of the landlords and *bourgeois* counter-revolutionaries; on the White officers, big Tsarist officials, and the most prominent figures among the nobility, the clergy and the capitalists." Although I was not in Russia at the time of the Kirov assassination in 1934, I have no reason to doubt that the executions which followed it were prompted by the same motives as in 1918; that is to say, that many of those shot were not implicated in the plot to assassinate Kirov, but were "hostile elements" whose elimination was meant to strike terror; it was not even an act of revenge, but a symbol and a warning.

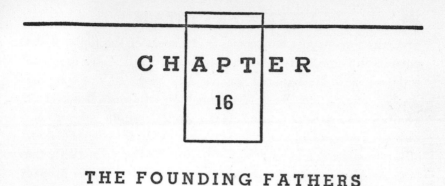

CHAPTER
16

THE FOUNDING FATHERS

ALL things considered, I believe that the eighteen months from the spring of 1922 to the end of 1923 were the pleasantest period I have spent in Moscow, and the proof of it is that I passed fifteen months of that time without once going abroad, or "out," as foreign residents of Moscow put it, as if they were making an escape. (Unless I am mistaken, the first gold-rushers to Alaska used the same expression.) Living was cheap and comfortable enough; the shops were well stocked with immediate necessities and I could obtain "luxuries" like candy, American cigarettes and razor blades from the A.R.A. canteen, or order them from Europe. I had a little T-model Ford and a chauffeur who was not too Russian for safety, a comfortable apartment and an excellent cook, whom I had taught to prepare meals as I like them, which is simple but good. Food cost less and less, not only because the rouble was steadily depreciating, but because food grew daily more plentiful. For friends there were my colleagues and the foreign diplomatic corps, which was gradually increasing, and last but far from least, the A.R.A. staff in Moscow, which must have totaled by then seventy or eighty Americans, lodged by batches in three or four large houses. The A.R.A. had several hundred Russian clerical employees in Moscow, all of whom had to speak English, French,

or German, and many of whom were feminine and fair. On
Saturday nights there was always a dance-party at one or another of the A.R.A. houses, to say nothing of the cafés, restaurants and *nacht-lokalen* which flourished all over Moscow. For
some reason the latter were never *nakt-lokalen,* to use the pun
on the German words for "night" and "naked," which spawned
like fungi across Berlin in the years from 1922 to 1927. The
latter were salacious and often vicious, which is a reproach that
can rarely be leveled against Russians. Russians think nothing
of mixed naked bathing—or did not until foreigners told them
how dreadful it was—and they are what we should call casual
about the less pleasant natural functions; they have, too, little
sense of what is known as sexual morality, perhaps for the excellent reason that they feel that sex has little, if anything, to do
with ethics. But the fact remains that in all my fourteen years
in Russia I have rarely seen a show or dance or other forms of
public performance which could be termed unpleasantly suggestive by the most prudish spectator. I did attend, in the summer of 1922, a parade of nudist enthusiasts of both sexes who
wore no more beyond the traditional fig-leaf than would hide
their shame, and of course I have seen thousands of men,
women and children bathing as Nature made them. There was
nothing "suggestive" in either case, although the nudists were
quietly but firmly discouraged from further public demonstra-
tions.

My work was immensely interesting, but far less arduous
than it became later. It was true that the Foreign Commissar,
Chicherin, had the strange habit of turning night into day and
constantly arranged appointments for two or three in the morning: I myself once had an interview with him at 3.15 A.M.,
which lasted until half-past four. The cable service to America
was slow—we filed most of our stuff through Riga in those days,
and 6 or 7 P.M. was the latest hour at which a story could be

sent from Moscow in time for the same night's "deadline," despite the seven-hour clock difference between Moscow and New York. Which meant that one could dine in peace and play bridge or dance or seek other amusement afterwards with the comforting assurance that no matter what might "break" in the evening, no news of it could reach New York until the following day. Things are very different at present. Cable transmission has been so greatly improved that it is possible to file as late as 6 or even 7 A.M. Moscow time, and still reach the last edition of the morning paper in New York. The Soviet Press Department, moreover, has developed a horrible habit of issuing news—sometimes in the form of badly multigraphed typescript reports of speeches by Soviet leaders eighty pages long in the original Russian—at eleven, twelve, or even one o'clock in the night. No foreign correspondent in Moscow to-day dares to go out anywhere to dinner without leaving a message to say where he can be reached and even the soberest and most respectable reporter who seeks his lonely couch at ten o'clock never knows when he may be roused from slumber and plunged into a frantic scuffle to get hold of his chauffeur and interpreter and reach the Foreign Office and receive the "handout" and translate it, write it, and have it censored and delivered to the telegraph office—and then trail wearily back to bed. *O tempora! O mores!* Where are the good old days of early N.E.P.?

. . . .

In addition to Lenin's illness, the Treaty of Rapallo and the appointment of Stalin, there were three other notable events in Soviet Russia in 1922: The power of the Orthodox Church was broken—it was deprived of its ancient treasures and rent by a Bolshevik-fostered schism; there was a plenteous harvest; the Soviet Government decided to form the U.S.S.R., or Union of Soviet Socialist Republics.

Bitterly as the Bolsheviks hated the Church and all that it stood for, they had not done more before 1922 than "disestab-lish" it and nationalize its wealth in land and financial invest-ments. Although a great number of monasteries and convents had been seized in and near the chief urban centers, many of them continued to function in rural districts. There was some looting of churches during the Civil War but no organized at-tempt by the Soviet Government to expropriate the reputedly vast treasure in gold and jewels which adorned the shrines and icons of the myriads of churches throughout "Holy Russia." In every village the church rather than the *château* of the landlord was the obvious landmark, with colored or gilded towers, domes and minarets rising proudly above the squalid huts of the peas-ants. During the period of Civil War and Militant Communism the Church and the Bolsheviks seem mutually to have avoided open conflict. The former prudently "lay low and said nuffin'," while the latter had other fish to fry although both of them knew how deep and unbridgeable was the gulf between them. The coming of N.E.P. made a radical change. As long as Mili-tant Communism lasted the Bolsheviks could think that they had defeated all the forces of the old Capitalist régime, amongst which the Church, cowed into passivity, was not the least im-portant. But N.E.P. was an admission that Capitalism was still undefeated; nay, more, it was a forced reversion to much that was meant by Capitalism particularly in regard to the peasants who were the section of the Russian population most subject to religious influence. Henceforth, as Lenin had said, the struggle was not against the old Capitalists or foreign Capitalists, but against the multitudinous small new Capitalists that N.E.P. was producing like weeds on a prairie. In this struggle the Church might again begin to play a preponderant rôle. The Bolsheviks realized this in 1922 and attacked the Church at its weakest points.

At the time I failed to understand the reasons for this attack, but now I can see that it was a sign of the deep Bolshevik resolve to create a Socialist State in Russia no matter what might be the temporary retreat of N.E.P. Or in other words, a proof, if I had been wise enough to know it, that N.E.P. itself was no more than a temporary expedient. The Bolshevik offensive against the Church proceeded along two lines: First they induced an ambitious or perhaps simple prelate, Archbishop Yevdokim of Novgorod, to demand that the Church should sacrifice all its wealth in jewels, gold and precious robes for the benefit of the 25,000,000 famine sufferers. Yevdokim based his appeal upon a comparison with a similar sacrifice made by the Church in the "troublous times" of the Middle Ages when Holy Russia seemed no more than a nut between Polish hammer and Tartar anvil. The Church leaders were forced to yield with the best grace they could muster and thus lost their potential sinews of war. Here and there a churchman, bolder than the rest, opposed this "voluntary" spoliation and was shot or exiled for his pains. The next phase of the Bolshevik attack was deadlier still. There was formed with official approval a schismatic ecclesiastical organization called "The Living Church," which professed to be a sincere reform movement—the Greek Orthodox Church had known no such reformation as Luther inspired in Western Europe—and perhaps was justified in its pretensions. Whether that was the case or not, the Living Church played into the hands of the Bolsheviks. It split in twain the direction and nerve centers of the Church and enabled the Bolsheviks to play the Living Church against the more orthodox faction, and *vice versa,* until both groups were reduced to impotence. The central control of the Church was thus destroyed and has never again emerged as a spiritual, much less political, force. Some years later, when the great Cathedral of Christ the Saviour, Moscow's premier fane, was blown to pieces to provide a site for the projected Palace of Soviets, there was no echo save the rumble of the explosives used. When the most sacred monument in all Russia, the little shrine of the Iberian Virgin at the entrance of Moscow's Red Square, was ripped to pieces in four hours, no crowd collected, no voice was raised in protest. So fatal and effective had been the blow that the Bolsheviks struck at the leadership of the Church in 1922.

Catherine the Great once said that one good harvest in Russia atoned for ten years of bad politics. Her aphorism was singularly correct in 1922 after the country had passed through eight years of stress and struggle such as even stormy Russia had not known for centuries. The bumper crop removed all further danger of food shortage, and the surpluses everywhere in the hands of the peasants after paying the "single tax in kind" to the State, which then amounted to fifteen to twenty per cent of the total yield, were so abundant as to satisfy the needs, not only of the peasants themselves but of their animals. Save in the model farms of a few progressive landlords in the old days and in similar establishments under the Soviet régime, Russian livestock, from horses and cattle to pigs and poultry, has always been poor in quality, for the simple reason that the peasants as a body could not afford to give their stock more than the bare minimum of anything but natural food like hay and grass and whatever swine or chickens might pick up for themselves. In a "prosperous" Russian village pigs, geese, ducks and chickens roamed at will and fended for themselves from the time when the snow melted in the spring until winter had set in. In the same way horses and cattle were turned out to grass. Conditions were the same in less prosperous villages, with the difference that there were fewer birds and animals, or hardly any at all if the village was really poor. During the winter, and in the other seasons when natural food failed through inclement weather, the stock was fed with hay and grain or, in the case of pigs and poultry, with scraps left over from the meager peasant larder. But in most years the peasant's subsistence margin was itself so narrow that he was forced to choose whether to stint his stock or his family. The 1922 harvest left a surplus which made this choice no longer necessary, with the result that the petty food supply of the country increased to a remarkable degree. This, however, was not enough to explain the extraordinary rapidity of recuperation shown by the Russian countryside in 1922–23. The fact was that the Civil War was largely fought along the main lines of communication, the railways and high roads, and did not directly affect the vast number of small towns and villages which were located thirty miles or more from any railroad. I had already seen in Latvia that the armed forces engaged in the fighting there were much smaller than generally reported, and that their operations did not stray far from the lines of easy communication. I am certain that the same was true of the Civil War in Russia, and I know, moreover, that when soldiers of any faction were reported in the neighborhood of the average Russian village, the first act of its inhabitants was to drive their cattle off into the woods or some other place of refuge. After that scouts were sent to report whether the soldiers were Red or White. If the former, the local priest made himself scarce and the new-comers were "hailed with delight" by the Village Soviet. If the troops were White, they received an official welcome from the Council of Elders led by the priest bearing a holy icon. The consequence was that the destruction of livestock was far less great than might be imagined, especially by anyone who thought of the Civil War in terms of the Western Front from 1914 to 1918. I am equally convinced that the casualties in the Civil War, at least from actual fighting, were absurdly exaggerated by both sides, although there was much indiscriminate killing of "class enemies."

The good harvest had a further effect of strengthening the

middle and upper peasants who profited by the sale of their produce at relatively high, although progressively decreasing prices, and of increasing the difference between them and the poor or landless peasants, who had no surplus to dispose of. The latter were forced to seek employment from their wealthier brethren and there was thus again created a kulak class of "exploiters of labor," as the Bolsheviks called them. Class distinctions in the villages had been largely wiped out during the years of Militant Communism; indeed, contemporary Bolshevik announcements that the kulaks had been completely crushed and "liquidated" make strange reading side by side with the speeches and articles about the new anti-kulak drive in 1928 and subsequent years. In point of fact, however, there was no discrepancy, because the so-called kulak was really no more than a peasant who was more energetic and intelligent than his fellows, or who had a large able-bodied family to work his land. If the truth be known, it was the natural ambition of every peasant to become a kulak, and under the rural Capitalism of N.E.P. it was inevitable that this ambition should be gratified in many cases. The Bolsheviks realized that this self-perpetuation of kulakism in the village could never be checked until the last remnants of Capitalism were replaced by Socialist forms; the years from 1923 to 1928 witnessed the hardening of Bolshevik sentiment on the subject into a determination that rural socialization must be undertaken at all costs.

* * * * * * * * * * *

The Constitution of the U.S.S.R. was drawn up and published in the winter of 1922, although the new State did not come formally into being until the early summer of the following year. The Constitution contained a clause which puzzled American correspondents to the effect that any of the six (later a seventh was added) Sovereign States of the Union had the free right of secession. Our surprise led a junior official of the Press

Department of the Foreign Office to suggest that there might be a clerical error in the copies issued to us. Prudently he decided to make further inquiries. He came back smiling. "The text is correct," he said. "You must understand that the framers of our Constitution are not thinking about the possibility of secession by any of the present six States. They are looking forward to a time when other countries, perhaps not immediately adjacent territorially, like Germany or England or even perhaps America, may wish to become members of our Soviet Union. It is clearly necessary to provide that they should continue to enjoy full rights of self-determination."

There was a moment of stupefied silence, then someone said indignantly, "Do you really think America will ever go Communist?" "I admit it seems improbable at present," replied the official urbanely, "but the men who framed the Constitution of the Union of Socialist Soviet Republics"—he rolled the words with unction—"are not thinking of to-day or to-morrow; they are planning for the future."

Most of my colleagues considered this an impudent remark but I was secretly impressed. I sat thinking that night by my fire, and the more I thought the more I began to wonder whether these Bolsheviks might not after all go a damn long way on the path that they had chosen. I did not particularly ask myself whether it was a right path or a wrong path; for some reason I have never been deeply concerned with that phase of the question. Right and wrong are evasive terms at best and I have never felt that it was my problem—or that of any other reporter—to sit in moral judgment. What I want to know is whether a policy or a political line or a régime will work or not, and I refuse to let myself be side-tracked by moral issues or by abstract questions as to whether the said policy or line or régime would be suited to a different country and different circumstances. I sat that night and thought about the Bolsheviks and reached the conclusion, which had arisen in my mind before, that, short of a disastrous foreign war, which seemed most unlikely, or a Kilkenny-cat fight among themselves, which was a less remote possibility than I imagined, the Bolsheviks were bound to succeed, at least as far as Russia was concerned. For the first time, too, it struck me that McManus might be right, that N.E.P. was after all no more than a temporary expedient and that the future path that Russia's feet must tread was the path of Socialism.

The Foreign Office official had spoken of the framers of the U.S.S.R. Constitution. Like every important act of the Soviet Government it was of course a composite achievement; it had been prepared by many hands and submitted to discussion by the Politburo and the Central Committee of the Party and had received the final seal of approval from Lenin. But everyone knew that it was mainly the work of one man, the Commissar of Nationalities, Stalin, whose Commissariat had been created chiefly to perform the spade work for the new Union and was abolished when the Union came into being. My old friend and colleague, Ernestine Evans, first drew my attention to Stalin; of that I am sure although I don't remember exactly when it was. I think it must have been in the spring of 1922, after Stalin's appointment as Party Secretary and after Lenin's illness, when Moscow was full of wild surmise. Ernestine wrote an article for the *Atlantic Monthly* or *Scribner's* called "After Lenin What?", in which she predicted that, despite the brilliance and greater renown of Trotzky, Stalin was Lenin's most probable successor. I am not sure when the article was published, but I do know that I had heard, and been influenced by, Ernestine's views on Stalin before I wrote my own first piece about him, which was in the middle of January, 1923. At Christmas-time there had been a recrudescence of pessimistic rumors about Lenin's health, and I got the impression that Lenin's recovery had been less complete than his friends had hoped. There was a feeling of nervousness in the atmosphere, which I learned to recognize and detect in France during the War. Such things are not part of a reporter's training but every experienced reporter knows what I mean and can sense a period of strain despite the strictness of censorships or the absence of definite news. I had talked with Trotzky twice and had the greatest admiration for his brains and executive ability, yet it had occurred to me that Trotzky, who was essentially an intellectual aristocrat, not to say an intellectual snob, was somewhat out of place in a Bolshevik *milieu*. Stalin I had never met, but I knew a good deal about his character and life. I knew that he was intensely stubborn, that he had refused to leave Russia after the disaster of 1905, and had led a forlorn hope for the next nine years with little time for the polemics and ideological discussions which engaged the enforced leisure of Bolshevik exiles abroad. In that bitter struggle, Stalin the man of action learned to know and trust his fellow-fighters and they learned to trust in him. Thus, when he was appointed head of the Party Secretariat, he not only was in a position to arrange the movement and appointment of Communist executives from this post to that but had at his disposal a nation-wide network of hard men proved by fire upon whom he could rely. This combination, in the hands of a shrewd and patient politician, was to prove irresistible.

On January 15, 1923, I sent a cable to *The New York Times* from Moscow in which I said that five men, Trotzky, Stalin, Kamenev, Djerzhinsky and Rykov had the whole weight of Russia on their shoulders. I added that Lenin and Zinoviev, then President of the Communist International, were resting by doctors' orders. After a brief explanation of the work being done by Trotzky, Kamenev, Djerzhinsky and Rykov I continued: "Finally there is the Georgian Stalin, little known abroad but one of the most remarkable men in Russia and perhaps the most influential figure here to-day. Stalin is officially the head of the Ministry for the nations that constitute the Soviet Union, and more important still is General Secretary of the Communist Party, but his influence is not measured by his official position. Of these five men Trotzky is a great executive, but his brain cannot compare with Lenin's in analytical power. Djerzhinsky goes straight to his appointed goal without fear or favor and gets there somehow, no matter what the obstacles, but he also is inferior to Lenin in analytical capacity. Rykov and Kamenev are first-class administrators and hardly more . . . During the last year Stalin has shown judgment and analytical power not unworthy of Lenin . . . Suppose to-day Stalin outlines a policy that he thinks should be adopted; others criticize it—Stalin answers."

To-day, twelve years later, I think that the above passage gives me the right to say that I did pick the right horse on which to bet in the Russian race. I owe the accuracy of my choice primarily to Ernestine Evans, but I myself already had a firm belief in the strength of Stalin's "key position" as Party Secretary. Just after I left college I met in New York Charles Murphy, who had recently become Tammany Boss but was far from the height of absolute authority which he reached later. He impressed me greatly, perhaps because he was the first big political leader I had ever met personally. I followed his career with passionate interest and saw how he utilized a key position to move men where he wanted them like pieces on a chess-board and play this group against that, or both ends against the middle. Georgians are regarded by Russians much as the Irish by Americans. Georgians are fiercer than Russians and quicker to anger, but less stable; Georgians are volatile and ebullient, easy speakers and deep drinkers, fine riders of horses, gay and ready with women. All this is true of the Irish. Yet Russians know that there is another type of Georgian, colder and more subtle, slow to speech but with an uncanny gift for the psychological moment when words draw blood; hard, and ruthless, reluctant to make any play that might reveal weakness but ever on the alert to take advantage of false moves by opponents. Such, I imagine, was Charles Murphy; such, I thought in 1923 and think to-day, is Stalin.

CHAPTER
17

A PROPHET WITH HONOR

THE spring of 1923 gave a flagrant illustration of the abyss which divides the methods and mental processes of Soviet Russia from those of the Western World. After fourteen years in Moscow I am not yet sure whether the Soviet or Russia is responsible for this gulf, but there is no doubt of its existence, as was demonstrated by the trial of the Roman Catholic priests in 1923. All of them were of Polish origin and the charge was high treason, which was alleged to include espionage activities during the Russo-Polish War of 1920. There was also at issue the old question, which caused so much conflict in medieval England, whether Roman Catholic priests had the right to invoke the authority of Rome against the law of the land. The most eminent of the priests was Monsignor Buchkevich, whose position was graver than that of his co-accused because he alone amongst them had not opted for Polish citizenship but was technically a Soviet national.

To the best of my recollection the majority of foreigners in Moscow were not unduly excited by the trial, because they thought that it was primarily a part of the general drive against religion which was then in progress, and secondly a device to obtain the exchange of Communists imprisoned by the Polish Government. It was expected that the majority of the accused would be found guilty according to Soviet law and that there would be a number of capital sentences, but I did not meet anyone before the trial or indeed until its final hours who believed that any death sentence would be carried out. Monsignor Buchkevich and his companions defended themselves with dignity and restraint against the savage attacks of the Soviet prosecutor, Krylenko, who frequently introduced evidence that would not have been admitted in a Western court. As the trial drew to a close it became evident that the Bolsheviks had failed to reckon with the power of the Roman Catholic Church and the interest with which proceedings had been followed abroad. Here, I think, the Soviet phase of the separation in thought-ways from the West was active. It is difficult for convinced atheists and anti-clericals to recognize that others regard with awe and veneration ideas and institutions which they themselves detest and despise. The Bolsheviks received proof of this immediately after the verdict, which, as generally foreseen, sentenced Monsignor Buchkevich and a number of others to death. Poland immediately issued a protest against this "judicial murder" and churchmen throughout the world added their voices to the Polish protest. The Primate of the Established Church of England, the Archbishop of Canterbury, launched a vigorous attack upon the Soviet judicial system, and a thunder of disapproval echoed from Germany, France and the United States. The Bolsheviks were impaled on the horns of an unexpected dilemma; if they carried out any of the sentences they must incur universal opprobrium; on the other hand if the sentences were commuted it would seem that they had yielded to foreign pressure, which was a thought they could not brook.

At this point the difference between Russian and Western mentality came into play. What was the life of one man or a group of men, they asked in Moscow, for such a fuss to be raised? And who were these foreigners anyway who dared to tell Russians how to conduct their own affairs? I am not the first to find that the attitude of Russians towards foreigners is paradoxical. Foreign countries on the whole are regarded with distrust and suspicion—this has been the rule in Russian history no less than it is to-day—but individual foreigners, whether residents or visitors, are treated with a respect, consideration, and kindness worthy of the highest laws of hospitality. If a foreigner commits a minor transgression or misdemeanor in Russia, it is condoned as a matter of course, but should he be considered guilty of a major crime the fact that he is a foreigner is rather a hindrance than a help to him; his crime is twofold because he has abused Russian hospitality. There is a certain logic in this view which prevails throughout the Orient, but it does not take into account the fact that Oriental jurisprudence and methods of justice are so different from those of the West that Western nations, if strong enough, have always insisted that their nations should be tried by special or mixed tribunals for any serious charge. To take a simple example of the difference between Eastern and Western juridical methods, it is a principle in the West that any accused is innocent until he has been proved guilty, whereas in Eastern countries and in Russia the presumption is that the accused is guilty, because otherwise he would not be brought to trial. The question of guilt or innocence has been predetermined by a preliminary inquiry. This is precisely the point against which the Anglo-Saxon race has fought most savagely, especially when, as is the case in Russia to-day, the authority which initiates the accusation and arrests the accused also conducts the secret preliminary inquiry to decide whether he be brought to trial or not. In such circumstances foreign public opinion cannot fail to be roused by what it considers injustice in the true sense of the word, but I have yet to find a Russian, much less a Russian Bolshevik, who is willing to agree with this.

So it was in the case of the Roman Catholic priests. Angered by the foreign protests the Soviet Press was unanimous against clemency, and factory meetings in Moscow and the provinces voted resolutions demanding "merciless punishment for the Polish traitors." There was, however, a different state of mind in the Soviet Foreign Office, whose anxiety was ill-disguised. Chicherin gauged foreign public opinion far better than the majority of his countrymen and did his utmost to obtain a mitigation of the sentence. His efforts were futile; Monsignor Buchkevich was executed on the night of March 31st. The storm of world-wide indignation which followed surpassed Chicherin's worst forebodings; indeed he was reported to have said bitterly that the life of this one man had robbed the Soviet of the fruits of two years of patient diplomacy. Feeling ran especially high in the United States, and New York presented the unusual spectacle of dignitaries of the Roman Catholic, Jewish and Protestant faiths uniting in a tremendous denunciation of the Bolsheviks. So strong was American sentiment that it is not unreasonable to assume that the Buchkevich execution did more than anything else to retard American recognition of the U.S.S.R. for ten years.

Twenty-four hours before the execution I conceived a bright idea, so I thought, that the German Ambassador, Count Brockdorff-Rantzau, whose personal relations with Chicherin were excellent, apart from the post-Rapallo collaboration between the Soviet and Germany, should make a final appeal for the life of Monsignor Buchkevich and support it by an offer to exchange for the prelate the Saxon Communist, Max Holtz. Communist influence had been strong in Saxony and for a time Holtz was something like an "underground" dictator, organizing strikes and seizures of factories, attacks on the estates of landlords and raids on banks. For upwards of a year he exercised a veritable reign of terror, but he had been captured in the winter of 1922 and was now in prison awaiting trial.

I knew the German Ambassador well enough to put my idea before him, but he refused to entertain it for a moment. He said that merely to imply a comparison between the distinguished prelate and a murderer and bandit like Holtz was insulting to the former, and that deeply as he deplored the inevitable effects of an execution he felt that it would be a breach of diplomatic procedure to intervene personally save upon instructions from his Government. I ventured to say that the life of another robber, Barabbas, had been offered for one higher than Buchkevich, to which the Ambassador replied curtly that he was not Pilate. I suggested that Max Holtz was a political offender rather than a common criminal, that his depredations, like the bank robbery engineered by Stalin in Tiflis in 1905, were carried out for the Communist cause, not for personal gain, and that in Soviet eyes at least the positions were reversed—Monsignor Buchkevich was the criminal and Holtz the martyr. At this point the Ambassador looked at me so forbiddingly that I made hasty excuses and fled, ill-pleased with the results of my first incursion into diplomacy.

Honesty compels me to add that from a newspaper point of view I mishandled the whole trial. To begin with I underestimated its news value at home, which is an unpardonable sin for a reporter to commit; secondly, I was convinced that it was a more or less formal affair which would end quietly with an exchange of prisoners. At the outset I may have been right in this opinion but I held on to it too long and played down a story that I should have written up. My New York office dealt with my shortcomings more in sorrow than in anger, but I realized that I had failed them and asked myself why. I found an answer which was as true as it was comforting, to wit, that I had been too long in Soviet Russia without a trip abroad. For twelve months I had lived in Moscow learning the Russian language and trying to understand the Soviet viewpoint and absorb the Soviet atmosphere. I had succeeded, I thought ruefully, too well; in the Buchkevich case I allowed my American sense of news values to be influenced by what I thought was my inside knowledge of Soviet-Russian viewpoint and Soviet-Russian methods. In other words I had become affected by my environment and was beginning to lose the perspective and critical detachment which every foreign correspondent must retain at all costs. To-day, if I were a managing editor of an American newspaper or agency, I should not allow any of my correspondents abroad to stay more than six months in the country to which they were accredited, without a change of scene. A correspondent should not necessarily go back to America every six months, although I think that the advantages of such a trip would outweigh its cost, but at least he should have a change of environment and a chance to look at the country where he works from the outside in instead of from the inside out. This is particularly true of a post like Moscow, where ideals and standards are so extravagantly different from those of America. A reporter who stays too long in Russia at one time is liable either to lose sight of this difference and to accept as natural and normal events and circumstances which are unnatural and abnormal to his readers, or else to find that the difference gets on his nerves to such a degree that he swings over to the other extreme and reports everything from a sour and jaundiced angle. Ever since the Buchkevich affair I have made it a point not to spend more than four consecutive months in the Soviet Union, with full approval, I may add, of my chiefs in New York.

.   .   .   .

Count Brockdorff-Rantzau was the highest type of Prussian aristocrat, with all that the phrase implies of good and bad. A man of commanding physique, inflexibly cold and haughty, he

ruled his embassy with a rod of iron, and subordinates jumped
like frightened rabbits at his word. He despised the Bolsheviks
as *parvenus,* with the exception of Chicherin, whose family was
as old as his own and with whom he shared the peculiarity of
preferring to work at night. The two statesmen used to meet two
or three times a week in the early hours of the morning and
engage in long conversations of the friendliest nature. The key
to Rantzau's character was an intense and burning patriotism.
He believed that with the aid of Russia Germany might one day
atone for the crowning shame of Versailles, so that for purely
German motives he was as ardently pro-Soviet as the rest of his
colleagues, save the Turkish and Persian envoys, were the reverse. On this account his relations with the diplomatic corps,
of which he was the official *doyen,* were correct rather than
cordial.

I had heard Brockdorff-Rantzau fling magnificent defiance at
the representatives of the Allied and Associated powers at Versailles, although he was at the time so broken by sickness as to
be unable to stand. As head of the German delegation summoned
to sign the Peace Treaty, he had denounced its injustice and
declared in the name of his country that Germany would never
accept this disgrace of mutilation and surrender or consent to
bind her people for two generations to come with the golden fet-
ters of Reparations-tribute. That Germany later yielded to the
direct threat of invasion is a matter of history, but the name of
Graf von Brockdorff-Rantzau was missing from the list of signa-
tories. When I first met the Ambassador I referred to his speech
at Versailles with such obvious sincerity that he was touched
and pleased. I cannot say that we became friends, for Rantzau
was too unbending and too formidable for that, but I used to
lunch with him every three or four weeks during the years he
spent in Moscow, generally *tête-à-tête* discussing the affairs of
Europe in general and of the U.S.S.R. in particular until nearly

dinner-time. We always talked French, which he spoke without
a trace of accent, and as our acquaintance progressed he spoke
more and more freely, especially with regard to individuals of
whom he disapproved. I learnt much from him, not only of the
undercurrents of European affairs during the past two decades
but of German mentality and its strange core of "authoritative
romanticism," as it has been termed by the Italian historian,
Guglielmo Ferrero.

I think that Count Brockdorff-Rantzau was the first non-
Bolshevik to foresee that N.E.P. would be much more shortlived
than other foreigners believed. He told me this in the autumn of
1923 at the time of the so-called "Scissors" crisis, when the
relatively abundant food supply, as a result of two good har-
vests, had forced the purchasing power of food in terms of manufactured goods down to one-eighth of what it had been before
the War. "The peasants are screaming to heaven," said the Ambassador, "and threatening to reduce the production of food.
The workers must have low food prices and there seems little
chance of solving the problem by any great increase in the out-
put of goods. Meanwhile the N.E.P.-men, who to-day control
four-fifths of the country's trade, are making enormous profits
and if the State does try to curb them by throwing its goods on
to the market at lower rates, there is so much graft that they
are able to buy up State goods themselves and sell them at a
bigger profit than ever. Another thing is that some of the richer
N.E.P.-men are throwing their money about in a most reckless
way. The gambling hells and night cafés and luxurious restaurants have aroused deep resentment among the workers and the
rank and file of the Party, who are asking whether they made
the Revolution to enrich a host of private profiteers. Personally
I believe that if Lenin had retained his health he would have
curbed the N.E.P.-men before this. Don't forget that in his last
public speech ten months ago he spoke of the necessity to trans-

form the Russia of N.E.P. into a Socialist Russia. As it is, I hear that the authorities are determined to take action before long. This is confidential for the present, but I was told yesterday that the Party leaders feel that N.E.P. has done what was required of it by reviving agriculture and setting the wheels of industry and commerce turning again." Rantzau swallowed his tenth glass of benedictine—we generally finished a bottle in the course of the afternoon, which never affected him, and of course drinking is part of a reporter's business—and concluded, "Mark my words, *jeune homme,* these Bolsheviks are determined fellows. One of these days N.E.P. will go out 'pouf' like a candle, and then will come the real fight when they tackle the peasants a second time. That will happen afterwards but I tell you it is inevitable."

Rantzau was a true prophet as was shown a few weeks later by an extraordinary incident which occurred at the great Hermitage Restaurant on the Trubny Square in the center of Moscow. For nearly two years this had been the main A.R.A. feeding station in Moscow, where upwards of 10,000 meals were served daily to undernourished or ailing children. But the A.R.A. had brought its work to a successful conclusion in the previous July, and the Hermitage was rented by a private corporation and lavishly refitted as a restaurant. Its main dining-hall, which could accommodate nearly a thousand guests, was a riot of white lights, gold and imitation marble, gilded cornices and statues in the lushest Muscovite manner. A gala program was arranged for New Year's Eve at which tables had to be reserved beforehand at the incredible rate—for Soviet Moscow—of five dollars gold a head including food but not champagne, which was served at six to ten dollars a bottle. In the early hours of the morning the scene resembled a New Year's Eve in New York in the days before the Crash, except that most of the men wore business suits instead of evening dress. Their fair companions were less cautious and the lights gleamed on flashing arms and shoulders ablaze with jewels. A jazz band blared in the gallery and the air was full of multicolored balloons and streamers. Some ingenious citizen thought of tying a wisp of lighted paper to the balloon string so that it burst, if rightly gauged, just when it reached the ceiling. In an instant his example was followed all over the room and the thud-thud-thud of exploding balloons sounded like a distant cannonade. Suddenly the music ceased and the whole room froze into silence as a high Gay-pay-oo officer entered followed by two guards. In complete silence he moved from table to table and asked the same question, "Who is the host here?" then, "What is your position?" If the host was a foreigner the officer moved on; if Russian he was asked, "Do you work for the State or private business?" If the latter, as was mostly the case, the next question was, "Have you paid your taxes?" The reply was always affirmative but in each case the officer retorted, "We shall look into that matter." A score of luckless citizens, however, muttered nervously that they were in State or coöperative employ. "Ah," said the officer, "and what is your salary?" They named sums equivalent to fifty or at most a hundred dollars a month. "Not enough for banquets like this," was the stern comment. "Go stand over there in the corner by the door." Within half an hour the wretched men were led away by the guards and the rattle of the auto trucks into which they were loaded was clearly audible. There was no more gayety in the Hermitage that night and within a few weeks its lease was rescinded. It is now used as a club and "guest-house" for peasant delegations to the Soviet capital.

To the 250,000 private traders who were estimated to have flocked into Moscow in the past two and a half years the Hermitage incident was a knell of approaching doom. I did not witness it myself and it is possible that my foreign informant made more of it than the facts warranted, but the whole affair was in keeping with the Russian sense of drama and with the Latsis theory of Red Terror as a warning and example.

I heard a strikingly similar story from Perceval Gibbon, one of the best-known English war correspondents, who had spent the first two years of the War on the Eastern Front. In the winter of 1915 the Russians by heroic and costly efforts saved Warsaw from the Germans, but the invaders had thrust deep into Polish territory and the front line was less than fifty miles from the capital. The Commander-in-Chief of the Russian Army was then the Grand Duke Nicolai Nicolaivich, uncle of the Tsar, a giant of a man six-feet-eight in height, who, though popular with the army and the nation, was an inflexible martinet. He had given orders that Christmas leave on the Polish Front should be restricted to a minimum, but the Germans showed no sign of aggressiveness and many a high-born young Russian officer could not resist the temptation of an hour's run in a high-powered car to Warsaw. According to Gibbon, the Grand Duke in full Cossack uniform with high astrakhan shako, which made him look nearly eight feet tall, attended by four guards as big as himself, made a sudden visit on Christmas Eve to the dining-room of the Hotel Europe, Warsaw's foremost restaurant, and demanded that all officers in the room should justify their presence by documents. Those who had left the Front without leave were arrested on the spot, taken to the citadel and shot at dawn.

·   ·   ·   ·   ·   ·   ·   ·   ·   ·   ·

Towards the end of 1923 I began to get wind of other happenings of the greatest future significance, although at first only in the form of half-hints and cautious whispers about grave disagreements in high places. Communist secrets were well guarded, but I think it was in October that I was told in the strictest confidence that Trotzky had walked out of a Plenary Session of the Central Committee of the Party some weeks be-

fore after delivering a furious attack upon the organizational
methods of the Secretariat, that is to say of Stalin, and that he
had later presented a statement to the Politburo criticizing the
Party leadership and declaring that it was ruining the country
—that was the period of the alarming "Scissors" crisis to which
I referred before. What I did not know until much later was
that Trotzky's salvos had been followed by a regular broadside
known as the "Statement of the Forty-Six," signed by forty-six
prominent members of the Party, most of whom had taken part
in former opposition movements. The forty-six made a direct attack upon Stalin and claimed that he was abusing the powers
conferred upon him as General Secretary of the Central Committee. Looking backwards it is easy to see that these were the
first guns of the battle which was to rage within the Communist
Party for the next four years, but in the winter of 1923–24
their portent was hidden from foreign observers in Moscow. In
my own case I had small comprehension of what was happening, although I believe I was better informed than most foreigners. There were many reasons to account for this lapse.
However officially friendly might be my relations with individual Russian Bolsheviks, there was always a certain barrier between us. There was, moreover, an abundance of anti-Bolshevik
gossip in Moscow, mostly inspired by members of the former
ruling class who at that time were less afraid of contact with
foreigners than later became the case. They naturally hated the
Soviet régime and were always talking of strife in the Communist Party, which they hoped would follow the suicidal course
of the French Revolution. I had learned to discount such rumors
and to believe that, although discussions amongst the Soviet
leaders were often acrid and prolonged, they were not allowed
to degenerate into serious conflict. I had been told, for instance,
that Trotzky as a former Menshevik did in a sense represent a
kind of minority section in the Bolshevik Party, which he had

joined only in 1917, and that although Lenin never doubted his allegiance to the cause of revolution he knew that it was something different from and more independent than the loyalty of old members of the Bolshevik Party, and might at times border upon what the English mean when they speak of "His Majesty's Opposition," which is a phrase no Russian Bolshevik I have ever met has been able to understand. I am confident that Lenin would have understood it, as he understood Trotzky, although he never spared Trotzky in argument and did not hesitate, on occasion, to refute him with the utmost vigor. Finally, the very gravity of the disagreement and the importance of the personalities involved tended to make for secrecy, and although the fact of disagreement might leak out, its details were studiously withheld. Should a parallel situation present itself to-day, I do not think that I should be taken unawares a second time, not because I know more people in Russia than I did twelve years ago, although that of course is true, but because I have learned to read between the lines of the Soviet Press and to "feel" the interplay of currents and counter-currents. In 1923 I had no such knowledge; it was all I could do to grasp the literal meaning of a Soviet editorial without the aid of an interpreter. Throughout the first five years of my work in Moscow I was in the most precise sense of the phrase "trying to find out," groping my way through the fogs of lies and rumor, of my own ignorance, and of the bewildering difference between Russian and non-Russian mentality in the first place and Bolshevik and non-Bolshevik mentality in the second place.

During the long intra-Party controversy there was never any great disagreement about the goal at which all were aiming; the struggle was to decide who should determine the policies of the Soviet State, what those policies should be, and how they should be carried out. It is easy and natural to dramatize the situation by stressing the personal rivalries involved, to make it simply a struggle for power, or more simply still, a duel between Stalin and Trotzky. Too natural and too easy because the personal conflict motive fails to take into account the fanatical devotion of all the Bolsheviks, including Trotzky and the other oppositionists of one category or another, to their Cause. Everyone concerned in the controversy or in the series of controversies, from Stalin downward, was so devoted to the success of Bolshevism that he could not believe that any policy that he himself considered wrong could be other than damnable and dangerous heresy, to be avoided, nay, extirpated, at all costs. Stalin and Trotzky disliked each other, that is certain; but their antagonism would have been far less bitter had not each believed so whole-heartedly that to question the rightness of his own views was a sin against the Cause.

It is easy to be wise in retrospect and to recognize a dozen minor indications which should have afforded clews to the course events were taking, but when the Party controversy began I was handicapped, firstly, as I have said, by ignorance, secondly, by my conviction that reports of quarrels in high places had been vastly exaggerated in the past. I knew that the Bolsheviks allowed themselves freedom of argument about measures and policies prior to their adoption; it was only when a decision had been reached and a majority vote cast that the rigid discipline of the Party compelled the defeated minority to accept that decision without reserve or qualification.

Nevertheless there was one indication that I ought not to have missed. Not long before Christmas it was announced that the Thirteenth Party Conference had decided that 100,000 "workers from the bench" should be invited to join the Party without delay. The inference was obvious that this new membership, which amounted to nearly twenty per cent of the total strength of the Party at that time, would be hand-picked by the Secretariat, through its subordinate personnel in Moscow and

the provinces. When it subsequently became known that the new
members would have a right to vote for delegates to the next
Party Congress (in May, 1924), the full import of the maneuver became clear; the Secretariat had boldly added twenty per
cent of the total electorate to its own supporters in what bid fair
to be an evenly divided contest. Several years later a veteran
Communist told me that he thought this to have been the turning-point in the struggle between Stalin and Trotzky. "Prior to
that," he said, "the odds were in Trotzky's favor. He was popular with the Army from the lower ranks to the high command,
and his prestige at home and abroad was indubitably greater
than that of Stalin." It might, of course, be argued that the latter's chance came when he was appointed General Secretary of
the Party, but under Lenin, the Secretariat had far less influence and importance than it later acquired, and it must not be
forgotten that Lenin was apparently in good health when
Stalin's appointment was made. The problem that Stalin had
to solve was how far he could utilize the Secretariat to counter-
act Trotzky's greater popularity. In the admission of the 100,-
000 he found a solution. In other words, the first round between
the two redoubtable adversaries had gone strongly in Stalin's
favor and had ended with a knock-down blow. It is not unreasonable to suppose that Trotzky was aware of this himself, because he left Moscow on sick leave early in the new year (1924)
and spent the next three months in the Caucasus. To the amazement of all he did not even return for Lenin's funeral in the
following January.

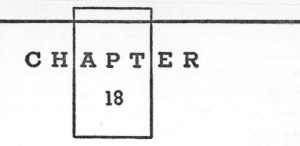

CHAPTER
18

LENIN'S FUNERAL—AND TROTZKY'S

LENIN died on January 21st, 1924. The official bulletin stated briefly, "On January 21st the condition of Vladimir Ilyich suddenly underwent a sharp aggravation. At 5.10 P.M. his breathing was interrupted and he lost consciousness; at 6.50 Vladimir Ilyich died from paralysis of the respiratory centers."

The news was a tremendous shock to the people of Russia; few save his closest intimates knew that he was afflicted with a mortal sickness, but even to those with him on the last day of his life his end was sudden and unexpected. That very morning he had gone out on a hunting party with Bukharin and some workers on the estate near Moscow where he had been staying for the last ten months, not taking part in the sport but sitting propped up with pillows in a sleigh to watch it. His condition had been improving during the past two weeks and it was thought that the outing would do him good. He came back in good spirits but appeared tired and the doctor in attendance advised him to go to bed. He ate a hearty meal about three o'clock and went to sleep. During this sleep the third and fatal attack of paralysis appeared, and he never recovered consciousness.

To the best of my knowledge his last words were wholly irrelevant to his remarkable career. They were: *"Vot sobaka,"* which may be translated: "Look at the dog." (There is no exact equivalent in English for the Russian *vot*, which corresponds to the French *voilà*.) I mention this point because it indicates how little was known outside the inner circle of Lenin's true condition. A few days after his death I received an account of that last morning from someone who was in a position to know the facts. He said, "Lenin was evidently in good spirits when they lifted him into the sleigh to go hunting. He sat watching with the keenest attention and when a young retriever brought back a bird to Bukharin, who was standing near the sleigh, Lenin raised his good hand and said, *'Vot sobaka.'* Everyone in the party was delighted, which made the blow all the more dreadful when it fell a few hours later."

To me the implications of this naïve account were staggering, but I do not doubt that it was authentic because it coincided with a semi-official version of Lenin's last hours that I obtained from the Soviet Foreign Office. I wrote that as follows: "Lenin had talked at his meal about the morning's sport, especially of one young hound which was nervous and untrained but showed remarkable aptitude. 'She is all right,' said Lenin, 'if you give her time and do not hustle her too much. She is young and stupid still and over-eager, but she will learn if you give her time.' " I added that these were practically his last words, which seemed to me symbolic in that he might have been speaking of Soviet Russia. Which marks the difference between poetry and fact. The *"Vot sobaka"* account showed that Lenin's second attack of paralysis must have smitten him with complete aphasia, for otherwise there would have been no cause for his friends to rejoice when at last he pronounced clearly two simple words. Admitting that they hoped desperately against hope, and that, as I was once told by an intimate friend of the great Chinese leader Sun Yat-sen, "He was so strong and big in our eyes that we refused to believe that death itself could conquer him," the fact remains that Lenin's condition in 1923 was far graver than foreigners in Moscow, or the great majority of Russians, were ever allowed to know.

I have the same memories of the week of Lenin's death and funeral as of the last days of July, 1914, which preceded the World War. Feverish, flurried hours blurred by lack of sleep, overwork, and the thrilling excitement of being able to report one of the moments in human history, with the signal difference that Paris in July, 1914, was so hot that I dripped and gasped and drank iced gin fizzes, whereas Moscow in January, 1924, was so cold that I froze and gasped and drank hot mulled wine. In both cases the sense of time was lost; there was no longer any idea of getting stuff in "below the deadline" or "to make to-morrow's paper," but just a roundabout of chasing the news and writing it, and writing it and chasing it. It rarely so happens that a reporter loses distinction between night and day and thinks only of getting the story and sending it. In such cases, it seems to me, he does not have to think of writing it; the story writes itself, an exhausting experience but incredibly exhilarating. My reports were published from day to day in *The New York Times* and later republished in a book so that I hesitate to repeat them here. A few excerpts may convey the stress and color of those historic days.

"Moscow, January 22nd, 1924. Lenin died last night at 6.50 o'clock. The immediate cause of death was paralysis of the respiratory centers due to a cerebral hemorrhage. For some time optimistic reports have been current as to the effects of a previous lesion being gradually cleared up, but Lenin's nearest friends, realizing the progress of the relentless malady, tried vainly to hope against hope.

"At 11.50 o'clock this morning President Kalinin briefly opened the session of the All-Union Soviet Congress and requested everyone to stand. He had not slept all night and tears were streaming down his haggard face. A sudden wave of emotion—not a sound, but a strange stir—passed over the audience, none of whom knew what had happened. The music started to play the Soviet funeral march, but was instantly hushed as Kalinin murmured brokenly: 'I bring you terrible news about our dear comrade, Vladimir Ilyich.' (Lenin was his pen-name.)

"High up in the gallery a woman uttered a low, wailing cry that was followed by a burst of sobs.

" 'Yesterday,' faltered Kalinin, 'yesterday, he suffered a further stroke of paralysis and—' there was a long pause as if the speaker were unable to nerve himself to pronounce the fatal word; then, with an effort which shook his whole body, it came '—died.'

"The emotional Slav temperament reacted immediately. From all over the huge opera house came sobs and wailing, not loud or shrill, but pitifully mournful, spreading and increasing. Kalinin could not speak. He tried vainly to motion for silence with his hands and for one appalling moment a dreadful outbreak of mass hysteria seemed certain. A tenth of a second later it could not have been averted, but Yenukidze, Secretary of the Russian Federal Union, thrust forward his powerful frame and with hand and voice demanded calm. Then Kalinin, stammering, read out the official bulletin."

"Moscow, January 23rd. Two unforgettable pictures stand out from this day of Russia's sorrow. First, Lenin lying in state —such simple state amid such grandeur—in the columned hall of the former Nobles' Club; second, the face and shoulders of Kalinin, the former peasant-worker, helping to bear Lenin's coffin from the station, when two steps down from the platform its weight was suddenly thrown on him in front. During those moments of strain he symbolized the struggle of Russia's 140,-

000,000 peasants against the blind enmity of nature and human oppression. For two nights he had not slept and, as the level ground relieved part of the burden, he staggered from sheer exhaustion. But on he went like an old peasant plowing the stubborn earth, with sweat pouring down his cheeks in an icy-flecked gale, until he reached a gun caisson with six white horses waiting in the station-yard to carry the coffin to the Nobles' Club.

"Back to the Kremlin barracks those gunners drove disconsolate, for Lenin's friends—members of the various central committees—insisted that they and only they should bear the glass-covered coffin through the five miles of snow-bound streets at the head of the gigantic procession. Every half-mile or so the *cortège* halted to change coffin bearers. Both sides of the route were lined with troops shoulder to shoulder and above them every house was crowded—windows, balconies and roofs—with a black swarm of spectators with bared heads beneath black-edged red flags that fluttered wildly in the storm."

(Later.) "In the central hall of the former Nobles' Club Lenin lay on a high couch with four columns that gave the effect of a sort of old-fashioned four-poster bed without curtains. Over his feet was a gray rug with something stenciled on it, over his body a dark red blanket; and his head rested bare on a white pillow. The face was a yellow-white, like wax, without the slightest wrinkle and utterly calm. The eyes were closed, yet the expression was of one looking forward, seeking something beyond his vision.

"At each corner of the couch stood members of the Central Committee of the Communist Party and of the Council of Commissars who will replace each other at intervals of ten minutes day and night for the next seventy hours.

"Never have I seen men so completely still. Not a muscle in their eyelids flickered, and they hardly seemed to breathe. They

wore ordinary dress, as simple as the couch itself, while round
them passed slow-footed mourners, who will continue to pass
for seventy hours between the lines of khaki-clad soldiers."

(Later.) "A mile and a half of people were waiting to-night
six deep in Moscow streets with the temperature 20 degrees below zero to pay their last respects to Lenin. From all over Russia special trains are hurrying tens upon tens of thousands
more to the capital. As I write, the echo of revolutionary hymns
which this waiting multitude is singing comes through the whirl-
ing snow-storm to my windows. So they will pass all night and
day for the next seventy hours, through the many-columned hall
where Lenin's body lies."

"Moscow, January 26th. All to-day and all last night crowds
flowed towards the House of Columns in, it seemed, greater volume than before. The doors were to be shut at noon to-day, but
before the eagerness of the multitude twelve hours more were
conceded until midnight. All this in the grip of the bitterest cold
—28 below zero Fahrenheit. One wonders how they stand it.

"Last night even the ponies of the guards outside the House
of Columns were white from head to tail with congealed per-
spiration as they halted for a few minutes to rest. The soldiers
stamped and waved arms around big log fires, but the long
black lines of people crept forward regardless, with scarcely a
sign of life save singing at intervals.

"This morning I watched a group of children, aged six to
eleven, pass through the Hall of Columns. Each triad of little
ones had an elder child or teacher with them, all four hand in
hand. With wide, astonished eyes they stared at the couch where
Lenin lay. As rank after rank moved across the room past the
body, their heads turned to the right as though held by an irresistible attraction. On the farther side of the hall the red carpet
turned sharply at right angles leading to the exit.

"Each rank of the children, and many older folks, too, went on straight ahead as though hypnotized and would have marched blindly into the wall had not the teachers been there to guide them round the corner. As it was, a guard at the corner was forced to intervene again and again, so lost were the people in their first and final contemplation of Lenin.

"The effect on the children and the simpler section of the public was extraordinary—a sort of veritable hypnosis that lasted two or three minutes after they reached the street again. The sudden bright lights in the hall, the dazzling white walls, and the heady perfume of flowers doubtless were responsible in no small degree, but there was something more—mass suggestion or crowd psychology perhaps.

"Most of all the children seemed struck by the utter stillness of the figure on the couch and the watchers beside it.

" 'Was it really Lenin,' asked one little girl, 'or was it only an image of him?'

" 'Of course it was he,' said an older friend, 'but he could not move, he is dead.'

" 'But the others standing by his bed did not move either,' persisted the little one. 'Were they dead, too?'

"Strangely enough, none of them seemed frightened. One small boy was weeping bitterly, and I asked him if he had been afraid. He shook his head.

" 'No,' he gulped at last. 'I'm sorry for poor Lenin—he looked so lonely there in the middle of the great big room with people passing around. . . .'

"What is happening here emphasizes the religious aspect of Bolshevism with Lenin as the central figure. How else can one explain the gigantic mass movement to see his body—a movement not of Communists and their sympathizers alone, but of the rest of the population, despite such agony of cold? The Bolsheviki can organize much, but it is not their propaganda which draws these hundreds of thousands to Lenin's feet."

"Moscow, January 27th. The climax of an amazing week of national emotion was reached at four o'clock to-day under the ancient wall of the Kremlin, where, as bells tolled and guns thundered, Stalin, Kamenev, Zinoviev, Bukharin, Rykov, and Kalinin bore Lenin's red-draped coffin from the high dais where it had lain all this afternoon to the mausoleum in the Red Square, still covered by a wooden construction shed, under the shadow of a huge plaster statue of a workman.

"Massed bands played the *Internationale* to slow time, and from the vast multitude in the Square rose in the icy air a fog of congealed breath, like the smoke of sacrifice. So cold was it —35 degrees below zero Fahrenheit—that beards, hats, collars, and eyebrows were white like the snow-clad trees in the little park close to the Kremlin wall. Few dared to take off their hats as Lenin's body passed to its last resting-place. The majority stood at salute with raised hands.

"In the streets leading to the square tens of thousands more, lined up under mourning banners, were waiting admission. At the corners soldiers built log fires, round which each squad, relieved hourly owing to the intense cold, stamped and beat their arms against their bodies.

"The most striking feature of the last moment was its utter absence of ceremony. Lenin's disciples took the Master's body and laid it in its appointed place. No word was said."

· · · · · · · · · · ·

To everyone in Moscow, whether Russian or foreign, the absorbing question in that week of strain and sorrow was the absence of Trotzky. It was a period of intense popular emotion and we all knew that to nine-tenths of the Russian masses Trotzky was second only to Lenin in popular esteem. He was said to be sick and traveling to a cure in the Caucasus, but nothing could condone his absence save the fact that he was so near death that it would have been fatal for him to make the return journey, which was not the case. Whatever may have been his reasons, Trotzky's failure to pay his last tribute to the dead leader horrified the people of Moscow as a want of respect and good taste. It was, moreover a political error of the first magnitude and dealt a fatal blow to Trotzky's prestige, which his adversaries were quick to see and turn to good account. To this day I cannot imagine why he did not come. The night after the funeral I discussed the problem with my friend Rollin, the only French correspondent in Moscow at that time, who had held an important position in the French Navy as personal aide and adviser to the Admiral commanding the French forces at Constantinople and was one of the chief editorial writers of the Paris *Temps,* which ranks as the semi-official organ of the French Government.

Rollin agreed with me that Trotzky's absence was inexplicable. "From all I can learn," he said, "Trotzky is not even dangerously ill, although I won't accept the view that his illness is wholly, or mainly, diplomatic." He paused and rubbed his high, broad forehead. "Yes," he said, "it's extraordinary— worse than any surrender. How pleased Stalin must be!"

"Don't you think that rivalry stuff has been exaggerated?" I asked. "After all you must admit that the Bolshevik leaders are sincere, and surely Lenin's death will induce them to iron out any personal differences that may have existed before."

"For the time being perhaps," said Rollin sagely, "but that effect of Lenin's death may be no more than temporary and emotional. Unless I am mistaken, the divergence between Trotzky and Stalin is fundamental. I'll admit that both of them are sincere, but now that Lenin has gone there is bound to be a clash between them. Until now I would have picked Trotzky to

win. I know that he is more popular than Stalin and I thought
he was much cleverer, but now I have begun to doubt it. My
God, what an opportunity to miss! Achilles sulking in his tent.
Quel idiot! As if he couldn't understand that the whole strength
of his position was his reputation with the masses as Lenin's
chief aide and supporter. Surely you've heard the story that
peasants in outlying villages talk with awe and reverence of the
new Tsar called Leninandrotsky, who has come from the East
to regenerate Holy Russia. As a matter of personal respect to
Lenin, Trotzky should have risen from his death-bed to be present; it was his duty and obligation, and there isn't a man or
woman in the whole country who doesn't think so. It is a blunder that will cost him dear. Think too of what he missed; if he
had come to Moscow, he couldn't have failed to be the central
figure in the funeral ceremonies. No one would have dared to
interfere with him; he would have stolen the show, as you say
in America, whether Stalin and the others liked it or not. But he
did not come. Henceforth, I tell you, my money is on Stalin."
"So is mine," I said, "but it was already."

. . . .

Trotzky's own explanation in his autobiography of his absence from Lenin's funeral is thin and unconvincing, and does
small credit either to his heart or head. He declares that a code
message from Stalin announcing Lenin's death was delivered to
him in his private car at the station in Tiflis on January 21st,
that is to say a few hours after Lenin died. He continues, "I
got the Kremlin on the direct wire. In answer to my inquiry I
was told: 'The funeral will be on Saturday; you cannot get back
in time and so we advise you to continue your treatment.' Accordingly, I had no choice. As a matter of fact, the funeral did
not take place until Sunday and I could easily have reached
Moscow by then. Incredible as it may appear, I was even deceived about the date of the funeral."

This final accusation was as unjust as it was ungenerous. Lenin died on the afternoon of Monday, January 21st, and his funeral was originally set for Saturday, the 26th, but the number of people who wished to see him was so great—thousands came from places more distant than Tiflis—that it was postponed twenty-four hours. The journey from Moscow to Tiflis by ordinary express takes three days and three nights—allow four or even five days and nights in 1924 in winter-time. Trotzky's private car was in the station when he received the news on Monday night. Tiflis is one of the biggest railroad depots in south Russia and there is not the slightest doubt that the Red war-lord, whose authority was still unquestioned, could have ordered a special train and been back in Moscow within seventy-two hours. Trotzky's account continues theatrically, "The Tiflis comrades came to demand that I should write on Lenin's death at once. But I knew only one urgent desire—and that was to be alone. I could not stretch my hand to lift the pen." He then adds that he wrote a "few handwritten pages." Strangest of all, there is no word in Trotzky's recital of any surmise on his part, much less compunction, as to what people in Moscow might feel about his failure to return immediately. Any thought of the duty he owed to his dead comrade seems to have been as remote from his mind as perception of the political effects of his absence. Instead he writes of spending those days before the funeral lying on a balcony in the sun at Sukhum, a twenty-four-hour train journey from Tiflis which apparently caused him no physical distress—facing the glittering sea and the huge palms—and of his own "sensation of running a temperature" with which mingled, he says, thoughts of Lenin's death. To make the picture complete Trotzky quotes a passage from his wife's diary: "We arrived quite broken down; it was the first time we had seen Sukhum. The mimosa were in full bloom, magnificent palms, camellias. In the dining-room of the rest-house there were two

portraits on the wall, one—draped in black—of Vladimir Ilyich, the other of L.D. (Trotzky). We felt like taking the latter
one down but thought it would look too demonstrative." Later
Madame Trotzky wrote: "Our friends were expecting L.D. to
come to Moscow and thought he would cut short his trip in order to return, since no one imagined that Stalin's telegram had
cut off his return." (This refers to the message from the Kremlin saying that the funeral would be on Saturday and that
Trotzky could not get back in time.) "I remember my son's letter received at Sukhum. He was terribly shocked by Lenin's
death and, though suffering from a cold with a temperature of
104, he went in his not very warm coat to the Hall of Columns
to pay his last respects and waited, waited, and waited with impatience for our arrival. One could feel in his letter his bitter
bewilderment and diffident reproach." On these extracts from
his wife's diary Trotzky makes no comment at all.

Such a combination of personal callousness and political in-
sensitiveness does more to explain Trotzky's downfall than a
hundred books by Stalin's warmest supporters. To suggest that
he was sulking, like Achilles in his tent, is perhaps unfair. His
autobiography states that he had an attack of influenza in October, 1923, which passed into a chronic fever aggravated (at this
point he cites his wife's diary in confirmation) by his losing
struggle against opponents in the Politburo. A month's stay at
Prince Youssupov's former country house near Moscow brought
no improvement and his doctor ordered a trip to Sukhum,
which restored Trotzky's health but ruined his career. From
that time onwards, although he had many devoted adherents in
the Party, he had irretrievably "lost face" with the mass of the
Russian people. His adversaries in Russia have not failed to
question the genuineness of his illness at that time; they have
claimed that it was sickness of spirit rather than sickness of
body, that Trotzky had made an ambitious bid for Lenin's suc-

cession and that when he failed his wounded egoism turned on itself like a scorpion and poisoned him. They point to the long comedy of his plea to enter Germany "on grounds of ill health and for no other purpose than medical treatment" at the time of his exile from Russia, when no country save Turkey would give him harborage. Even there, from the pleasant island where he lived in the Bosphorus, he poured out a continual stream of complaints about his health. In short, they imply, Trotzky was either a liar or a hypochondriac or both, but what they really mean is that he "worked himself into a fever," as the saying goes; and that may well be true. It is clear from his own account that it was not the state of his health which prevented him from taking part in Lenin's funeral. As for his sojourn in Turkey I can only say that two of my friends visited him on the Bosphorus island and both of them remarked on his robust physical condition. In the spring of 1930 I went to Alma Ata in Central Asia, to which he had first been exiled. During his stay there Trotzky's sympathizers in Moscow wailed loudly that his health was being ruined by the extremes of heat and cold. He refers in his autobiography to the prevalence of malaria and leprosy. I saw the house where he lived in Alma Ata, which is far more comfortable and spacious than my own apartment in Moscow; I saw the pleasant villa in the mountains where he spent the summer; and I heard everyone, from the local Gay-pay-oo men to the man in the street, talk warmly of Trotzky's hunting trips and how hard he worked and how cheerful and friendly he was to one and all.

A great man Trotzky, of that there is no doubt, a man of superlative mental ability, and a most competent executive withal; a man of proven courage, both physical and moral, a splendid writer and orator with the rare power of equal appeal to an intelligent and to a popular audience. In all history there are few careers so romantic as that of Trotzky: to have risen from so low to such a height, to have shone so bright in the sun, and to have done brave deeds in a quaking world—and then to have fallen again to nothing, to spend his declining years in spiteful twilight. What a tragic fate for this man who was gifted with intelligence and force beyond his fellows, yet cursed by the folly of selfishness and pride.

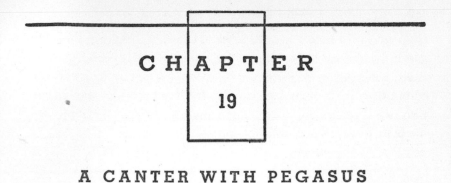

CHAPTER
19

A CANTER WITH PEGASUS

LENIN's death was followed by a period of truce in the intra-Party controversy. This gratified me—quite unduly as I now see —because I had been writing a lot of sentimental twaddle about "Lenin's old comrades burying the hatchet in the grave of their lost leader," and so forth. I do not mean to suggest that the popular sentiment evoked by Lenin's death and funeral was anything but genuine; throughout the country there was a rush of enthusiasm to join the Communist Party and 250,000 new adherents were enrolled between January and June. But sentimental considerations had small place in the hearts of the Bolshevik leaders. The official historian of the Communist Party, Comrade Popov, in handling this phase of the Party controversy misses the point little less completely than I did. He ascribes the truce to the smashing defeat that Trotsky and his associates had sustained in the summer and autumn of 1923. The truth of the matter was that Trotzky was prostrate and broken, not by "the smashing defeat" or even, as he himself suggests, by illness, but by the sickening realization of what his absence from Lenin's funeral had done to him and his career. They say that Hell is paved with good intentions, but the white-hot plowshares of opportunities missed and advantages lost make cruel treading for ambitious feet. Trotzky lay on his balcony in Sukhum facing the sun and the sea and the mimosa and palms and camellias, reading letters or receiving friends. Little comfort either brought him and no good medicine for distress of soul. I have already suggested that the cause of his illness was psychological as well as physical. In what torment he must have writhed when letter after letter, friend after friend, told him, albeit unwillingly, the plain and sorry truth. At first, I have been informed, he refused to believe that his tremendous popularity had not only faded but was changed in no small degree to resentment. Gradually, despite himself, he was forced to understand that this was the case, and, worse still, that he had missed the heaven-sent opportunity of confirming in the mind of the masses the position that he claimed—and indeed had held for six full years—of Lenin's right hand and destined successor. The cabal of his adversaries, of which he speaks so bitterly in his autobiography, might defeat him in the Politburo or the Central Committee, but they never could have robbed him of his hold over the masses. As Rollin said, Trotzky would have "stolen the show" at the funeral in the teeth of Stalin and the rest of them.

In twenty years of newspaper work I have been present at many scenes of national thrill and color—the day War was declared in Paris when a frenzied mob surged down the Grand Boulevard singing the *Marseillaise* and shouting *"à Berlin,"* and Armistice Night in Paris, and the Victory Parade—but all of them are dwarfed in my memory by Lenin's funeral week. I have known, too, popular figures and spellbinders of many races but never one to surpass Trotzky in the flame and power of his appeal to any audience. Lenin's funeral was literally made for Trotzky. Whether Stalin liked it or not, Trotzky could have delivered a speech in the Red Square that would have electrified not only Russia but the whole world and established his supremacy beyond any doubt or question.

In justice to Trotzky it may be supposed that Lenin's death had caused him deep personal sorrow. Nevertheless, that sorrow can have been nothing in comparison to the despair that he felt at seeing himself blacked out of the Russian picture in which he had played so prominent a rôle. No wonder that his health did not improve and that he took no active part in politics until the late autumn. Whatever he might write about being "deceived" as to the date of the funeral he must have known that he himself was responsible for his fatal blunder. By his own act he had ostracized himself, and there was no more spirit in him.

Stalin was not slow to take advantage of the situation thus created. To him too, Lenin's death provided a golden opportunity—indeed if Trotzky is to be believed it was more than that; it prevented an attack inspired by Lenin which Stalin might not have been able to resist. Personally, I am inclined to question Trotzky's version at this point. I think that drowning in the deep humiliation which followed the knowledge of his own mistake he clutched at the straw of a half-expressed or tentative intention on Lenin's part and made of it a beam to buttress his weakened self-esteem. Unlike Trotzky, Stalin seized opportunity with both hands. On one side he used his power as Party Secretary to shift Trotzky's adherents from key posts and replace them by men of his own choice; on the other he took advantage of the enthusiastic influx of new blood into the Party. The most decisive of the shifts in personnel was the replacement of Sklanski, Trotzky's right-hand man at the Commissariat of War, by Frunzé, who later succeeded Trotzky as Commissar. This was approved by the Thirteenth Party Congress in May, 1924, which Trotzky did not attend, but it was only one of a series of such changes which showed that Stalin knew and was utilizing the strength of his position as Party Secretary.

In the months between Lenin's death in January and the

Thirteenth Congress in May 241,000 men and women applied for admittance to the Communist Party, in addition to the 127,-000 new members who had joined after the decision of the previous autumn to enroll 100,000 "workers from the bench." The total membership at that time was 736,000. Thus the new members, all of whom, as I said earlier, had been hand-picked by the lower ranks of the Secretariat, that is to say by the Stalinist machine, were exactly half of the total. Trotzky in his autobiography says that three-quarters of the Party were new members, but his error has no importance in view of the fact that the Party was almost evenly divided between him and Stalin in the middle of 1923 and that almost all of the new members could be relied upon to support the Stalinist platform. Indeed, what Trotzky probably means is that three-fourths of the Party were against him in May, 1924, which was perfectly correct. What he fails to say, however, is that prior to Lenin's death more than three-quarters—probably not less than nine-tenths—of the Soviet proletariat were for him. Comrade Popov in his official history of the Communist Party may choose to ignore the fact that the Moscow Gay-pay-oo and the Foreign Office itself voted pro-Trotzkyist resolutions at their meetings in the summer of 1923, but it is true and bears witness to Trotzky's popularity. The army was devoted to him and he had a glamour for the working masses which Stalin never rivaled. Trotzky begins one of the later chapters of his book by saying that he is often asked how he came to lose power. His answer consists partly of an analysis of the reaction that is liable to follow any revolution amongst the masses and their leaders, partly of a diatribe against the "conspiracy" led by Stalin, Djerzhinsky, Ordjonkidze, Kamenev and Zinoviev, of which he claims he was the victim. This explanation is as confusing as it is voluminous. Trotzky "lost power" because on the afternoon of January 27, 1924, he lay in the sun on the balcony of the rest-house at Sukhum and felt "the sensation of running a temperature," mingled, as he says, with the thought of Lenin's death, instead of appearing in uniform in the Red Square of Moscow and helping to carry Lenin's body to the mausoleum.

.   .   .   .

During 1923 and the first half of 1924 the Bolshevik leaders had been too much occupied by anxiety about Lenin and by their own quarrels to pay proper attention to what was happening in the country. When Trotzky was for the time being disposed of and they had time to look around them, what they saw was not reassuring. The N.E.P.-men still handled two-thirds of the nation's trade; the production of factory-made goods and of iron and steel was barely a quarter of its pre-War volume; and last but not least a new class of prosperous farmers employing labor, that is to say kulaks, had arisen in the villages. In a typical Bolshevik manner Stalin replied to this unsatisfactory situation indirectly and with violence. He launched a savage drive against grafters in State service and it was said that in the months of March and April, 1924, there were 30,000 arrests in Moscow. In a preceding chapter I told how a Gaypay-oo official "purged" the Hermitage Restaurant on New Year's Eve. What he so demonstratively began was continued on a steadily rising scale, because for every grafting State official who was arrested there were three or four N.E.P.-men accomplices who shared his guilt in a greater or less degree. The Bolsheviks themselves were appalled by the extent of the corruption they found. Heads of State Trusts, Party members, some of them of long standing, were living in scandalous luxury with country villas, fancy women, and elegant carriages drawn by thoroughbred trotters. There had grown up a widespread illicit coöperation between State and private trade, as profitable to individuals as it was damaging to the community. Dishonest State employees were punished without mercy but the drive begun against them only brought home to the authorities the fact that their worst enemy was not graft or corruption but the anomalous coexistence of State and private trade, which made that corruption possible and profitable; in other words, N.E.P. itself. The anti-graft campaign was followed by a series of measures against private traders, that is to say a heavy increase in taxation and the erection of strong barriers against their purchase of State-produced goods. Many of the N.E.P.-men saw what was coming and hastily sold out to coöperatives, and some were fortunate enough to escape abroad with the proceeds. I knew one of them who still lives luxuriously in the South of France and tells all and sundry how he escaped from the Crimea in 1920 with his "family jewels" sewn into the lining of his coat. I doubt if this particular citizen ever had a father who was willing to acknowledge him, much less a family or jewels. He skipped abroad *via* Riga in the summer of 1924 with a couple of hundred-thousand-dollar bills plastered in a red woolen chest-protector above his quivering heart. This reminds me of a story I was told last year by a Russian *émigré* in Paris. He said, "I don't need to tell you that there are more Russian nobles, princes, counts, and generals, in Paris alone than there ever were in Tsarist Russia. One night a group of these 'distinguished' fellow-countrymen of mine sat talking over old days. 'Oh dear,' said one, 'when I think of my splendid *château* in the country and the parties I used to give, 200 guests with fifty flunkies and all the vodka and caviar that the greediest could desire.' 'Yes,' said another, 'and my four-in-hand coach which I had imported from England at a cost of 20,000 roubles; do you remember that, how I used to drive to the races in Moscow like King George at Ascot? Alas, those days are gone for ever!' A third chimed in, 'And my mistress, the famous dancer to whom I gave a necklace of pearls that a Grand Duke had tried in vain to buy. Yes, my friend, you are right; those days are gone for ever.' While they talked an old gentleman was sitting in the corner with a tiny Dandy Dinmont terrier on his knee. He, as it happened, had been a real grandee of Tsarist Russia, General in the army, Governor of a province, owner of 50,000 acres with full *entrée* to the Imperial Court. 'Yes,' he said reflectively, 'those were the good old days, which now are gone for ever. Don't you remember, Dandy my dog'—he tweaked the terrier's ear affectionately—'those good old days before the Revolution when you were a great big borzoi wolf-hound and won prizes at the Imperial show.' "

In 1924 the Russians experienced the sorrows of deflation. They learned, as did Americans after 1929, that there is an almighty difference between a balloon going slowly up and falling headlong down. That the Russian inflation had been one of currency when the rouble soared to astronomic heights, whereas America's was a credit inflation when the weekly bank turnover of checks amounted to fifty times more than the total currency in circulation, made no real difference. In both cases the balloon went up and up and was over-inflated; in both the balloon fell down, down, down—deflation as it is termed. In both cases, too, the results were identical—hard times and unemployment. In Russia with a population of 150,000,000, unemployment was comparatively negligible, not more at the peak than 1,250,000, as compared with 12,000,000 or more unemployed in the United States; but Russia was a poor country with no resources or accumulated fat, and its 1,000,000 unemployed were a heavy burden. This too was a problem for the Kremlin leaders to solve, and they did not see where a solution could be found under the system of N.E.P. It was then that the Bolsheviks first began to think of a system of planned economy and to envisage the choice that lay ahead of them; either they must let Nature take its course and allow unemployment to depend, as in capitalist society, upon the financial and economic situation, or they could

strike out boldly upon a new socialist course and find employment for anyone who wanted it in the development by the State
of the natural resources belonging to the State. This was another
nail in N.E.P.'s coffin. The fact is that N.E.P. had done what
was required of it; it had reëstablished agricultural production
and set the wheels of industry aroll once more, but the Bolsheviks were not yet quite resolved to throw N.E.P. overboard. That
they were approaching that resolve even I could see but they had
not reached it, and in the meantime the fruits of N.E.P. remained for a rapidly diminishing minority to gather. Foreign
residents of Moscow were numbered in this minority. Little they
cared when one private store after another shut down through
the imprisonment or ultra-taxation of its owner so long as other
stores remained where they could buy what they needed. They
grumbled of course about rising prices but none of them, including myself, seemed to understand that what was happening to
the N.E.P.-men was not a series of accidents but a historical
process, whose conclusion must mean that N.E.P.-men would be
eliminated.

Nevertheless life was pleasant in Moscow that summer. I had
come to know a number of poets and writers and artists, who
used to meet in the evenings at a café on the Tverskaya opposite
the Hotel Lux which bore the extravagant title of "Stable of
Pegasus." It was a favorite haunt of Isadora Duncan—she had
a school of dancing in Moscow at the time—who had just married what seemed to me an extremely worthless poet named
Essenin. Of all the people I have known I think Isadora was
the most picturesque. I saw her dance once in London while I
was still in college, and ever afterwards the memory of her
grace and beauty and slim, flashing limbs stayed with me as
something rare and wonderful. Then I met her in Moscow, a
stout middle-aged woman married to this pimply Essenin, and
strange to say I was not disillusioned in the least, because Isa-

dora had a flame inside her whose brightness had nothing to do with her body. I knew that she was fat and lazy and drank to excess and did not much care whether she was ill-kempt or sloppy, but I knew also that she had a hole in her heart which excused everything. In all human experience there is nothing so devastating as a hole in the heart, no matter what it comes from. In Isadora's case it was caused by the tragic death of her children in Paris when a taxi-driver drove them and their governess and himself suddenly into the Seine, because his steering gear went wrong on the corner of a bridge, and all of them were drowned. After that Isadora did not care much about anything. She told me so herself and I said, "Did you ever care much about anything anyway? You're an artist, aren't you? What do artists care about anything ever?" Isadora said, "You're damn clever, Walter Duranty, and you're a damn fool. Can't you understand that there's all the difference between what you feel as an artist and what you care about as a person?" Isadora was lonely in Moscow and I think she liked talking to me because she knew that I admired her terribly and thought her conversation wonderful.

One night in the fall of 1923 I spent an hour in her dressing-room at a theater where she was going to dance with some of the children from her school. Kollontai, the first woman ever to be appointed Ambassador—she had served in Norway or Sweden, and Mexico—was there too. It was a ceremonial evening in honor of the Fifth Congress of the Women's Section of the Communist Party, and the preliminary speeches took more time than had been expected. Isadora grew impatient and sent me out for a bottle of vodka, then she and Kollontai sat and talked about life and love and men and what they thought of them. Kollontai had fully as much experience as Isadora and had written some interesting books on relations between the sexes, from a highly modern and radical viewpoint. I remembered a little rhyme that someone in the American Army used to remind men on leave of the danger of talking too much about troop movements and where battalions or divisions were stationed, and so forth:

> *There was an owl who lived in an oak:*
> *The more he heard the less he spoke:*
> *The less he spoke the more he heard:*
> *Soldiers, imitate that wise bird.*

Like the owl I sat tight and listened. I would give much for a stenographic report of that conversation, delivered at high tension by two past masters in the Art of which they spoke. To my sorrow the vodka on top of a hearty dinner was too much for my memory, but I know that I have rarely had an hour of greater entertainment, and I am certain that the transcript of their dialogue would have made a marvelous book. I heard a story about Kollontai when I first went to Moscow which illustrates Lenin's humanity and sense of humor. In the early days of the Revolution she had a violent affair with Dybenko, the idol of the Red fleet, who had brought the cruiser *Aurora* up the Neva from Kronstadt to Petrograd, at the time of the Revolution in November, 1917, to fire on the Winter Palace which was then the headquarters of the Provisional Government. He and Kollontai were so absorbed in each other that they forgot about the Revolution whose fate still hung in the balance, and rushed off to the Crimea for a honeymoon. This caused acrid comment amongst the Communist leaders, who were a puritanical lot, and finally the matter was brought up seriously in a meeting of the Central Committee. One speaker after another demanded the severest penalties against the erring couple for what they called "desertion in face of the enemy." It was soon clear that the meeting wanted to have them shot, no less.

Then Lenin intervened. "I have listened, comrades," he said solemnly, "to your just and weighty remarks, with which I fully concur. No punishment can be too harsh for this unworthy pair; death itself is inadequate. I therefore suggest that we vote upon the following resolution: 'Sternly repudiating the behavior of Comrades Kollontai and Dybenko the Central Committee of the Communist Party decides that they be punished in an exemplary manner, to wit, that they are jointly and severally condemned to be exclusively faithful to each other for the period of five years.' " The motion was dropped in a gale of laughter, but my informant added that Kollontai never quite forgave Lenin for saving her life in that way.

I was sitting with Isadora Duncan one evening in "The Stable of Pegasus" café when the poets were having a party; that is to say one after another got up on a little stage at the end of the room and recited his own verses. That, it seems, is the poet's ideal of a party. Essenin had been sitting there rather drunker and more offensive than usual, which was saying a good deal, and when he left us just before his turn I couldn't help asking Isadora why on earth she married that one. She was not in the least offended. "He's not at his best to-night, poor Sergei," she admitted, "but there's one thing I'd have you know, and it's this; that boy's a genius. All my lovers have been geniuses; it's the one thing upon which I insist." Mentally I raised my eyebrows but I did not attempt to argue. A minute or two later Essenin reeled on to the stage to speak his piece. The café was full of a motley crowd, poets and their girl friends all talking at the top of their voices; just behind me a couple of prostitutes from the Tverskaya bargaining noisily with a reluctant client; in a corner near the door two drunks were having a wordy battle with a hack-driver who demanded payment on account before he would agree to wait for them indefinitely. Then Essenin began to recite one of his poems called *The Black Man*. At first his voice was low and husky, but as the swing of the verses caught him it deepened and grew stronger.

The poem was raw and brutal but alive and true. It described the feelings of a drunkard on the verge of delirium tremens, who was haunted by the face of a negro grinning at him. The face was not unfriendly but it was everywhere—looking over his shoulder in the mirror when he shaved, beside him on the pillow in his bed, poised between his shoes in the morning when he got up to put them on.

I knew the story of this poem. The negro face was that of Claude McKaye, the colored poet who had visited Moscow a year or so before and had been a friend of Essenin. Essenin was then close to delirium tremens, and his verses were real; they expressed what he had felt and known.

As his voice rose there came utter silence in the café. Line after shattering line banged the consciousness of that motley crowd and froze them into horror. It was tremendous and ter-rible to hear the agony of the haunted wretch, and Essenin made us share it. A triumph of transmitted emotion from the Artist to the Public.

When he stopped there was not a sound. Everyone—cab men, speculators, prostitutes, poets, drunkards—all sat frozen with pale faces, open mouths, and anguished eyes. Then Isadora, whom nothing could dismay, said to me quietly, "Do you still think my little peasant boy has no genius?"

CHAPTER
20

I WRITE AS I PLEASE

IN THE summer of 1924 I witnessed a still more striking instance of the power of human personality. This was real drama and a man's life was at stake, but I always think of it as the greatest theatrical performance I ever attended. It began theatrically; I was sitting at home one evening about 9.30 when there came a telephone message from the acting chief of the Press Department of the Foreign Office, asking me to meet him there at once with my car. That was all, but his voice was full of excitement. When he got into the car he fixed me with a glittering eye. "I am taking you to a trial," he whispered impressively, "only two other foreign correspondents will be admitted. It is the trial of our greatest enemy; we have caught him redhanded. To-night the Supreme Military Tribunal of the U.S.S.R. will pass judgment on its arch-enemy, Boris Savinkov, Kerensky's War Minister, who planned the killing of Count Mirbach and the attempted assassination of Lenin and the revolt at Yaroslavl in 1918; the man who more than anyone brought about the Franco-British Intervention and the Polish War. He came into Russia secretly, in disguise and with false papers, but we caught him; and to-night he will be judged."

I had not been two seconds in the room where the trial was to be held before I felt the terrific excitement of everyone present. There were only 200 or so of this "*élite* first-night audience" but they were the ranking men and women of Soviet Russia. Stalin was not amongst them, nor Djerzhinsky, Zinoviev or Trotzky, but with these exceptions everyone who was anyone in Moscow was in that hot packed room, all tense and eager as hounds when they sight their laboring quarry and rush forward to the kill. Save myself and two colleagues no foreigners were present, which infuriated the diplomatic corps when they heard of it and won me a dozen invitations to dinner in the next three days.

The real work of the trial, it appeared, had been done *in camera;* all that remained that night was the "last-word" speech of the defendant and the verdict. Savinkov was worthy of his audience and his stellar rôle. His final speech, not in his own defense because he did not attempt to defend himself, but to explain himself to them and perhaps even more to explain himself to himself was the greatest piece of oratory I have ever heard. I say this deliberately, although I have heard speeches by men who are reputed great orators. The best speech I ever heard, or so I thought until I heard Savinkov, was by Viviani in Paris at a lunch of the Anglo-American Press Association, where he, as ex-Premier of France, was the guest of honor. It was in the early 1920's at a time when all the members of the Anglo-American Press Association were thoroughly tired of the theme of heroic France. Many of us had written it and all of us had heard it, *ad nauseam,* and beyond. Viviani must have known that, but the knowledge could not diminish or detract from his gift of oratory. Before beginning the speech he gulped down two double benedictines, then spoke for twenty minutes with such vehemence, skill and beauty that when he had finished there was hardly a dry eye at the table. He had moved that hard-boiled crowd of newspaper men to a passion of flame and pity on behalf of France. Viviani was a Southerner and he got his

effect by the use of the right word and by releasing the exuber-
ance and fervor of his Southern heart. Savinkov's position was
different. His was nearer the last speech from the scaffold with
which condemned criminals about to die in old Britain, whether
they were kings or highwaymen or poor devils who had stolen a
sheep, used to regale an appreciative audience. Savinkov played
no oratorical tricks. Standing alone amongst his enemies, he
spoke in a low voice in which there was no tremor. He told them
in substance, "I am more of a revolutionary than you Bolsheviks. When you were hiding underground in Russia or talking
Marxist ideology in the cafés of Geneva or Paris, I carried out
the shooting of Tsarist governors and smashed Grand Dukes to
pieces with bombs." With superb egoism he added, "I was an
active revolutionary while you were plotting revolution. While
you hid or fled I was playing on death's door-step." Savinkov
said more than that. He went on to a magnificent peroration
which saved his life from that vengeful court. He was formally
condemned to death, but the sentence was commuted the next
day to a term of imprisonment.

What impressed me most in the Savinkov case was that phrase
about playing on death's door-step. It conveyed to me the
thought of mortal danger as a permanent companion, which
was something that hitherto had been beyond my ken. During
the War I had undergone some occasional risks of death, which
terrified me at the time but were not frequent enough to affect
my mind. It was the same thing in the Baltic; the fact that a
sentry's bullet flicks the wall a foot above your head or that you
miss a train which was blown up is little more than a line for
future conversation. It makes you more interesting to people
who listen to you and possibly also to yourself, because there is
nothing more elevating for the average man—except maybe
opium and religion, both of which any philosopher must regard
as artificial stimuli—than the knowledge that his ego has been

preserved from extinction at a moment when by the rights and laws of chance it should have been extinguished.

In November, 1924, I enjoyed this elevating experience plus a long period, not of playing, as Savinkov had said—and I think for him the word was true—but of lingering or being dangled on death's door-step. A train on which I was traveling from Paris to Havre ran off the rails in a tunnel and another train ran into it and knocked me twenty-five yards through the air, with no worse injury than a splintered shin. It might just as well have been my neck or my spine, and the strange thing was that I did not lose consciousness when I was flying through the air or feel any fear, although timid by nature, but had only a grotesque reminiscence of a story I once heard about a colored parson who was mending the roof of his church and suddenly slipped and rolled down towards the gutter, and while he was rolling prayed quickly to his God, "O Lord, save thy servant; O Lord, let me stop rolling or catch on something." And then as the Lord failed to save him and he came to the gutter, cried out despairingly, "O Lord, now for a bloody bump." If I had any conscious sensation during the nightmare while in the tunnel it was precisely that; "Now for a bloody bump." I found myself on the ground, as far as I knew unbumped, but when I tried to stand up I saw that my left leg was splintered, with white pieces of bone sticking out above my shoe. Mind you, I felt no pain thus far, which any soldier who was injured by a shell in the War will corroborate. The shock to the nerves is too great for their immediate reaction. My first thought was, "By God, how lucky I am!" As I said before, this gave me an elevation of spirit beyond compare.

I paid for that elevation by several months of torture, because they took me to a hospital where the surgeon was better than most, and so, instead of amputating my foot immediately, he tried to save it. He gave me an injection against tetanus and

three days later I would have preferred tetanus, whether it
meant certain death or not. The after-effects of an anti-tetanic
injection make you itch to a point of frenzy. My hands and my
legs and my head were all tied up in bandages, but that did not
stop me itching. If you have ever read the Book of Job you will
know that the sorrows with which that patriarch was afflicted
were many and terrible; his children were killed by raiders and
his cattle looted, but his soul was steadfast. Then he was plagued
with boils and other nasty complaints, but the thing that troubled
him most, unless my memory of Holy Writ betrays me, was
that he had itching sores. I can sympathize with Job.

I did not get tetanus, so the injection may have been valuable. I also had an anti-gangrene injection, but I did get gangrene. It stayed with me for several months until at last they
chopped my foot off, and through all those months it held me
dangling on the edge of death. During that time I had something
which most of the human race lacks always but which nevertheless is the true foundation of art and thought and beauty—in
short, for what is known as culture; namely, leisure. One of
the reasons why the Soviet Revolution has not yet produced
anything good as Art is that there has been no leisure in Russia.
The *tempo* of life, by which the Bolsheviks mean the rush of
their progress, the haste of their desire to catch up and surpass
the capitalist world in material achievement, has been too swift
to allow any of them to pause awhile by the wayside, and think.
But I had leisure to think, and galore. I had, too, a less kindly
teacher than leisure, whose name is Pain. There is nothing so
dreadful as Pain; She is more to be dreaded than her brother
Fear, and together they form a hard grindstone to sharpen human wits. I learned much from those twin teachers with all the
leisure I could wish.

In the first days after my accident I thought how lucky I
was that I had broken my shin instead of my spine. That was

what I thought because I was still young and was glad to be alive. Later I learnt what gangrene meant—is not the word itself a menace, or have words no power?—and how a skillful surgeon can hold in torture a patient whom he hopes to cure outright instead of the swift mercy of letting him go crippled. In my pain I came to hate my lucky escape and grew weary of my tortured flesh. Then I thought to myself, "I am probably going to die, but if I do not die, I shall act differently in the future. I have too often been afraid in my life, but now I am facing the *ultimate fear*, beyond which there is nothing. None of the things I have been afraid of before, complaints by my boss or the loss of my job or the opinion of my friends or any danger, are as bad as the thing I am facing now, which is death by slow torture. Than that there is nothing worse; if I escape it I can say to myself that I at least can no longer be frightened by anyone or anything. Now, facing death, I regret few of the things I have done, but I regret not doing a great many things I might have done and not saying or writing things I might have said or written. Henceforth," I thought to myself, "if I *do* get back I shall do as I please and think as I please and write as I please, without fear or favor." I was half delirious, but that was a good thought, which stayed with me and strengthened me. Of course it was impossible, as I found out later. One may try to think as one pleases, although that is more difficult than it sounds, but one cannot talk as one pleases, much less write as one pleases, still less act as one pleases. I had not been back at work in Moscow for a week before I found that, despite all my "death-bed resolutions," it was out of the question for me to write news-paper dispatches "as I pleased." I found that out without any harsh remarks from the Soviet censor or my New York office. The utmost I could do, I found, was to substitute a fraction of independence for my dream of complete intransigeance. I took solace from the thought that newspaper writing was more or less

stereotyped, but that in books there was real freedom of expression. I thought, "One day I shall write a book and call it *I Write
as I Please*. I shall say what I please, how I please, with no care
for syntax or the opinions of other people." That thought stayed
with me, too, but it was not really much better than the half-
delirious thought I had before. There are *always* limitations.

Take my own case. Here I am writing a book with the title
I chose, but I am enmeshed in and encompassed by limitations.
First, I can see that the title is misleading; it suggests that I am
writing a "Now-it-may-be-told" book to give the "inside dope"
about Soviet Russia. My second limitation was of time and
space and selection—my three old enemies in newspaper work
from whom I thought I might escape by writing a book. Thus
I am left with the melancholy conclusion that my title ought to
be *I Write as I Talk*, by which I mean that I try to express my
thoughts simply without much care for euphony or grammar,
with less attention than is meet to time and space. To take an
example, I am here at this very moment talking about myself
writing this book in the summer of 1935, when my narrative
declares that I am lying in bed in a hospital in France in the
winter of 1924. Is this freedom or license? I don't pretend to
know, but the two are connected in my mind by a story about
the celebrated Dr. Porson, who was the greatest classical scholar
of his day, a hundred years ago, at Trinity College, Cambridge.
A student brought him a set of Greek verses. The doctor read
three lines and arched his portentous eyebrows. "Where, young
man, did you find this word to be written in iambic lines?"

"In Pindar, sir," said the youth brightly. "I know that Pindar
employed Doric archaisms, but he was a great poet."

The Doctor read on and found another word. "This, too, I
presume, is Pindar?" he queried.

"Yes, sir," said the student meekly.

The Doctor read some more, then his eyes flashed fire. "Is

this too Pindar?" he cried, placing a long thin finger on a word of which Sophocles or Euripides had never dreamt.

The student nodded.

"Get thee hence, sirrah," thundered the Doctor, "and come into my presence no more. Pindar was a bold fellow, but thou art an impudent one."

I had nightmares about that story in hospital, in which I was the student, always trying to think of an answer to the redoubtable Doctor.

I thought about Dr. Porson until he grew big as a house in my fevered brain, like the great Agrippa in *Strubel Peter*—

Whose head it was so high that it nearly touched the sky—

who drowned little boys in inkpots because they annoyed him, one of the improving tales for children I read in my early formative days. I was unkind to Trotzky a few chapters back, but I have to admit that few things are more debilitating than continuous high fever because it has the horrid effect of making you doubt your own thoughts until you wonder whether you are thinking them or whether they are just coming from somewhere out of the void, independently, to torment you like the grinning negro face that Essenin saw under his bed. It is not good to lie in pain and fever and be unsure whether your thoughts are your own children or bastards in whose birth you have had no part, or to put it more shortly, it is not good to lie in pain and fever. One night the nurse left on the table by my bed a little box of morphine tablets, twenty tablets each five centigrams, each tablet a moment of release from pain or all of them together one swift painless death. My leg was a river of pain in which I lay drowning, wave after wave of pain, ninety every minute, one for each hurried heartbeat. I knew far better than De Quincey the just and subtle potency of morphine. How well

I knew that Socrates was right, that no pleasure, not even love's orgasm, can compare in joy and splendor with release from pain. To swallow one by one the bitter tablets, slowly, in delicious anticipation; the pain beats would grow less sharp, less frequent, be lulled soon to nothing and their victim would float away on rosy clouds of peace and happiness—to peace and death.

I did not want to die so I let the morphine alone, but I have often wondered since whether the nurse forgot it or left it there on purpose. Lord knows she had reason to, because my leg was so painful that I could not bear it in any position for more than ten minutes and could not change its position myself, which meant that I kept ringing for her every fifteen minutes all through the night. I did not ring because I wanted to but because I *had* to, and must say for her that on no occasion in those three bad weeks when I kept ringing for her so often in the night did she show any sign of annoyance. It is easy to become morbid under the combined effects of pain and fever, and perhaps I was quite wrong to imagine that the box of morphine tablets was left deliberately by my bedside. Unhappily for me I was in a French hospital and had read De Maupassant, who knew his fellow-countrymen.

It is easy to have morbid thoughts when you have gangrene and pain and fever, but what disturbed me most was the fact that this nurse was a Norman. I kept thinking of Maupassant's story about the Norman farmer who hired an old woman to watch his dying wife. They were both Normans and very avaricious and argued long about the rate of payment. The old woman wanted ten cents an hour, which the farmer thought was too much, so finally they made a bargain that she should receive a lump sum of fifty cents. The farmer knew that his wife was tough and thought she would probably live ten hours at least, so that he would save money, whereas the old woman who had watched many dying persons gave her only two or three hours more and was delighted with the bargain. The farmer went about his work and the hours slowly passed, two, three, four, but the patient lingered with no sign of change. The old woman grew furious; at this rate she would soon be losing ten whole cents an hour. She looked venomously at the poor creature in the great feather bed. For a moment the thought crossed her mind how easy it would be—but no, that was a temptation of the Devil. The Devil—she remembered that the dying woman, whose life had been none too exemplary, had a terrible fear of the Prince of Darkness. Then her eye fell on a round black two-legged stool. Quietly she got up and passed into the kitchen carrying the stool. She burnt a cork and blackened her face with it, and took flour and made large white rings around her eyes. Then she tied the stool, legs upwards, on her head and crept cautiously back into the room to the foot of the bed. She rose suddenly to her feet with a loud cry, "I have come for you."

The farmer's wife opened her eyes and saw a frightful apparition with long black horns. She half raised herself in bed with a convulsive scream of terror and fell back dead. The old woman tiptoed back to the kitchen, untied the stool and washed her face; then came back smiling with satisfaction to prepare the corpse for burial. The clock marked exactly four hours; she had gained ten cents.

No pleasant story this to haunt the wakeful hours of pain and fever, but try as I might I could not drive it from my mind. I believe it did more than anything to make me insist that the surgeon should abandon his latest idea of grafting a piece of bone from my other shin, which would certainly have killed me, in favor of immediate amputation, which nearly killed me, but not quite. Within four weeks I was lying in the hot sun by the blue Mediterranean drawing new life from each breath of air and each plunge in the clear warm water. I stayed there a month

until I could hop around easily on a peg leg, then went back to
Paris to get a regular one, complete with foot.

It was early July and the three weeks that followed were the
best of all my life. To have come back alive from the darkness,
to have passed into sunlight from the shadow, gave me a sense
of personal triumph. Never had Paris looked so beautiful, never
were friends so gay and entertaining. I had a studio in Mont-
parnasse and made my headquarters at the Café Select on the
corner next to the Rotonde. That year, 1925, the Select was like
an Anglo-American Club where everyone knew each other. We
used to meet about noon for an *apéritif*, then to have lunch and
go on the river or to the races; then perhaps cocktails on the
Right Bank, and dinner, followed by hours of conversation on
the Select Terrace once more. It seemed to be a rendezvous for
all the most interesting people I knew. There was Hemingway,
who talks as well as he writes; and Cooper and "Shorty" Shoed-
shack, who had just returned from the Bactrian uplands between
Persia and Mesopotamia, where they had been making a film
they called *Grass*; and Judge Wells of New York, who had recently sailed a thirty-foot ketch from Copenhagen to America
following the route of Leif Ericsson. The Judge was less fortunate than Leif the Lucky, for his voyage ended on the rocky
coast of Halifax, where his ship was wrecked and he and his
companions, his son, another boy, and a Danish sailor, had a
miraculous escape from death. Floyd Gibbons showed up for a
week or two full of conversation and gigantic schemes. I have
known Floyd a long time and consider him a pirate with face
and nerves of brass but a heart of gold, and the best company of
any man I ever met. Unless I am mistaken, he was planning that
summer a tour across the Sahara Desert on Citroën caterpillars,
which were said to have cost his employer, Colonel McCormick
—Floyd then worked for the *Chicago Tribune*—250,000
francs. Perhaps I am wrong, and the tour had already been

made and Floyd's new scheme was intended to divert the Colonel's mind from that prodigious and vain expenditure—it does
not matter. I have forgotten, too, the purpose of Floyd's Saharan
expedition, but I think it was inspired by a book which some
Frenchman had written about a hidden city in the desert, ruled
by a lovely queen of ardent and romantic character.

Bolitho paid a flying visit from the little *château* that he
had just bought near Avignon, where I had stayed with him for
a couple of days on my way up from the South. It was called
La Préfete, because it was said to have been built by Napoleon's
Préfet de Police, Fouché, for one of his mistresses, a lady of
such dauntless character that she insisted on being addressed as
Madame La Préfete, despite the notorious absence of her marriage papers. That whole section had formerly belonged to a
great monastery, whose monks had constructed a marvelous system of irrigation and planted fences of towering cypress trees
eighty or a hundred feet high for shelter against the mistral.
Anything would grow there and Bolitho, who was born in South
Africa, set eagerly about acclimatizing African fruits and
plants. He planned to make a garden that would be the wonder
of France, regardless of cost. A year or two later, after his book,
Twelve Against the Gods, had made a hit in America, and he
could look forward with certainty to an income of $20,000 a
year, he said to me one day, "I'm determined not to spend more
than $5,000 in any year away from La Préfete. I shall put the
rest of the money into the ground here and make it a place of
wonder and beauty, no matter what it costs." Poor Bolitho! He
did not know that it would cost his life. An attack of acute ap-
pendicitis wrongly diagnosed by a local doctor, then a last-
minute rush in a local ambulance to the operating-table in Avignon, where he arrived too late; and death from peritonitis after
thirty-six hours of agony.

No foreshadow of this tragedy darkened the evening we spent

together in Paris. After dinner we sat on the Select terrace and Bolitho talked. "Do you know, Walter," he said, "this leg business of yours is luckier than you think. I mean that really it's a blessing, not a curse. First of all, you are getting $10,000 compensation from the French Railways; you know what that means —a full year's security. The trouble with newspaper men is that they're paid well enough but never save any money. You know as well as I do that all our friends, whatever their salaries may be, are always about $500 in debt. The result is they are never independent or able to talk back at their offices, that is to say, they are wage-slaves in the worst sense of the word. If they had more sense it would be different, but if they had more sense they wouldn't be newspaper men."

"Oh, shucks," I said, "there's no better job in the world for a man without money of his own, or family influence or what not."

Bolitho shrugged his shoulders. "For a time," he said, "don't forget that, for a time. Look at the French saying, 'Journalism leads to everything as long as you get out of it.' That's the point —newspaper work is a stepping-stone but not a real career, except for the one per cent or less who work up to be executives of some sort. How many reporters here in Paris do you think will ever be executives in their newspapers at home? Perhaps your friend Jimmy James, who is as hard as nails and has ambition in every strut of his cocky little body, and maybe Paul Scott Mowrer, who takes life seriously, and that's about all. I maintain that there's an essential contradiction between what's needed to make a man a good reporter and to make him a competent executive. Reporting is all right when you are young and energetic, but don't forget there are other men coming along younger and more energetic than you. A reporter's job is two-thirds in his legs and one-third in his head. Experience may enable him to balance two-thirds head against one-third leg, but sooner or later as he gets older he will find that the reporting job requires physical energy that he no longer possesses."

"Well, what's the answer?" I asked.

"To get out of it, as the French advise," said Bolitho without hesitation. "I don't mean a movie publicity job or whatever they will pay you as contact man for a bank or oil company, but to exchange the newspaper game for the thing we are trained to do, namely, writing. Books or plays, or what have you; in other words, to capitalize your knowledge and experience and capacity for putting words on paper in a way that will interest your readers. I don't care whether it's fact or fiction, but it's got to be done somehow unless you want to end up like old 'Whiskers'—you know who I mean—as a burnt-out reporter cadging drinks and dead-dog assignments from his younger friends." Bolitho sipped his cognac and resumed with greater vehemence. "As far as you are concerned, that isn't half of it. $10,000 gives you independence, but your missing leg gives you distinction. By distinction I don't mean merit or eminence— that's another matter—but simply that people distinguish you in a crowd, which is what counts in our business. We meet hundreds of people all the time, many of whom are important, and do you think any of them remember us? Mighty rarely. The only thing the average man has got is himself, and who takes notice of the average man? If he is unusually tall or good-looking or ugly as sin or fat as a barrel, people will notice him and remember him. But then he is no longer an average man. You, Walter, were just about the average, perhaps a little under height and mentally more alert, but otherwise completely average. When you came into a room no one ever noticed you particularly. But now you are lucky, and I'm not trying to comfort you, I'm stating facts. Henceforth people will say, 'Who's the little man with the limp who asked an intelligent question?' Even if you don't open your mouth, they are liable to say, 'Who

was the little man with the limp?' If you have to make your
way in the world, as we do, brains are probably the most im
portant thing, but brains alone are rarely sufficient; you have to
supplement them by impressing your personality on people, and
some physical form of impression is of course the easiest. Look
at your friend Woollcott; I'll admit that he's smart, but his great
fat tummy is worth at least half as much to him as his brains."

"I hope you are right," I said. "I don't much mind being
crippled because it doesn't seem to matter except for games
or dancing. I don't care about games any more and I never
could dance well anyway, so that's no loss, and as far as I can
see it doesn't make any difference with men, or girls either for
that matter, except that maybe they are more friendly, or perhaps that's just because I feel so good these days that all the
world and everyone in it are bright and gay to me."

Bolitho rubbed his nose with a funny Jewish gesture. He
claimed that he had caught it from one of the leading Zionists
at the Paris Peace Conference, and when I kidded him about
it one day he made a casuistic rationalization. "To the Jew
his nose is a badge of Race. Race is still the strongest factor in
human affairs. When the Jew rubs his nose he is unconsciously
appealing to the accumulated strength which has maintained
Jewry intact throughout twenty centuries of persecution. It is a
form of ancestor worship or prayer to the Lares and Penates of
the Family. It also serves the more immediate purpose of giving
the nose-rubber time to think." So Bolitho rubbed his nose in
the ritual Jewish way, there on the terrace of the Select, and said
after due reflection, "Of course I'm right; I tell you that you
gained by this accident in every way. If you don't think so
you're a damn fool, because everyone ought to know that the
most important thing in life is not to capitalize your gains—any
fool can do that—but to profit from your losses. Which requires

intelligence and marks the difference between a man of sense and the damn fools."

That was what I liked about Bolitho; he was always so sure and categorical. "All right," I said, "but what about your other idea of getting out of the newspaper game; how's that to be done?"

"Write a book," he said simply.

"What book?" I asked.

"Any book, provided that it is *your* book, that's to say, the book that comes from *you* out of *your* consciousness and is not something that you are writing as you think you ought to write or as someone else wants you to write. The only books which matter must be written with conviction and must be true to the people who write them, however untrue their truth may be. Look at Elinor Glyn, for instance, and Harold Bell Wright and the Hull woman who wrote the piece about an Arab sheik, and the *Scarlet Pimpernel* and all the goddam tripe about the Foreign Legion from Ouida upwards or downwards. The reason this stuff gets across is that it's true to the people who write it—that, I'm telling you, is the basic principle. The second is that a book should be actually true and well written, but there are more true and well-written books which fail than hokum-plus-conviction ones which succeed. When you have the two together—a book written with conviction but true and without hokum—the result is bound to be right. The better you write it and the more interesting the subject the more right is the result. It is not easy to do, especially if you have an inner critical faculty, as you and I have, but I am going to do it and you should also. I tell you again, don't write what they want you to write; write what *you* want to write, as *you* want to write it."

"All right," I said again, "if I ever write a book I shall follow your advice."

CHAPTER

21

RETREAT FROM MOSCOW

In August, 1925, I returned to Moscow and found the country in a state of bewildering confusion. I had been absent a full year, and although I had tried to keep in touch with Soviet affairs through the Moscow newspapers I soon saw that much had happened and was about to happen to which I had no clew. I felt lost, like a blind man groping. Thereupon I determined to test my new resolutions about thinking for myself and to see whether I could not turn my disadvantage into profit, as Bolitho had advised. The weakness of my position was that I had been too remote from the Soviet scene to gauge the meaning of events, but surely that gave me the advantage of detachment? Unable to distinguish separate trees I ought therefore to see the wood more clearly as a whole. And so, before running round to see people and get facts second-hand, I sat down to think things out for myself, and reached four major conclusions, which I have never had reason to change, as follows:

1. That inside the Bolshevik Party there was a hard central core which had never wavered from the intention to create and develop a successful proletarian State upon Socialist foundations.
2. That the Party controversy did not affect this determina-

259

tion, but was concerned with three points: by whom, how, and at what speed the socialization process should be conducted; and that all these points were of vital moment.

3. That N.E.P., it was now clear, was no more than a temporary measure, the ostensible purpose of which was to give the whole country a breathing space, but whose real purpose was to enable the Bolsheviks to build up enough industry and commerce, and store up enough reserve to enable them to tackle the work of building a Socialist State with greater success than in 1918–21.

4. That a new reckoning with the peasants was inevitable and not far distant.

Having reached these conclusions, I thought about them. My first conclusion was chiefly important as background; I must never lose sight of it for a moment, but it was henceforth to me too axiomatic—as it was too fundamental—to have much practical news value. My second conclusion, I thought, was the most important thing in my world from the point of news and everything else, because, until the problem it presented was solved no other problems could be solved. N.E.P. I thought was doomed, at least as far as urban private traders were concerned, and all the rest of the private enterprises which had danced like grasshoppers in the sun during the past four years. N.E.P., therefore, had a diminishing value, both politically and as news. Finally, the peasant question was not, I could see, yet acute, but, I told myself, I must keep it also in mind as a big future issue and more immediately as a key pawn in the merciless chess game that was being played between Stalin and Trotzky. Continuing my thought, I concluded that there was no reason for me to change my opinon that Stalin would beat Trotzky in the long run —had not the latter been removed from the Commissariat of War a few months earlier and replaced by Frunzé?—although I had read and admired Trotzky's pamphlet called *The Lessons of October* which he had published in the previous fall. It was a strong and subtle piece of work, which the Stalinists not only found it difficult to answer but which later disintegrated their forces considerably.

In this pamphlet Trotzky called for a return to the fundamental principles of Marxism, of which he said the Bolsheviks were losing sight. His main thesis was that the Revolution must be dynamic, not static, that it could not mark time but must always, everywhere, push forward. Trotzky utilized this theoretically sound Marxist basis for a telling attack upon the home and foreign policies of the Stalinists and more particularly upon the theory, which they had not yet fully adopted, although it was in process of formation, that it was possible to "build Socialism in a single country." This theory, be it said, Marx had once described as rank heresy, although Stalin's apologists later argued with evident justice that in speaking of "a country" Marx had in mind the comparatively small States of Europe rather than such vast and economically self-sufficient continental units as the United States and the U.S.S.R. Trotzky thus appealed to Marxist internationalism and the ideal of World Revolution against Stalin's policy as ruler of Russia; he was trying to drive a wedge between the Bolshevik as Bolshevik, that is Marxist revolutionary, and the Bolshevik as statesman directing the destinies of a nation. To this apple of discord flung into the midst of his victorious opponents in the Central Committee, Trotzky added a grain of mustard seed, which later grew and flourished exceedingly, in the shape of a question about class differentiation in the villages and the right course to be adopted towards the kulaks and middle peasants.

I thought about the pamphlet for a long time, and the more I thought the more I felt sure that the Party controversy was big news. The next day I went out to gather information. I have

found since that there are two dangers in the practice of "doping things out" for yourself; first, you are liable to twist facts to
suit your conclusion; secondly, if your conclusion is erroneous
the deductions you draw from it are more erroneous still. In
this case, however, it seemed that I had guessed right, especially
about the Party squabble. I heard that the Kamenev-Zinoviev
group in the Stalin *bloc* were showing signs of restiveness, partly
because they saw that Stalinism was progressing from Leninism
(as Leninism had progressed from Marxism) towards a form
and development of its own, partly because they were jealous
and alarmed by Stalin's growing predominance. All my inform-
ants agreed that the Party fight would be the news center for
the coming winter.

Sure enough, as events proved, Zinoviev and Kamenev spent
the autumn in creating inside the majority *bloc* a new opposition movement and, what is more, they concealed their doings
so dexterously that it was not until the delegates to the December Party Congress had been elected that Stalin perceived how
the wind was blowing. Kamenev's case was relatively unimpor-
tant; he had a fair measure of support in the Moscow delegation but nothing like a majority. Zinoviev, however, had long
been undisputed boss of Leningrad and had packed the delegation from top to bottom with his own henchmen. It was too late
to change the delegations, but the Party Secretariat (*i.e.,*
Stalin) lost not a moment in cutting the ground from under
Zinoviev's feet. There was a radical change in personnel
amongst the permanent officials of the Leningrad Party machine, particularly in the Communist Youth organization, where
pro-Zinoviev tendencies were most marked. The editorial staff
of the two Party organs, the *Leningrad Pravda* and the *Leningrad Communist Youth Pravda,* were sweepingly reformed;
and a vigorous "educational campaign" (*i.e.,* propaganda
drive) was begun in every factory and office in the city. These

measures were decided at a secret meeting of the Central Committee of the Party in November and embodied in a resolution of twenty-four points, carried *nem con,* but with half a dozen significant abstentions. At this point I myself, inadvertently, came into the game. Among the newspapers I read daily was a little sheet in tabloid form called *The Workers' Gazette.* One morning I was startled to find on its back page, unheralded by headlines, the report of a Central Committee resolution in twenty-four paragraphs "concerning the administrative organization of the Leningrad Party and Communist Youth organization." It was strongly worded; phrases like "grave ideological errors," "weakness of discipline and Party control," "failure of the Party executives to appreciate correctly," and so forth were followed by the blunt announcement that the Leningrad Party machine and Press would be reorganized; individuals "dismissed with blame" were named and their successors appointed. This document, I understood, was a direct frontal attack upon Zinoviev and the administration of the Leningrad Party; which could only mean that Zinoviev and his chief colleagues in the Leningrad Party, who had been Stalin's strongest supporters against Trotzky, were now themselves in opposition. This was interesting news, although of course I did not dream that it was the first step towards the formation of the *bloc* of all opposition movements, however mutually disparate, which developed in the following year. That I could not guess, but I did know, to my regret, that the "somewhat Byzantine squabbles of the Bolsheviks," as a *New York Times* editorial had cuttingly described them, were of little greater interest to the mass of my readers than the Arian heresy which convulsed the early Christian Church. Nevertheless, I wrote a restrained but powerful piece giving the facts and explaining their significance. Hearing nothing from the censor about it, I presumed that it had been passed, which was far from being the case.

I went to New York shortly afterwards and forgot all about the incident, until I was abruptly reminded of it by Rakovski, then Ambassador in Paris, on my way back to Moscow two months later. I knew Rakovski well and liked him; he had been a member of the Trotzky opposition, but I thought, wrongly, that he had not taken a prominent part in it because of his absence in Paris. We had been talking for twenty minutes about conditions in America, then I said, "By the way, Mr. Ambassador, would it be possible for me to get a Soviet visé here at the Embassy instead of going around to the consulate and filling in forms?"

Rakovski raised his eyebrows. "A Soviet visé?" he asked. "Surely you do not propose to go back to Russia."

"Of course I do," I said with equal surprise. "I'm on my way there now. Why on earth shouldn't I?——"

"But it's impossible," Rakovski said. "Surely you know that. It's out of the question."

"Impossible? Why? What have I done?"

Rakovski stared at me a moment without reply. "I'll tell you," he said at length, "although you must know. It's that Central Committee resolution about Leningrad." Again he paused. "From whom did you get it anyway?"

I stared back at him. "You mean that resolution about the Leningrad Party apparatus?" (That's what they call "machine" in Russia.)

"Of course," snapped Rakovski. "Who gave it to you?"

"No one. I read it in the paper, that little tabloid, *The Workers' Gazette.*"

Rakovski shrugged his shoulders. "All right," he said, "have it as you please. I suppose you'll say you don't know anything about your expulsion or how you got the exact wording of the resolution or——"

This was too much for me; was he crazy or was I? "Listen,"

I said, "I don't know what on earth you are talking about. Of course I had the wording of the resolution because, as I told you, I read it in the paper, but I didn't have to write that in my dispatch; and as for this talk of expulsion, it's Greek to me."

"Is it?" he asked incredulously. "You filed a dispatch last November giving precise information about an event of the gravest importance which was known only to fifty men in the Soviet Union and the two secretaries, both of the highest integrity, neither of whom had been outside the Kremlin. They accused Trotzky and me of giving it to you, then Zinoviev. They were so furious that they decided you should be expelled immediately under guard to the frontier. You would have gone that night if it had not been for Bukharin. He said that you were leaving soon on vacation, and that if you knew so much as that the wisest thing was not to antagonize you unnecessarily; you should go when you pleased, but of course never be allowed back again. They settled it like that, so why talk to me about your visé?"

"Good God!" I cried, really startled. "How amazing! Why didn't they *say* anything? Why didn't the Press Department ask me, instead of stopping the story without a word? I'd have told them where I got it and shown them the newspaper. Really, Mr. Rakovski, this is ridiculous. You must see that I have no reason to lie to you; this is Paris and you're not the Gay-pay-oo." I think that shook him.

"Well," he said slowly, "it's easy to find out. I'll cable Moscow to-night and of course if—I mean, as you say—it sounds like the truth, but I simply can't believe it."

Two days later I saw Rakovski again. He was all smiles. "It's all right," he said, "and you can have your visé any time." It appeared that the first intention had been to publish the resolution in the Moscow Press and that copies had actually been sent out to the newspapers. Then the order was countermanded and the letters were all recovered undelivered except that, in a typical Russian way, someone forgot about *The Workers' Gazette*. The *Gazette* ran the story as a matter of routine and it was actually published in the early edition for workers going to their jobs—most Moscow newspapers aren't sold on the street until 9 A.M. or later—when someone belatedly remembered the *Gazette's* existence and hastily killed the story. It is quite likely that the *Gazette* said no edition containing it had appeared and that the forgetful comrade in the Kremlin did not mention his lapse. I asked the Press Department when I returned to Moscow why they had not questioned me at the time. They looked grave and said that the facts and personalities involved were too serious for that. All is well that ends well, but this incident illustrates the Russian faculty for putting two and two together and making ten of them, which has cost the lives of men less fortunate than I.

At the December Congress Zinoviev and Kamenev played possum, but in the following spring they joined Trotzky to form a united opposition *bloc* which concentrated its assault upon Stalin's agrarian policy, demanding that the kulaks be expropriated immediately. Stalin refused to yield; he met blows with double blows and used all the weapons in his armory, from control of the Party machine and the Press to police regulations about public meetings. It availed his opponents little to say that he forced them into a position of illegality, into holding secret conclaves or using "underground" printing-presses to disseminate their views. The news of a secret meeting which they held in the woods near Moscow in the autumn of 1926 produced such a furore that Trotzky, Zinoviev and Kamenev were expelled from the Politburo without a voice being raised to defend them. The six chief opposition leaders yielded to public indignation and issued a formal disavowal of "underground tactics" and "illegal factional meetings," but in the following spring and summer they returned to the charge in the belief, which perhaps was justified, that the Party masses were really stirred by the kulak danger. Again Stalin muffled the attack by control of the Press and public meetings. The opposition leaders lost their heads; on November 7th, anniversary of the Revolution, they "came out into the streets" in Moscow and Leningrad and appealed to the people from balconies or in the public squares. The attempt was a fiasco; the public was indifferent; there was no excitement, much less rioting or violence. But in Soviet law this was counter-revolution. For the last time Trotzky had played by his own act into Stalin's hand; this error was fatal—political suicide. On December 18th the Fifteenth Party Congress expelled the seventy-five leading members of the opposition from the Communist Party; its adherents followed, neck and crop. In January, 1928, the oppositionists great and small were scattered in exile across Siberia and Central Asia.

The exile of Trotzky, who was sent to Alma Ata, formerly Verney, on the borders of China in south-east Kazakstan, gave rise to an extraordinary incident. I witnessed it myself in the company of Paul Sheffer, correspondent of the *Berliner Tageblatt* and am certain about the facts. One morning early in 1928 Sheffer and I learned that Trotzky with his wife and two secretaries, and I think his son, was to leave Moscow that afternoon on the Tashkent train at four o'clock or thereabouts. An hour before train time we went to the Kazan Station and found the central hall and the approaches to the Tashkent platform packed with people. The crowd was orderly, but there was excitement in the air; a large force of police and "special" (G.P.U.) railroad troops kept narrow aisles through the crowd open for passengers. Sheffer and I showed our credentials and were admitted to the Tashkent platform without difficulty. Here, too, a line of guards faced the train at a distance of four or five feet to maintain a "gangway." Behind them the platform was a solid mass of people, mostly young men, but there was no pushing, noise or disorder. Hundreds more were perched on the roofs of a train in the adjoining track, and Sheffer and I were fortunate to secure a place on a flat-car attached to it, about twenty-five yards diagonally from the door of the international sleeping-car of the Tashkent train. We thus had a clear view. At intervals there was singing, the popular *Budyonny March* and other army songs, and fragments of the *Internationale*. About ten minutes before train time there was a stir and buzz of voices from inside the station, no shouting or actual noise, but what is described in parliamentary reports as "movement in the audience," followed by a ripple along the crowded platform as everyone craned forward eagerly to see. Down the narrow gangway hurried a little procession, two uniformed guards, then a woman and three men with porters carrying baggage and two more guards in the rear. The third man was a short erect figure wearing an astrakhan cap pulled down over his ears, a thick muffler, and a heavy fur coat—it was bitterly cold weather. He carried his head high, but looked neither to the right nor to the left, nor said a word. In a moment all four passengers had disappeared into the sleeping-car. As they had passed along the platform a low wave of sound followed them, as everyone breathed simultaneously, *"Vot* Trotzky." Strange to say, there was no cheering or booing, although one group sitting on the carriage next to our flat-car did sing a few bars of the *Internationale* just after Trotzky's party boarded the train, to which there was no response from the rest of the crowd. Sheffer and I agreed that the prevailing sentiment of the crowd was interest, mainly sympathetic interest. We thought it probable that most of those present, say 2,000 people in all, were Trotzky's admirers or adherents, but that they had not ventured to show their feelings openly for fear of getting themselves into trouble or causing trouble for him. This was largely surmise on our part, but it seemed to be confirmed by the cautious replies we received to our numerous questions. I went home and wrote my dispatch along those lines, and it was duly passed by the censor. Two days later Sheffer came to me in great excitement. "Did you send that Trotzky story?" he asked. "Of course," I said, "didn't you?" "Naturally," he nodded, "but tell me, are you sure it was Trotzky we saw?" "Of course I'm sure," I said; "everyone at the station saw him." "So did I," said Sheffer, "but we didn't. You and I and all the rest of them were wrong; there was no Trotzky at the Kazan Station. Trotzky and his wife were taken from their home the next day, put into an automobile and driven to Lubertzee, twenty miles from Moscow, where they entered the Tashkent train. That is the real truth—I know it from an unimpeachable source."

At first I refused to believe it, but of course he was right, and if any doubt were possible Sheffer's version is confirmed by Trotzky's own biography. So there it was—the authorities, presumably fearing that Trotzky might attempt to address the crowd and cause a disturbance, or at least an undignified scuffle, which they wished to avoid, had deliberately arranged a "Potemkin" or bogus Trotzky for the sake of the public peace. I heard afterwards that the central figure was an actor who had impersonated Trotzky in one of the Civil War films. Am I not right, when people ask me how I handle news in Russia, to reply that my first rule is to believe nothing that I hear, little of what I read, and not all of what I see?

Another curious story about an opposition exile was brought to me a year or so later by an American tractor expert who had made a tour of Siberia giving addresses to explain how tractors should be treated and used. He knew only a smattering of Russian and as his lectures were technical, he had some trouble with interpreters. "But at one small town," he said, "I had a crackerjack, a thickset, middle-aged man wearing black shirt and breeches and high boots. That was the most successful address I ever gave, because he really put it across and roused their interest; they asked questions for more than an hour. When it was all over, I told the interpreter how grateful I was for his splendid translation. He said modestly, 'Oh, I do not speak English very well, I have not known it very long.' 'Do you know any other languages?' I asked. 'Oh, yes,' he said, 'French, German, Italian, Roumanian, Bulgarian and some Spanish, the latter about like English, not very good.' 'Good God, man,' I cried, 'you ought to get a job in Moscow or abroad; a man like you would be invaluable abroad.' He smiled. 'I have had jobs abroad, and in Moscow too.' 'What were they?' I asked. He smiled more broadly, 'Plenipotentiary representative of the Soviet at the Court of St. James, England, in Paris, and in Geneva. You see my name is Rakovski, so I do not think I shall soon get a job abroad, or even in Moscow.' "

In point of fact, Rakovski, who was one of Trotzky's closest friends, "stuck it out" longer than any of the other oppositionists. It was only at the end of 1933 that he finally asked forgiveness of the Central Committee, and even then his appeal, which was granted, was dignified and simple without any of the gross self-abasement exhibited by his fellow-exiles.

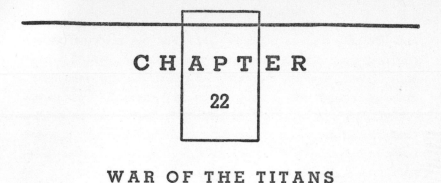

CHAPTER

22

WAR OF THE TITANS

THE intra-Party controversy occupied the time and energy of the Soviet leaders for nearly four years and left scars that are not yet healed, but in the end its credit balance far outweighed the debit, because *it settled things* in the only way which Asia can understand, that is, by the survival of the fittest in a conflict without mercy. Most foreigners who go to Russia or try to analyze it fail to understand that Russia is Asiatic; if by luck or good judgment they hit on that salient fact, they do not know what Asiatic means. Whether the multifarious peoples of the U.S.S.R. are racially more European than Asiatic is an open question, but there is no doubt that they are Asiatic-minded. The Romanov dynasty led by Peter the Great laid a veneer of Western culture over Russia, but the Tsar whose name stands highest in Russian history is not Peter but Ivan Grozny, called Ivan the Terrible, although the word *grozny* really means "dread" in the sense in which the Bible speaks of "the most dread God," that is to say, a term of intense respect. As contact with the West grew easier in the nineteenth century the ruling class of Russia became more Western-minded and thereby widened the breach between themselves and the mass of the nation; they "lost contact with the masses," as the Bolsheviks say, and dallied with the un-Russian ideas of democracy and parliament and freedom

of speech and elections by secret ballot. Or as Holy Writ puts it
more succinctly "They went awhoring after strange inventions,"
and paid the penalty therefor. Whatever the Bolsheviks may
have thought or wanted when they seized power, one of the
effects of their success was to rip to pieces the Western veneer
and its shoddy un-Russian fabric of "democratic freedom,"
which the peoples of Europe had created for themselves, by centuries of struggle, but which in backward Asiatic Russia was
alien, unnatural, and unwelcome to the vast majority of the
nation.

What the word Asiatic means has always been a problem for
Westerners, who are wont to speak of the mystery and inscruta-
bility of the Asiatic mind, but in the matter of politics, which is
all that concerns me for the moment, the problem of Asia was
solved seventy-five years ago, at the time of the great Taiping
Rebellion in China, by an old English civil servant who had
lived in China so long that the sense and feeling and spirit of
China had permeated his mind and body. I read his book—it is
called *The History of the Chinese People and Their Rebellions*,
or some such title—on a long dreary journey from Moscow to
Peking in 1927. I spent three months in China and said afterwards that those three months had taught me more about Russia
than the previous six years I had passed on Russian soil. I now
see that I was wrong; what I had learned came from Meadows'
book. It is little known, but I am convinced that it is a "key to
understanding" of Asiatic problems. Meadows' thesis was simple: The Emperor was the Son of Heaven, therefore it was
blasphemy and damnation to raise a finger against him or his;
but sometimes Heaven grew tired of Its son or doubted his legit-
imacy, and turned away Its face from him. This only could be
proved by results, that is to say, by a successful rebellion. If the
rebellion did not succeed, the Emperor *was* Son of Heaven and
rebellion was blasphemy, to be punished by the worst tortures

that Chinese wit and leisure could devise; if it did succeed
the rebels were not blasphemers but the chosen instruments of
God. There in a nutshell is the key to Asia and the spring that
winds its clock.

Applying Meadows' theory to Russia, Lenin held power because Heaven had turned its face away from Kerensky as earlier
it had disavowed Tsar Nicholas. When Lenin died what ignorant mortal could know whether Stalin or Trotzky was the chosen
son? Only results could prove that, for the wisdom of China is
as hard and immutable as the law of nature which decrees that
the fittest must survive. Stalin rose and Trotzky fell; therefore
Stalin, inevitably, was right and Trotzky wrong. That is the
wisdom of Asia and it is perhaps not wholly an accident that
Stalin's blood is Asiatic—did he not once greet a Japanese correspondent with the words, "I too am Asiatic"?—whereas Trotzky and his opposition colleagues had drunk deep of the un-
Russian waters of the West. It is no less significant that there is
not a single member of the Politburo to-day who has spent more
than three consecutive months outside the boundaries of Russia
(or U.S.S.R.) or has anything save contempt for Western ideas
of freedom and democracy, or that the Politburo thinks what
Stalin thinks and does what Stalin orders. Not one of them, ever,
begins or ends a public speech without reference to their leader
Stalin who ranks higher than any Tsar because he has been
proved by conflict "the chosen Son of Heaven."

I do not for a moment suppose that the eminent Meadows
really believed that God in his Heaven selected this one or that
one to be ruler of the Chinese people, any more than the Bolsheviks would believe it now. What he wrote was an attempt to
convey to Western readers in a manner they would understand
the utterly different fashion of Chinese thoughts and methods
from their own. I have followed his example, not only because I
think it is wise and right, but because it is the only way to ex-

plain what is otherwise inexplicable. The fundamental point of
the Meadows thesis was that when things were unsettled, conflict settled them and gave the Asiatic mind what the Asiatic
mind requires, namely, a clearly defined line to follow and an
absolute ruler to define it. In this conflict victory went to the side
which deserved it most (which is what Meadows means by his
reference to Deity), that is, by being the strongest and most fit.
Stalin deserved his victory because he was the strongest, and
because his policies were most fitted to the Russian character
and folkways in that they established Asiatic absolutism and
put the interests of Russian Socialism before those of international Socialism. Trotzky may use his brilliant pen to prove by
all the Marxist texts that Stalin is no Marxist, and lesser scribes
may follow him and prate of ruthless methods and the iron age
and lament the brutality of purpose which drove through to its
goal regardless of sacrifice and suffering. Stalin is no less of a
Marxist than Lenin who never allowed his Marxism to blind him
to the needs of expediency. When Lenin brought in N.E.P., he
jettisoned Marxist principles more thoroughly than Stalin ever
did, and when Lenin began a fight, whether the weapons were
words or bullets, he showed no mercy to his opponents. It was
Lenin who said savagely to the Party Congress of 1921 which he
had bludgeoned into accepting the policy of N.E.P., "I am fed
up with those oppositions; I am going to put the lid on opposition and clamp it down." Lenin always insisted—and Stalin followed him implicitly—that the worst mistake for a leader, especially a revolutionary leader, was to lose touch with the masses,
who, he claimed, were instinctively right about the line that
the leader should follow. To Westerners, who have accepted the
philosophy of Gustave Le Bon that crowd psychology—*i.e.*, the
crowd mind, is on a level with the mind of its lowest units,
Lenin's dictum sounds incredible. I think there is here a confusion of terms, that what Lenin really meant was, as Meadows

would have agreed, that the "chosen" leader was he who gave
to the masses what was truly best for them in the sense of being
most suited to their needs, however unformulated, and to their
aspirations, however unconscious, and that this was a prime
element of his success.

The Party conflict gave a mandate to Stalin to steer the
U.S.S.R. towards Socialism by any means he might choose.
Meanwhile, the struggle had been of value in threshing out
every detail of home and foreign affairs and canvassing every
policy that could possibly be adopted. In the fire of controversy
all the angles of national life had been sharpened and defined
so that it was no longer difficult for Stalin to plan his course.
The cardinal fact before him was that N.E.P. had done its work.
To demolish what was left of the urban N.E.P.-men was child's
play. During the last three years their petty industry had been
eliminated by the withholding of supplies and raw material and
their trade crushed by taxes and privileged State competition.
Now they themselves received the *coup de grâce* in the form of
retroactive taxation, which in the cruel Bolshevik phrase "liquidated" them as a class. How this was done I saw myself.

I had moved to a new apartment, one of six in a small house
recently built by a group of N.E.P.-men who realized that the
days of private trade were over but thought that they could live
modestly on the proceeds of their investments in tax-free State
loans and in house property that they had constructed with
State approval and financial aid. All the other five of this group
lived in their own apartments, but the owner of mine was richer
than the rest and had a bigger apartment in another building.
One morning four youngsters about twenty, dressed in black
leather jackets and breeches, the favored unofficial uniform of
the Communist Youth organization, rang my door-bell. The
leader said curtly, "We have come from the financial department of the Moscow Soviet to estimate the value of your apart-

ment and its furniture and fittings. Have you any other valuables?"

"Wait a minute," I said, "I don't own this apartment; I rent
it. I am a foreigner, the correspondent of an American newspaper, and if there's anything you want to know about me or
my apartment, you can apply to the Press Section of the Foreign
Office."

He made some notes in a little book and went away. Ten minutes later there was another ring at the bell and there he was
again. "What is it now?" I said testily. "I have work to do and
I told you that if there was anything you wanted to know about
me, you could get it from the Foreign Office." "I want to use
your telephone," he said. "Oh, that's different," said I, "come
on in."

He rang up the nearest police station and said rather plaintively, "I am here with three comrades at such and such an
address with orders from the Moscow Finance Department to
value the property of certain citizens for the purpose of taxation. The tenants refuse us admission unless there is a policeman present. Send one along at once; my order is number so-
and-so, signed by So-and-so—all right?—then send him quick."
He thanked me and turned to go.

"Stop," I said, "what's the big idea?" The boy grinned.
"N.E.P.—men—fin—ish," he said slowly in English, then drew
his hand quickly across his throat, with the Russian gesture
equivalent to "thumbs down" in the Roman arena.

That was a sad day for those poor N.E.P.-men and for thousands of their ilk in Moscow, Leningrad and other cities. In one
apartment the four young vigilants found a bootleg knitting-
machine. The owner and his wife and her cousin from the country were producing stockings without a license and selling them
without paying taxes. He was arrested on the spot. Another had
$20,000 worth of foreign currency in a suit-case. He, too, was

promptly arrested for illegal speculation in foreign valuta. The remaining three fared little better; the next morning they were informed that a new retroactive tax had been imposed upon all N.E.P.-men of two or perhaps five or seven per cent upon the total turnover of their last business year. Whatever the tax was, it coincided neatly with the value of their apartments and furniture! Vainly they protested that they had retired from business after paying all their taxes. This, they were told, was a new tax, and retroactive. Within three days they were out in the streets with little more than the clothes they wore and some bedding. N.E.P. was good and gay for the N.E.P.-men while it lasted, but its end was glum.

If I was writing about Americans or any Western nation I should say grim instead of glum, but Russians are different. Nine-tenths of all Russians that have ever lived have never been able to call their souls their own or had any property worth fighting for, and the remaining tenth have always known that their Lord the Tsar could strip them of their wealth and power and titles at a moment's whim. Dear life itself was a hazard throw in Russia, but the Russian people, high or low, did not wilt or worry in circumstances that would have driven Westerners to despair or sword-in-hand revolt. *"Nichevo,"* said the Russians, shrugging their shoulders, "what of it?" That, too, is a philosophy of Asia.

. . . .

In 1928 there began for me a period which lasted nearly four years upon which I look back with mingled regret and pride. During much of that time I was in the position of seeing the wood so well that I did not distinguish the trees well enough. What I mean is that I gauged the "Party Line" with too much accuracy and when my opinion and expectations were justified by events, as they frequently were, I was so pleased with my own judgment that I allowed my critical faculty to lapse and

failed to pay proper attention to the cost and immediate consequence of the policies that I had foreseen. I had no intention
of being an apologist for the Stalin administration; all that I
was thinking of was that I had "doped out" the line that the
administration inevitably must follow, and when it did follow
that line I naturally felt that it was right. In other words, I had
tried to make myself think like a true-blue Stalinist in order to
find out what true-blue Stalinists were thinking, and had succeeded only too well. For instance, I had foreseen the final
extinction of the urban N.E.P.-men. When it occurred, therefore, my first reaction was one of pleasure. Instead of feeling
sympathy for the N.E.P.-men, or at least remembering that their
fate would seem worthy of sympathy to ninety-nine per cent of
my readers, I said to myself, "Well, they got what I knew was
coming to them, and that's that."

My office in New York made no remarks on the subject, but
I had a number of letters from friends which showed that I had
made a mistake. For a time, then, I was rather doubtful about
my system of trying to think like the Bolsheviks, but it worked
so well the next year that I was reassured. I deduced from the
action against the urban N.E.P.-men that there would soon be a
parallel move against the rural N.E.P.-men, namely, the kulaks.
Sure enough, in the fall of 1928, Stalin launched a nation-wide
campaign to collectivize the farms. I cared no more than he did
that he was accused of stealing his opponents' thunder, because the production of grain from State farms was now almost
equivalent to that of the kulaks, whereas two or three years before when Trotzky had demanded the expropriation of the
kulaks, their production could not be replaced. At this point I
thought that my further reasoning was clever. "They may begin
by gunning for the kulaks," I thought, "but they will end by a
wholesale attack on peasant individualists; that, after all, is the
logical conclusion to the destruction of the N.E.P.-men in the

towns, because the coexistence of socialism in the towns and cities with individualism in the villages is patently absurd. "What this means," I said to myself, "is a new period of Militant Communism or something like it. The last Militant Communism failed because the towns had been unable to supply the villages with goods. Therefore we shall soon see a big campaign for industrialization, because Lenin said when he introduced N.E.P. that rural socialization was impossible until State industry was properly developed." A week or two later the first Five-Year Plan was announced, and I felt pleased as Punch.

I do not mean to suggest that I simply sat and spun what I imagined would be Bolshevik thoughts without checking up my ideas in every possible direction. I used to form my theory on what seemed to be logical grounds, much as I have just described it, then try it on all sorts of people and watch their reactions. I also had access to the reports of the last Party Congress, which, after expelling the oppositionists, had indicated a line of policy not far removed from the conclusions I was reaching several months later. When the program figures of the Five-Year Plan were published there arose a chorus of derision in the outer world; not only were such terms as astronomic, fantastic, Utopian, generally employed, but it was suggested that the Plan was little more than an attempt to hoodwink public opinion both in Russia and abroad. In point of fact the Plan was far more ambitious than the most *farouche* of its critics imagined. It was not merely the first instance of Planned Economy applied to every branch of the life of a great country, but it was a major Socialist offensive along the whole Front, as Stalin termed it. The Soviet Planned Economy was not, as the term has been employed in Capitalist countries, merely a method of regulating the national economic system, but the instrument whereby industry, finance and commerce should be both developed and Socialized simultaneously, in harmony with the progressive Socialization of agriculture. The agrarian section of the Plan provided that one-third of the peasant small holdings should be collec- tivized by October, 1933, which presumably meant that, to- gether with the State Farms, for which rapid development was expected, the "Socialized Sector" of that year's harvest should contribute nearly half of the total crop-production.

It is a matter of history that the first Five-Year Plan succeeded far better than anyone abroad expected. The Bolsheviks claimed that it was "completed" in four and a quarter years instead of five and that its "global accomplishment" was ninety-seven per cent of the total program. Such a figure cannot be controlled be- cause many important sections of the Plan surpassed their orig- inal provisions, whereas others no less important—for instance the production of pig-iron, steel and copper—fell heavily below the estimated levels. Be that as it may, the results of the first year of the Plan, which came into operation October 1, 1928, were much better than the Bolsheviks themselves had anticipated. As events proved, the consequences of this success were disas- trous. Success is heady wine at all times for youthful stomachs to digest, and in this case its effects were intensified because the Bolsheviks had been forced to swallow large doses of hostile criticism. It turned their heads and made them reckless; instead of riding soberly in the long stiff race before them they began to rush their fences. Not only were the Plan's program figures sharply revised upwards in the autumn of 1929, but the whole "tempo" of its course was heightened. One might say that the Plan was "jazzed" almost beyond recognition, and this was the reef on which it was nearly wrecked. Stalin, who speaks rarely but always to the point, recognized this the following year in his famous statement called "Dizziness from Success." At the time stress was laid upon the word "dizziness," the results of which were already apparent, but it is now clear to me that "success" was the important word in Stalin's title, because it was the cause

and dizziness merely the effect. I remember a doggerel verse
that was taught me in childhood:

*Well did the ancient sages say, "To men the greatest bane
Is not the pinch of poverty nor bitter pangs of pain,
Not faithless friends nor kin unkind though sore such woes
     may be;
Far worse is fickle Fortune's smile, undue prosperity."*

Undue, or at least unexpected and ill-digested, prosperity had
turned the Soviet head to such an extent that the Five-Year Plan
was badly overloaded and driven at a speed to which it had not
been geared.

To use a simple illustration, everyone knows that a new car
should be driven at a slow, steady speed, not more than thirty
or forty miles an hour, for its first thousand miles. The Five-
Year Plan was a very new car indeed, which had never been
tested. It ran so smoothly in the first two hundred miles that the
Russians threw it into top and set off at ninety miles an hour,
and nearly shook themselves and their machine to pieces by
doing so. The Bolsheviks pride themselves upon what they call
"Bolshevik tempo," that is to say getting things done quickly,
but they are apt to forget that more haste is less speed. Their
attitude is natural enough; it arises from youthful impetuosity
and from the need to push and energize the sluggish mass of
their fellow-countrymen, but its effects are sometimes unfortunate. There was the case, published in the Soviet press several
years ago, of the enthusiastic young director of a poultry farm
who read the directions on his five new hundred-thousand-egg
American incubators. "What," he cried, "twenty days at a temperature of 96°!"—(or whatever the correct figures may be)—
"That may do for capitalist America but it is our duty to catch
up and surpass America." So he put the temperature at 105° to

get his eggs in eighteen days! And a General Electric engineer once told me that he had to argue all day and at last get an order in writing, to prevent the manager of a factory starting a newly mounted turbine at full speed immediately because some important visitors were expected and he wished them to see the turbine develop its maximum power.

In the Five-Year Plan it had been provided that private production-cum-distribution, which in the years 1925–27 supplied the Soviet population with fully two-thirds of the food and goods it consumed, should be gradually and progressively eliminated. Instead of that, private producers and distributors were "rushed" out of business in the first eighteen months, although no mechanism had yet been developed to take their place. Two further difficulties arose, for which the sponsors of the Plan were not responsible. First, the World Depression, which cut almost in half the prices of raw materials and foodstuffs whereby the Soviet had to pay for the machinery and means-of-production goods it had bought on credit at tip-top prices. Second, the Plan was a program of peaceful development, but in 1930–31 war clouds darkened the horizon in East and West alike, as Japanese designs upon Manchuria became more clear and were finally put into practice, while Hitler rose like a comet in the western sky. The Soviet Government found it necessary to graft upon the original Plan a fresh network of war factories and their subsidiary supply factories, which for strategic reasons must be placed in the center of Soviet territory in the region two hundred miles west and eight hundred miles east of the Ural Mountains, an area potentially rich in minerals but immensely remote and ill-provided with means of communication. Apart from the intrinsic weight of this added effort the strain it caused to an already overworked transportation system and a dwindling food supply was almost intolerable.

When all these factors are considered, it is little short of a miracle that the Plan was carried through. In the final issue the crux of the struggle came in the villages where an attempt was being made to socialize, virtually overnight, a hundred million of the stubbornnest and most ignorant peasants in the world, that is, to force them into new and unfamiliar ways and expect them meanwhile to go on producing food. The new post-N.E.P. kulaks did not yield without a struggle, and the mistakes and excesses of the hot-head Communists, which Stalin denounced so harshly, tended to throw the middle and sometimes the poorer peasants on to the kulak side. Scores, even hundreds, of Communist organizers were "kicked by a horse" or "hit by a falling beam" or "killed in accidental fires," as kulak resistance stiffened. There were more overt attacks and, in some of the Cossack sections, attempts at armed revolt. Despite opposition in high places and some wobbling by those to whom open opposition was repugnant, the central authority in the Kremlin never wavered. The kulaks and their supporters were crushed by main force and the peasants were collectivized willy-nilly. What the authorities overlooked was that they were producing a state of affairs similar to that of the "carpet-bag" era in the ex-Confederate States after the Civil War. The upper and middle peasants were the natural leaders of the village communities. With their removal—they were exiled in great numbers—the rest of the village was little more fitted to handle the complicated management of a collective farm than the colored population of the Southern States was capable of self-government. The results were identical; either the Collective was run into the ground by the sheer incapacity of those in charge, or it became the prey to "carpet-baggers," shrewd crooks from outside who wormed their way into leading posts and ate up the fruits of the earth like locusts. By the end of 1932 the situation was desperate. Not only was animal food reduced to a minimum, but grain itself, that age-old staff of Russian life, was rotting unharvested in the fields. Here and there a well-managed Collective flourished like an oasis in a desert of despair, but the mass of the peasantry were degraded and discouraged beyond belief. It mattered little that by this time the chief difficulties in the industrial section of the Plan were being overcome. What profit was there to build a steel city on the Siberian steppe if its inhabitants could not be fed?

Desperate occasions require desperate remedies, and by a curious coincidence the remedy Stalin found was not much different, save in terms of legality, from that adopted by the white inhabitants of the Southern States to end the intolerable conditions of the "carpet-bag" period. By the beginning of 1933 industry had progressed sufficiently to provide twenty-five hundred machine tractor stations of about twenty-five machines each. To each of these was attached a Political Section, as it was called, of veteran Communists, most of whom had had military experience as well as long years of Party discipline. They were appointed directly by the Kremlin and given full powers over any local authority to clean up the collective farm muddle. They chased the "carpet-baggers" underground, literally, and riding roughshod over local cabals, jealousies and cliques, forced efficient management upon the Collectives and stood by to see that it was maintained. They did more than that; their reports straight from the land convinced the Kremlin how grave was the plight of the population in the North Caucasus and the Ukraine. The sacred "iron grain fund" or army reserve was raided to provide seed—and food—for the coming spring. The dispirited peasants were galvanized into action, the crop was planted, and the harvest of 1933 was the greatest Russia had ever known.

I do not think it is too much to say that the Political Sections of the tractor stations literally snatched victory from defeat in the cause of rural socialization. If the collective farms had been left to themselves for another six months and to the tender mercies of local officials, whose chief desire was to make a good showing for themselves regardless of what might happen to the peasants, the richest grain lands of Russia would have reverted to desert and the agrarian problem might have been solved by the elimination of the peasants. In point of fact, the harm done by the bureaucrats was nothing compared to the basic evils from which the Collectives suffered—unwieldy and incompetent management, lack of organization, individual jealousy and feuds, and a perpetual alteration of rules and regulations until even an efficient directorate would have not known whether it was standing on its head or its heels. The Political Sections changed all that; they established order with curt vigor and, as a result of their recommendations, a "type system" of Collectives was evolved called the *artel*, which meant that the land should be owned and worked in common, together with a number of other communal enterprises—building, carpentering, stock and poultry raising, jam-making and preserving—but that, meanwhile, the members of the Collectives should be encouraged to raise their own animals, large and small, have truck gardens, keep bees or rabbits and otherwise contribute to their own improvement and support.

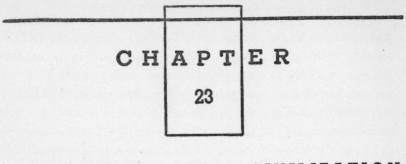

CHAPTER
23

COLLECTIVES SPELL CIVILIZATION

FUTURE historians—perhaps not Soviet historians alone—may well regard the Russian struggle for collectivization as a heroic period in human progress. As the world saw it in near perspective while it was happening, there was general sympathy for the kulaks, hard-working peasant farmers torn from their homes to labor under task-masters on alien soil, but this sentimental "close-up" omits the real point at issue, which was the attempt to regulate on an equable scale the old quarrel between the interests of Town and Country. Town wants and needs that the price of food be low and the price of goods high; Country wants and needs the exact reverse—a fundamental contradiction. Town in general is progressive, inventive, and tending inevitably towards coöperation, which is the first form of collectivism. Country is individualist and set in its ways; its methods are antiquated, but it does not like to change them. Every economist knows that the production of food, even in advanced countries, is wasteful as compared with industry. Yet farmers everywhere, through their voting power and numerical weight, have resisted change. The Bolsheviks said, as Henry Ford had said before them, that there was no reason why agriculture should not be run as efficiently as industry. In their case it was almost a matter of life and death because farming in Russia was far below Western standards. At the beginning of 1918 there were fifteen million peasant holdings in Russia. They had increased to twenty-five million in 1928, to correspond to the natural increase of the peasant population, without any great increase in the area of cultivated land. The average acreage cultivated on each of these twenty-five million "farms" was less than ten acres, that is to say barely enough, in the most favorable conditions, to provide a living for the holder, his family and stock, and the methods of cultivation were obsolete and cumbrous beyond words.

The Bolsheviks decided that if Russia was to be modernized, let alone socialized, there must be a thorough reform of the agrarian system, because 125,000 farms with an average of 2,000 acres, run on up-to-date lines with machinery and expert methods of cultivation, would not only be vastly more productive but would save an infinity of time and labor. Thus, the most backward section of the population would have the chance to obtain what it most needed, namely education, and its most hard-pressed section, namely the women, would have the chance for leisure and freedom as well. In other words, whether the villages preferred their dirt and ignorance to Progress or not, Progress would be thrust upon them. Many of those who mourn for the sufferings of Russian peasants torn from their homes have not seen the homes in question, which were often more like pig-sties than human habitations. "Be it ever so humble" is one thing, but be it ever so filthy, degrading and disease-breeding is another.

I first met exiled kulaks on a trip to Central Asia in 1930, when a carload of foreign correspondents went down to Kazakstan to see the "meeting of steel" on the Turk-Sib Railway, which had been built from north and south simultaneously to meet at a point just north of the Ili River. The Turk-Sib was one of the triumphs of the Five-Year Plan, and the exiles were its débris. The contrast was sharp and pitiful. Where steel met there were two huge trains of sleeping cars, bright with flags and garlands, a great wooden grandstand decked with red bunting and crowded with local dignitaries, shock-workers and their families, all happy and excited and dressed in gay colors, while the fields for miles were dotted with the round felt tents of Kazak nomads, who had come in thousands to see the show and stood gaping in amazement at the swooping aëroplanes or at the funnels of the loud-speakers. Then—a few miles down the track—a dark gray train on a siding, with foot-square windows heavily barred and armed guards lounging beside it. At the windows haggard faces, men and women, or a mother holding her child, with hands out-stretched for a crust of bread or a cigarette. It was only the end of April but the heat was torrid and the air that came from the narrow windows was foul and stifling; for they had been four-teen days en route, not knowing where they were going nor caring much. They were more like caged animals than human beings, not wild beasts but dumb cattle, patient with suffering eyes. Débris and jetsam, victims of the march to Progress. But I had seen worse débris than that, trains full of wounded from the Front in France going back to be patched up for a fresh bout of slaughter. In those trains, too, there were pale lineaments of woe and eyes of hopeless resignation. Patriotism and Progress are high-sounding words and noble as Ideals, but are they *always* worth the pain they cost?

The official purpose of our trip to Central Asia was to chron-icle the Turk-Sib conjunction, but for me there was a far more glamorous goal. I had known at Cambridge a strange, swarthy young poet, of equal ugliness and charm, named James Elroy Flecker, who later enchanted England with a play called *Hassan*, in which, unless I am mistaken, the poem which he had just finished when I met him found a place as a minstrel song or ballad. It was called *The Golden Road to Samarkand* and its chanting rhythm brought to me all the glory and magic of

Tamerlane's proud capital. Samarkand—the name itself is music and romance. Samarkand and fabulous Bokhara—those were the magnets that had drawn me to Central Asia, not the thought of my friend, the stout Bill Shatoff, driving the last golden spike into the railroad he had built. And beyond them another goal, more dim and distant yet—Khiva. When I was a child there hung over my bed the pictures of two unusual Englishmen—Gordon, Chinese Gordon, Gordon of Khartoum; and Burnaby, hero of the "Ride to Khiva," the only Englishman and one of the very few foreigners who had ever reached that ancientest of cities in its desert oasis, far south of the Aral Sea. At Khiva, they say, there are irrigation dikes that were built when the Sumerians ruled Mesopotamia, and land had been cultivated without intermission for ten thousand years. Khiva was six weeks' journey by boat down the Oxus and by caravan across the desert, which of course was out of the question for me, but I knew a young Lettish airman stationed at Tashkent who had flown to Khiva when its Khan rebelled, unsuccessfully, against the Bolsheviks in 1922. The Lett told me that there was a more or less regular service by army plane between Khiva and Samarkand, and I hoped, not greatly but most deeply, to find him and persuade him to take me for the two days' trip. The hope was vain; he was away scouting on the Afghan border, where there had been some trouble, but Samarkand and Bokhara were facts, not hopes—I could visit them by train.

How strange to see the name of golden Samarkand in dingy white Russian letters on a dull red background in the typical railroad station of a Russian provincial town! And stranger still to find beneath it a Red Army band and detachment of soldiers in khaki uniform and a crowd of workers and local officials drawn up to welcome our train. (I forgot to mention that in addition to foreign correspondents there were two carloads of Soviet newspaper men and writers and six cars full of shock-

workers, who were being rewarded for good work in Moscow
factories by this joy-ride through Central Asia. The welcome was
primarily for them.) After speeches of greeting, which seemed
interminable to my impatience, we moved at last into the station-
yard and embarked in rickety Fords. What a sight that was before my horrified eyes! Not a sign of ancient monuments or the
glories of the past, not even ruins to bear them witness; nothing
save tall locust trees and acacias in full foliage and an occasional native costume to show that we were in Central Asia,
much less in storied Samarkand. For the rest it might have been
a town on the Volga or the outskirts of Moscow itself—squat
stone houses, frowzy shops, an electric carline with ill-painted
cars, and an asphalt highway, of which the driver spoke with
pride. "But is this Samarkand," I asked him, "old Samarkand?"
He shrugged his shoulders. "Old Samarkand," he said, "oh, no,
that's over there." He pointed southwards. "That's three miles
away, but it's just a mass of ruins and native dwellings. This is
the Russian city, built when the railroad came thirty years ago,
now our Soviet city. We have still two miles to go but wait until
you see the new textile plant and the workers' club and the
movie theater and the hotel that has just been finished; it's a
regular new town we're building." That was a relief at any
rate; there was more of Samarkand than what I saw before me.
Suddenly our car swerved into the gateway of a park, rushed
down a gravel drive, and halted before a large stone building of
the pseudo-Gothic type so popular in Russia at the end of the
last century. "What's this?" I asked the driver. "Headquarters
of the Soviet," he said proudly, "formerly the Governor's palace. A reception has been arranged for you here." I felt like
Tantalus in Hades.

We had only two days to spend in Samarkand and it was
already ten o'clock, but for three long hours I sat perforce and
listened and listened to speeches. All the speeches were the same

speech except that those of the hosts began with words of welcome and those of the guests with words of thanks. Then both parties proceeded to eulogize the Five-Year Plan and to tell what they, whether hosts or guests, had done to help it forward. The conclusion was a pledge of further devoted service and "Hail to the Soviet State." This sounds short but they took a long time to tell it, and some of the speeches were in Uzbek or other Oriental tongues and had to be translated. It grew hotter as the hours passed, and I was drowsy—I had not slept much the night before because I was so excited to find one of my dreams come true. Suddenly I sat bolt upright as the clear, firm tones of an efficient-looking young female Party Secretary struck horror to my brain. "And now, comrades," she said firmly, "you will all go to see our greatest and latest achievement, the irrigation dam which contains umpteen thousands—or millions—cubic meters of concrete and will irrigate umpteen thousands—or millions—of acres of cotton land. It is only forty miles away and the road is being rapidly improved, so that you will have time to visit also the new tobacco factory seven miles further on and our model collective cotton plantation, which last year harvested umpteen centners of cotton per hectare. Then when you come back here in the evening we shall meet again at a banquet. The cars are waiting to take you to the dam." These dreadful words were greeted with hearty applause by all present save the foreigners, who looked at each other with greater anguish than any exiled kulak ever showed. It was more than I could bear—to have come from the ends of the earth to golden Samarkand and be rushed off in a mob of "udarnik" shock-workers to see an unfinished dam and a tobacco factory. I clutched frantically at the arm of the foreign office representative who had accompanied us to censor our dispatches. "Good God, Podolsky," I cried despairingly, "this can't be true. Do you mean to say that I have to go off and look at a *dam* when Tamerlane's tomb and the Registan, which Curzon called the most magnificent monument in the world, are waiting for me fifteen minutes away? I won't do it." He shrugged his shoulders. "You are their guests," he said, "and they are proud of their dam because they built it themselves." "Yes," I said passionately, "and Tamerlane built the Registan, but I suppose they've never heard of Tamerlane." Podolsky smiled. "They've probably heard of him but they know he's been dead a long time."

When France lay prostrate under Talbot's iron heel, a simple country girl stepped forth from her village in Lorraine to save her country in its hour of need and drive the English back to their foggy island. Her courage did not fail when the warriors of France shrank back. Amongst our party there was a young New York society girl named Molly Van Rensselaer Cogswell. She was no more a regular reporter than Joan of Arc was a regular soldier, and you wouldn't exactly call her a simple country girl—or at least you wouldn't have called her it twice—but she rescued three veteran reporters— Jim Mills of the A.P., Ed Deuss of Hearst's, and myself—from what then seemed worse than death. "Come on," she said quickly, "get into the car and don't argue." We followed dumbly. "You sit next to the driver," she said to me, "and tell him in your most violent Russian to drive straight to the old town and shoot the first man that tries to stop him." I obeyed and we started. Podolsky rushed forward, protesting. "Hey, stop," he cried. "You can't do that; where are you going; you must wait for the rest." "We are going to the Registan, Mr. Podolsky," said Molly with utter firmness, "and we shall give it your love." We went to the Registan. "Your ancestors weren't patroons, Molly; they were pirates," said Jim Mills, as we scattered the crowd at the gate of the park and swung round on two wheels into the straight road that led up to the hill on which Tamerlane's city was planted. "All right," she replied, "but

you wanted to be kidnaped, didn't you?" "Pirates nothing," I
cut in, "they were heroes and so are you; you're not Molly Cogswell but Joan of Arc, and I mean it."

As we breasted the hill I suddenly realized why they called
it Golden Samarkand. All the roofs of the adobe houses, flat as
that on which Bath-sheba bathed under David's eager eyes, were
a mass of yellow poppies blazing in the sun. We halted right at
the Registan itself, a towering three-sided square, its buildings
fronted with blue and white tiles, each front a mighty archway
curving upwards to a point, each archway flanked by two great
towers high as factory chimneys, also gleaming with tiles in
white and blue. The Registan was market-place and place of
worship; the buildings were mosques and behind them what
corresponds to colleges where students once numbered in thousands lived and learnt. Many of the tiles were broken, the tops
of two pillars had fallen and a third was supported by steel
cables, but more than enough was left to justify Lord Curzon's
praise. I have seen many buildings but nothing nobler or more
spacious. We climbed to the roof of the mosques and Jim and
Deuss scrambled up inside one of the towers to the top. We
found an old mullah in a little cell where his brothers, the servants of Allah, had lived before him for five hundred years. He
spoke to us and we could not understand him, but his tone was
peaceful and full of friendship. In a similar cell across the
square lived a Russian archæologist who spoke German, which
Deuss knew thoroughly. He had been there since 1890, he said,
and his chief regret was that he had not seen Samarkand before
the earthquake of 1886, which did so much damage to its ruins.
The mosque of Bibi Khanoum, which Tamerlane built in memory of his dearest wife, had suffered dreadfully—there was but
a shell left of its gorgeous sky-blue dome. Tamerlane built that
himself, the old man told us, but the Registan and most of the
monuments of Samarkand were erected by Tamerlane's grand-

son, Ulag Bek, surnamed "the builder." We asked how the Revolution had affected his work. He blinked, as if bewildered, behind his spectacles, then said mildly, "I heard some shooting and there was excitement for some months in the bazaar, but I think, you know, the Bolsheviks are fine people. They have done more in the last five years to maintain and, where possible, most carefully to restore these treasures of the past than was done in twenty years before them. It is late now, but perhaps to-morrow, if you are free, I will take you to Tamerlane's tomb where they have put me in charge of restoring the gateway. It is simple, you know, a small domed building like a mosque in a little garden down the hill. I am replacing the tiles of the gate that leads into the garden. Of course I only use the old tiles, and it is hard to find them unbroken, but we make progress . . ." he nodded absently, "yes, slowly we make progress. It will take a year or more but I hope I shall live to see it finished."

We took coffee and cakes in a low flat room whose beams were blackened with the smoke of centuries, wide open to the narrow lane of the silversmith's bazaar where brown men in multi-colored silk costumes sat tapping with little hammers at silver trinkets, as their ancestors had done to adorn the saddles and bridles of the Tartar horses when Tamerlane rode to war. It was indeed a dream come true; I have never known so sure a case of my anticipation equalled by reality. If one drop was needed to complete our cup of happiness, like the touch of absinth in the hands of a master barman, which can change an ordinary cocktail to nectar, it was provided by the sight of our colleagues an hour after our return to the shady garden round the house of the Samarkand Soviet. The banquet, we had heard, was set for six sharp, so we were prompt to time in the thought that our truancy might haply be condoned. It was cool in the garden and a white-clad comrade-waiter brought us light wine from the Bokhara oasis, fresh and fragrant as the Bokhara grapes that are large as greengages, with a soft pink skin like a peach. At seven-thirty the pilgrims arrived, and to look at them you would have thought they had walked from Samarkand to Mecca and back again. There was one Japanese—it is true he wore a gray suit—as like to a pillar of dust as Lot's wife was a pillar of salt, save for his round, gold-rimmed glasses. All the rest was one smooth dusty surface. The others looked much the same, but patchier where the heat had melted their dusty coating. Their faces were like a map of little rivers running in canyons through a gray plateau. The waiter who had served us wine brought one bucket of water for the twelve of them—it seemed that the Soviet press and the udarniks had rushed eagerly to a meeting—and we sat and watched them without a word. They were the drop of absinth, which means wormwood, in our cup of bliss, but it was they, not we, who provided the bitterness—of others—without which no human felicity is wholly perfect.

.   .   .   .

After Samarkand I thought that Bokhara would be an anticlimax, but it wasn't. Here were no ruins of great antiquity but an Oriental city with hardly any European-type buildings because the country had been nominally independent prior to the Revolution, like the native states of India, with no visible signs of Russian suzerainty save a Resident with a military guard attached to the Emir's court. A division of troops, however, was always stationed in the new Russian town on the main-line railroad nine miles from Bokhara proper, from which a branch had been built to old Bokhara, I think since the Soviet occupation. The Emir fled to Afghanistan when the Red Army advanced in 1920 or 1921. He was a thickset, Persian-looking potentate of unusual profligacy and great wealth. When the Reds advanced he found that he had only enough camels to take his treasure and half of his harem, which was equally composed of boys and

girls. He took most of the boys but left all the girls behind, perhaps thinking that it might delay the Red Army. Red discipline
was better than he guessed, and as pursuit grew hotter the Emir
dropped boy after boy until at last he reached the border in
safety, with only one mignon left but with all his gold and
jewels. He was welcomed by the Afghans and financed the abortive "Basmachee" religious rising against the Bolsheviks in 1922
but took no part in the fighting. I believe that he is still in
Afghanistan.

We visited the Emir's palace, a modern building of rather
gaudy Moorish architecture set in a charming garden full of
shady walks, fruit trees and running streams. The palace was
empty but the grounds and outbuildings were occupied by the
new Women's Lunatic Aslyum, for what reason I cannot tell. At
the back of the palace were marble steps leading to a large open
swimming pool, now empty save for two young piglets which
rooted about among the sand and weeds, squeaking sadly for
their mother. The Emir used to sit here on the steps in the cool
of the evening and watch his favorites disporting themselves in
the limpid waters; then he would choose this one or that, or
these and those, as companions for the night. Yet even this sen-
sual monarch, I was told, had moral scruples. At the end of a
long passage lined in crimson plush the Emir had two bedrooms,
one on either side, for boys on the left and damsels on the right.
He made it a point of honor never to mix the sexes.

On the day of my visit the Emir's place on the steps overlooking the pool was occupied by a somnolent Russian attendant,
reading a heavy book. Whether he was guarding the pigs or the
female lunatics I did not ask, but I did ask the title of his book.
Believe it or not, it was *The Economic Causes of Lunacy*. Between
that and the vanished Emir I could think of no wider contrast.
He could not inform me why the palace gardens and stables had
been allotted to the female lunatics, but suggested on second

thought that it was a sign of Soviet culture, as perhaps it was, although I prefer the theory that it was some subtle form of Oriental derision.

I have never been able to understand why the Bolsheviks, who are not squeamish about human life nor burdened with belief in God and the immortality of the human soul, have not set the world an example by killing off hopeless lunatics. To the best of my knowledge they don't even kill criminal lunatics, which is one of the things that baffles me entirely in our Western civilization. If you admit that it is lawful and meet to hang or electrocute a sane murderer, it seems to me infinitely more reasonable to kill a crazy murderer. Instead, their lives are spared and they are shut up in institutions more comfortable than any prison —from which they sometimes escape or are actually released— to live on with no profit to themselves and considerable expense to the State. I suppose that God-believing countries may retain some belief that criminal lunatics are "afflicted by Allah" as it were, but why the Bolsheviks should hesitate to shoot them or use them for medical experiment, I cannot for the life of me imagine. The same applies to hopeless cases of lunacy that are not criminal. Of course there is no reason why harmless "softies," the feeble-minded and persons who may recover should be summarily liquidated. For them sterilization would be sufficient, and little as I admire the present régime in Germany, I give it full marks for having set a precedent in this respect. It may be objected that killing is a violent measure and there are always doubtful cases. Very well, let the doubtful cases live, but every doctor knows that there are cases where no doubts are possible, and if anyone, whether he believes in God or not, has ever seen a coprophagous idiot in action, he can have no doubt that happy dispatch is the best and kindest medicine for the creature and its relatives. As the laws of America and England stand to-day a man can go out and kill somebody for the perfectly sensible reason that he needs money or hates that person bitterly. If he is caught and convicted he goes to the chair or the scaffold, but when in sadic frenzy he rapes and strangles a dozen little girls, they put him away in a nice asylum and keep him safe until he dies. If that is Civilization, give me Abyssinia.

The Bolsheviks have a modern and sensible view about murder. They regard it as the most serious crime one individual can commit upon another, but their criminal code is intended primarily for the protection of society rather than of the individual. Therefore, there is no death penalty for murder in the U.S.S.R., only the maximum prison sentence of ten years, that is for a single murder or at most two murders. If any citizen makes a habit of murder, then he becomes a menace to society and is shot as such. On the other hand, the Bolsheviks are ruthless in regard to crimes against the State—high treason or the murder of officials in pursuance of their duty, or a murder actuated by political motives, and, since 1932, even the theft of State property may be punished by what is called "the highest measure of social protection, namely shooting"—that is the formula in which death sentences are worded. This makes it all the more surprising that they do not consider an insane murderer to be a public menace, and shoot him without compunction.

I remember one case where this question was raised in a Soviet court and hotly debated by press and public. Several years ago a gang of footpads haunted the outlying villages in the woods around Moscow, where many people spend the summer months. This gang committed many murders and its victims were always killed in the same way, strangled with a cord or wire twisted tight round their throats by a small piece of wood at the back of the neck. When at last they were caught and brought to trial it was found that their leader was a boy of thirteen, who they declared planned all their operations but took no part in the attacks until the victim lay helpless with the cord round his neck. Then this engaging child twisted the cord or wire until the end had come. The boy made no attempt to deny the testimony of his accomplices, but the reports of the case declared that he eyed them so terribly that they faltered in their confessions. The adults were shot at once as a danger to society but the boy was remanded for psychopathic examination. He appeared perfectly normal, indeed of unusual intelligence and strength of character, as one might well imagine. He said calmly that all the evidence was true; he had been the leader of the gang and had ordered all its doings. "But why," they asked him, "did these hulking men obey you?" "I told them to," he said simply, "and they did what they were told." Asked why he finished the victims off himself, he replied, "Because I liked to see their eyes pop out." This was too much for the psychopaths, or for the police authorities, I don't know which. In any case the boy was shot.

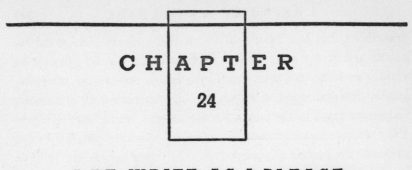

CHAPTER
24

I RE-WRITE AS I PLEASE

I CONTINUED, "To illustrate the vicissitudes of the long-drawn fight to socialize agriculture and industry, I shall now give the stories of a typical Russian village in the grain belt and of a typical provincial town." I went on to relate stories at considerable length. The first was about a village in the North Caucasus which was rushed into collectivization only to find that however desirable collectivization might be in theory, it meant in practice mismanagement and woe. At the eleventh hour the collective was rescued by a Political Section which came literally as a "god from the machine."

The second story was also a record of mismanagement and incompetence, also with a happy ending in that finally the town learned by trial and error to build and run its factories. Its people suffered greatly in the process which lasted from 1928 to 1933, but the net result was that the factories were built and that the freight-cars which they intended to produce were indeed produced, on a socialist basis.

Both stories were true enough, but when I was making a final revision of the manuscript in Moscow in August, 1935, they seemed to me a dreary and uninteresting, remote historical record rather than a living graphic picture of what happened. For the best of reasons: that I had not seen or shared what I was

300

describing, but had been told about it by others. Any good reporter can give a second-hand description of a brief episode as vividly as if he had seen it himself, but to convey the miseries, hopes, disappointments, struggles, and successes of a Russian village or town in the tragic yet wonderful years from 1928 to 1933 without having seen them requires a genius which I do not pretend. And after all, what I told in those stories could have been said in two sentences—the Five-Year Plan, not as it was conceived but as it was executed asked far too much of a backward people like the Russians. Nevertheless, by dint of enormous effort the Russian people did substantially what was asked of them.

I decided, therefore, that I would eliminate my stories and was not sorry to see them go. Even to a reporter who prides himself on having no bowels of compassion to weep over ruined homes and broken hearts, it is not always easy or pleasant to describe such wreckage, however excellent may be its purpose —or even its final fruits. But what matters to me is the facts, that is to say whether the Soviet drive to Socialism is or is not successful irrespective of the cost. When, as often happens, it makes me sick to see the cost, I say to myself, "Well, I saw the War and that cost was worse and greater and the result in terms of human hope or happiness was completely nil. Here at least it seems the results are better in that the Russian peasant who never was free and who had no more consciousness of what the American farmer means by freedom than a toad with or without a jewel in its head has of Æsculapius will within five years or less benefit enormously from being forced to accept a modern form of agriculture instead of the wasteful clumsy methods which he and his grandfather and great-grandfathers have followed since the days of Ham. It is the same with industry: the Bolsheviks want Russia to adopt a system of socialized industry

that Russia didn't like, but once again the net result in terms of
production shows startling gains."

That was what I thought and I thought too that in the course
of the last seven years, this country has made an unprecedented
capital investment in socialized industry and has simultaneously
converted agriculture from narrow and obsolete individualism
to modern Socialist methods. What is more both of these operations have been carried out with success. Their cost in blood and
tears and other terms of human suffering has been prodigious,
but I am not prepared to say that it is unjustified. In a world
where there is so much waste and muddle it may perhaps be true
that any plan, however rigid, is better than no plan at all and
that any altruistic end, however remote, may justify any means
however cruel. While I was thinking these things, and sore perplexed as Robinson Crusoe would say, how to replace my two
lost stories, I received orders from *The New York Times* to
cover the International Physiological Congress in Leningrad. It
was an unwelcome assignment because no newspaper man worth
his salt likes handling a story about which he doesn't know
anything. Physiology is one of the abstrusest of the sciences and
its mysteries are further veiled by its votaries. Physiologists
use words like enzyme and hormone in the same way as the
average American uses nickel—just small change in his own
currency. I know more about currency and its fluctuations than
most people because I have been forced so often to tread the
Mohammedan razor-bridge ostmarks from pengoes or English
pounds from Tsarist roubles. I understand the convolutions of
valuta and the gyrations of the Greek drachma, but I was completely baffled by the small change of physiological conversation and I did not choose to seek refuge in little trick stories
about making a cat's ear grow out of its left hind leg or about
a ram which could enseminate—artificially—thirty-six hundred
ewes. I didn't want such "human interest" chit-chat: I wanted

to do justice to the story of the Physiological Congress and write it down with the decorum and knowledge that it deserved. But I found I lacked that knowledge. It would have required many years of scientific training to explain adequately and correctly what the Congress was about.

For the first three days in Leningrad, therefore, I was more perplexed than ever, but on the fourth day I suddenly realized that "ex malo scilicet bonum," which is to say that instead of letting yourself be defeated by difficulties you must try to turn them to your own advantage. That, I think, was what Bolitho meant by saying to me that losing a leg need not be an unmixed misfortune, and after a life of considerable adventure and some disaster I believe that it is the most important lesson which human beings can learn. To get good out of good is easy enough, but inasmuch as it seems that more unlucky or ungood things happen to us than good and lucky ones, we ought to prepare ourselves rather for unpleasant than for pleasant contingencies. There is the alternative philosophy of "a stiff upper lip and keep smiling," which sounds to me like a contradiction in terms because how can one smile if one's lip is stiff, and anyway it does not get you anywhere. It is a "bite on the bullet" theory, which *au fond* is not far removed from the Oriental doctrine of Quietism and a passive acceptance of whatever evils it may please God to place upon you. I am not an Oriental, and I do not believe that any god is sufficiently interested in me to pester me with anything, from boils (like Job) to wooden legs. I am therefore interested in what I or anyone else should do when confronted by any unpleasant event or circumstance, and I follow Bolitho's idea in accepting said event or circumstance as it comes without protest or repining, and then trying to make use of it as best I can.

I applied Bolitho's philosophy to the Leningrad International Congress of Physiologists, and on the fourth day, as I have said, there dawned upon me a great light, as on Saul on the road to Damascus. Physiologists, I perceived, were incredibly akin to the Bolshevik rulers of Soviet Russia. They used language which perhaps by deliberate intent was incomprehensible to all save adepts. Their aims and ideals were magnificent, the ne plus ultra of human endeavor, but their methods were often distressing, not only to the subjects of their experiment—here was a further parallel—but to sentimental observers of their doings. There is a certain difference in that the Bolsheviks regarded the kulaks as enemies, not as subjects of experimentation, but in both cases cruel methods are held to be justified by the goal at which the experiment is aimed. In both cases that goal is the betterment of humanity, than which there could be no loftier aspiration. It may be objected that vivisection of living animals is a sad and dreadful thing, and it is true that the lot of kulaks and others who have opposed the Soviet experiment is not a happy one, but again, in both cases, the suffering inflicted is done with a noble purpose. Thus you come to the age-old question whether or not the end *does* justify the means. I am convinced that Bolsheviks and physiologists, whatever they may say in rebuttal, sincerely believe that it does.

Fortunately for me, I was only once faced by this problem in a matter of serious, personal importance. It was during the War in the summer of 1917 when I was called upon to write a story which I believed to be a fake, as a means to an end which, if not intrinsically noble because it was a matter of war propaganda (and I do not now think that war propaganda was noble), was at least considered so by people far more august than I, and by my own chiefs, and for that matter by me also. I was young and inexperienced, but I had to decide the question alone. I tried to persuade myself that the story *might* be true, but I did not believe it, and it was *not* true. I have never, except on that occasion, written a story I did not believe at the time I wrote it, although I plead guilty to adding a little local color on occasion. I wrote the story and got good marks for it, but I am still uncertain whether *I* was justified whatever the end or the means may have been. I was so much worried by this affair that I finally got rid of it by self-expression, in the Freudian sense, that is to say by writing a sort of prose poem in the e e cummings manner, as follows:

i sat and wondered whether the End justified the Means
as many another reporter has wondered before me
and whether that meant any end justified any means
i decided it didnt
or whether a noble end justified any means
i wasnt so sure about that
and finally whether a noble end justified somewhat doubtful
    means
at this point i fancied it might

i thought of the day when a foxy patriot named Creel
decided it would pep up the fighting spirit of the American
    public
to hear that the first American troop flotilla sent to Europe to
    win the war
(to win the war for those dear distinguished associates of
    theirs
who have never ceased to be grateful)
had been attacked by shoals or schools or coveys of German
    submarines
and only escaped by Miracles of Heroism and the Gracious
    Providence
which protects those who battle for a Righteous Cause

i remembered how excited the American public thereupon
    became

and how its excitement was nothing to the excitement of American newspaper offices
and how i received a cable in Paris rush triple urgent two thousand word dispatch
about thwarted submarine attack on first American troopships
and how my boss was "somewhere in France" welcoming General Pershing
and how it was all news to me about this thwarted submarine attack

so i phoned the French war office and got nothing
and phoned the French ministry of marine and got abuse
for interrupting their afterlunch siesta
and phoned in all directions and still got nothing
and it was three oclock and no cable filed in those days after seven
would reach New York in time for the next days paper
so i phoned in some more directions and finally got in touch
with the eminent aide of an eminenter American naval officer
who said the submarine story was bunk and hokum and a lot of naval remarks
that were not FIT TO PRINT
and i thought i was raw and inexperienced and this was a Great Problem
and i thought id face it HONESTLY and cable a flat Denial
(strangely enough the ranking American admiral thought the same and cabled HIS denial
but he had to wait a long time maybe until the war was over
before his denial was ever known to the American Public)
and then i had a second thought a startling but not unfounded thought
that some of my more experienced colleagues might be less honest than i

and it was halfpast three and the deadline for me was seven
then i thought a third thought a thought which i now realize
marked my graduation from apprenticeship as a reporter
a thought as i look back on it that would have baffled saint
    athanasius
to solve its subtle casuistry
and decide was i BLESSED or DAMNED

spurred by my thought i sped to the New York bar
and Henrys bar and the Chatham bar and a number of neigh-
    boring bars
all full of American soldiers and sailors whod crossed the
    ocean with Pershing
to make the world safe for the French
and i told them my woeful plight and i told them my startling
    news
and i said to them what will you drink have another the next
    rounds on me
but tell me the story of how did you act and how many you
    sank
IN THE TERRIBLE BATTLE AGAINST THE GERMAN
    SUBMARINES
and they told me they told me PLENTY how they shot and
    how they acted
how torpedoes slid along their bows like the velvet touch of
    safety razors
and scraped their sterns with bubbles close as the best of
    shaving creams
they told me enough for TWENTY thousand words
with oodles of facts and details
and it was nearly five oclock

i sped back to my office full of facts and details
and of multifarious toasts i had pledged to voluble warriors

and wrote me a powerful piece and sent it on its way

before the fatal deadline and went out to play auction bridge

with a junior naval officer and a junior diplomat and a senior
*   army officer*

none of whom had heard a whisper

of the terrible battle against the German submarines

and didnt believe it when i told them.

but before id FINISHED telling them with all those facts and
*   details*

they werent entirely sure whether some of it had happened

and i said of course you know im not an experienced reporter

but you cant doubt EYEWITNESS accounts not so many of
*   them i mean you cant*

not so many eyewitness accounts that had so many points of
*   difference*

but tallied so closely on the main important FACT

that there was this TERRIBLE BATTLE

and they guessed you couldnt doubt it tho the senior army
*   officer*

made a cynical remark about NEVER believing sailors

or even he added soldiers when THEYD been on the sea

well i ask you does a reporter not mean someone who reports

reports exactly what he sees verbatim what he hears

and did i not report it to my full two thousand words

and did it LEAD THE PAPER or not

and if Saint Peter asks unpleasant questions about it i shall
*   appeal to Saint Athanasius*

and if Saint Athanasius lets me down i'll shout for citizen
*   Creel*

and if they cant find him in heaven then i fear we'll meet in
*   HELL*

I suppose that the real answer to the problem of end and means is belief, and passionate single-minded earnestness. The Bolsheviks have that and I respect them for it, but I have not got it and do not want it. I generally see too many sides of a question to be quite sure which one of them is true, and in my heart of hearts I am rather inclined to pity single-minded people as being somehow deficient in unbiased judgment. I once said something of the kind to a master or teacher at school or college, and he replied severely, "You, Duranty, are afflicted by the curse of Reuben—instability. You may flatter yourself that you are seeking for truth, but the fact is that you cannot make up your own mind. Remember the curse of Reuben, 'Unstable as water thou shalt not excel.' " I was much cast down by this reproof until one day I thought to myself that I did not particularly want to excel. What I wanted, I thought, and what I still want, I know, is to see and hear new things, and to find out— to find out the great things of world affairs and the small things in people's minds, not for any profound purpose, good, bad, or indifferent, but for my own interest, entertainment and, in latter years, amusement. It is perhaps a selfish philosophy and somewhat negative, but it is neither greedy nor cruel; nor is it foolish or frightened. They used to talk of Seven Deadly Sins, but in my opinion there is nothing more deadly or more sinful than folly, greed, fear and cruelty, which I regard as the Four Horsemen of the Apocalypse who ride over our world to-day.

. . . .

Whether one approves of the Bolsheviks and their methods or not, the fact remains that they have applied, developed, and set going in a practical form the only form of complete national collectivism which the world has known since the Inca civilization was destroyed by the Spaniards. I should have said the only form that human beings have known, because ants knew it long ago, and bees. The bee collective corresponds to the Inca system, with its theocratic head, Son of the Sun, at once ruler and fount of life. The ant-heap, however is Communist in its purest and final form, a combination of all for all and each for each, a place for everyone and everyone in his place. But ants lived on the earth in their present form before Man had evolved from monkeys, so that they have had a longer time at their disposal to work out the Communist experiment, at which the Russians still are aiming as a distant goal, for all that they have built them a solid structure of Socialism.

It is generally admitted nowadays that some form of collective system is desirable. If the Depression did nothing else, it taught the world that "rugged individualism" in the old sense is an anachronism in a modern state. The upper classes, or vested interests, or money power, or whatever one cares to call them, are beginning to realize that there is no security for them, no permanent security, unless the working masses can also feel secure. This may involve some sacrifice on the part of the possessing class, but the logic of facts is irrefutable and unless some form of collective security—in an economic sense—is achieved, there is always the risk of an explosion.

The objection to Communism from the American viewpoint is that it is not only foreign but coercive and is therefore repugnant to our love of personal independence. The Bolsheviks claim that no permanent collectivism is possible so long as private interest has any control over production and the means of production, but to apply their system in America would undoubtedly cause no less violence and coercion than it did in Russia. The question arises whether it is not possible to develop an alternative collective system of our own. I believe that the "New Dealers" are aiming at something of the kind. Unfortunately, Messrs. Tugwell and Company do not seem to realize that the methods they are applying are socialist methods, that they are in effect putting the new wine of Socialism into the old bottles of Capitalism. Capitalism and Socialism are contradictions and the Bolsheviks are quite right in believing that the two cannot be successfully combined. On the other hand, it is not necessarily true that Capitalism and collectivism are contradictions. Surely it would be easier and wiser of Capitalism to seek a remedy for its ills from its own children rather than from Socialism, its enemy.

The most eminently practical and salutary creation of modern Capitalism is insurance. Why, then, doesn't Capitalism look to insurance for help instead of applying a lot of half-baked Socialist nostrums which may alleviate the pains for a time but are really poison to its system? I don't mean what is known as social insurance alone, although British experience demonstrated the benefits of that beyond any doubt. I'd go much further than that and suggest that everyone in receipt of income, salary, or wages from whatever source be compelled by law to take out insurance against the loss of a fixed proportion of said income, against loss of health, loss from fire or any crime committed against him or her, against accident, and finally against death. The rates would vary greatly in different cases just as they vary now in health insurance, for instance, according to the age and physical condition of the client. But this is merely a matter of actuarial calculation. Attempts at fraud might occur such as occur to-day in the case of health and fire insurance, but here too the insurance companies would take due precautions. I say insurance companies because an essential feature of my scheme is that it should be merely an extension of the present individualistic capitalist system with the only difference that it would be a legal obligation of every citizen in receipt of an income however small or large. This would require a certain degree of state control and the pledge of state support.

The state would have to guarantee the payment of benefits by the companies; insurance companies would be licensed by the state which would issue licenses only to companies that were financially sound; and the state would have access to the books of the insurance companies as to-day Federal Reserve examiners have access to the books of banks. But the state would be for-bidden to meddle with insurance companies or to remove any insurance executive unless improper conduct could be proved.

The point of my suggestion is that we should thus have a complete system of social insurance which would be run on busi-ness lines by business people without any interference from or admixture of politics. One of the most singular anomalies of American life is the abhorrence of a permanent civil service. It seems fantastic that the civil service of States and municipali-ties are liable to be changed wholesale every two years—and a great part of the Federal service every four years—by a swing of the political pendulum. The result is inevitably that politics dominate not only the civil service but even the judiciary which ought to be a solid block of principle in any well-organized state. The evils consequent upon the lack of a permanent civil service and judiciary divorced from politics are all too evident. Instead, however, of attempting to remedy this state of affairs, the present Administration is making gigantic additions to the political bureaucracy, that is to say is spreading evils rather than diminishing them. Introduction of social insurance by the state would simply mean that they were spread still wider.

To summarize the whole matter, let us take for granted that some form of universal security is necessary for rich and poor alike. If the security is provided by the state, there is no mech-anism yet available to provide it and any mechanism that might be created would be dominated by politics whereas insurance companies have a mechanism of their own which already works admirably and is capable of expansion. Obviously it would not be simple to work out the details of such a scheme, but it could be done and it would provide a bridge from "rugged individualism" to "capitalist collectivism" without involving coercion or violence or any of the sufferings which during the past five years have attended the birth-pangs of Soviet socialization.

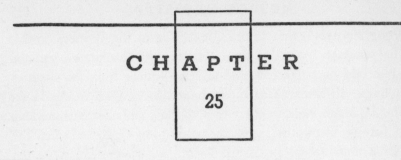

CHAPTER
25

MOSCOW REVISITED

THE question may well arise—and has often been put to me—
"Why on earth did the Russian people endure such hardship
without revolt?" An obvious answer is that they had no choice,
that the ruling forces of the régime—the Red Army, the Gay-
pay-oo and the Communist Party with its junior organizations
—were far too strong to be resisted, and that such sporadic attempts at revolt as did occur were nipped harshly in the bud.

I think, however, that the truth lies elsewhere. First, it would
be more correct to say that the ruling forces themselves had no
choice, that once embarked upon their program of socialization
it was a case of "*Kto Kavo*" (who beats whom) in the full sense
of the phrase, that no compromise was possible this time—Socialization must either win or lose. Second, the Socialist program was supported by the section of the population that was
strongest, morally, physically and politically; even in the villages that suffered most the percentage of poorer peasants who
had more to gain than lose from collectivization—if it once
could be made to work—was greater than those who had more
to lose than gain. Third, which is a peculiarly Russian explanation—both the industrial and the agrarian campaigns were carried on at a great height of tension, deliberately maintained by
all the devices of propaganda to create an emotional *sturm und*

314

drang similar to that of the Great War in the Western world. The sabotage trials that were a feature of this period and the stress laid on kulak hate and villainy—these were the enemies at home always waiting their chance for a stab in the back. The Japanese menace, the rise of Hitler, and the machinations of foreign Capitalists, were the alien forces against which the nation must accept any sacrifice for its own protection. In the war atmosphere thus created workers and peasants tightened their belts in the conviction that each stroke of hammer or sickle was a blow for the victory of a noble cause. This was particularly apparent at the crucial moment of the struggle, in the first months of 1932, when the urban and working populations throughout the country and the Red Army and all the Communist organizations were galvanized to fresh effort by the threat of Japanese attack, and the impetus thus given to the Socialist program served to carry the peasants willy-nilly through the tragic year that followed until industry was sufficiently on its feet to solve the problem as Lenin had formulated it—"Communist Party plus 100,000 tractors and modern farm machinery equals rural Socialism." In other words, the "war" was fought on two fronts, industrial and agrarian. As might be expected, the initial successes were gained in Moscow, Leningrad, Kharkov and the larger towns, where living conditions were less burdensome and where socialized industry had already a substantial foundation. One might thus say that the turning-point of industrial victory came in the beginning of 1932 and gradually spread outward to more distant sections; its effects were such as to turn the ebbing tide of agrarian socialization and snatch success from the very brink of failure. Be that as it may, I am sure of one thing, that when I left Moscow for New York at the end of April, 1932, I had few doubts about the ultimate issue, because I knew that the most determined and vital elements of the

Soviet people were united in support of their strong and resolute leadership.

I crossed the Atlantic with Bob Lamont, son of the then Secretary of Commerce, who had just made a trip to the North-east Caucasus at the request of the Commissariat of Agriculture to investigate the stock-raising situation and advise them what to do. I had seen a lot of him in Moscow before he went south and thought, when he came back, that I should get an interesting story about conditions in the Caucasus, which were said to be very bad. To my surprise he had seen few signs of distress at the dozen or more stock farms which he had visited, although he had heard, he said, dreadful stories of disease and want in other areas. I did not know what to make of it because I was quite sure that Bob was telling me the truth. My first thought was that this was a repetition of a report I read in *Pravda* during the Famine of 1921 about President Kalinin's first investigation committee being told in every village that conditions there were bad, though not intolerable but that in the next village the situation was awful and people were dying like flies. When the commission came to the next village they heard the same story, but never found the horrors of which they were told. My second thought was that Bob was being used for "whitewash" purposes on account of his father's position—a sort of modern "Potemkin Village" tour.

The facts of the case were simpler. The cattle-raising area in the foothills of the North-east Caucasus had suffered much less than the rest of the province, partly because the inhabitants had always practiced a system of collective herds for their own protection and convenience and therefore fitted more or less naturally into the Soviet collectivization scheme, partly on account of the courage and wisdom of one man, Kalmikov, president of the small autonomous republic of Kabarda in the heart of the cattle country. Kalmikov had handled the collectivization campaign with such skill and moderation that no one save a very few rich individual herd owners had been dispossessed or forced to leave Kabarda. He had, moreover, sufficient author- ity and prestige with Moscow to prevent the "hot-head excesses" which caused so much trouble elsewhere. During all the hard times and to this day Kabarda has been an oasis of happiness and plenty. Bob did see there soup kitchens and other forms of charity for peasants from surrounding sections, and this prompted a remark which startled the authorities at a large pig farm where valuable animals were dying wholesale. Bob told them, "The mistake you make is thinking you can treat your pigs the way you treat your peasants. A pig won't stand for that; he has to have plenty of sun and air and his feet kept warm and the right kind of food in proper quantities. If he gets all that he'll reward you richly, but if he doesn't you can't argue with him or coerce him with threats of exile; he'll just turn round and die on you."

In the less strenuous atmosphere of the smoking-room on the *Majestic* Bob told me that the real high-spot of his trip to the Caucasus was the discovery of some fifty-pound trout—he is an enthusiastic fisherman—in the River Terek, I think it was. To his horror these monsters, which he swore were true trout, al- though river trout of such a size were hitherto unheard of, were either netted or dynamited, but Bob said he would return one day with an assortment of salmon flies and show the natives something they had never known before. Before we landed he suggested that if I went to Washington I might like to stay with his father and mother; he thought he would be there himself, but in any case he was sure they would be glad to see me.

I had not been in New York since 1926, and found a very great difference, not only in general conditions (by the way they were infinitely better than I had been led to expect from reading the Soviet Press, although I heard more verbal woe and wailing in the single down-town section of Manhattan than in all of hard-pressed Moscow) but in the attitude of people towards the U.S.S.R. and the interest which it everywhere aroused. It seemed that everyone first wanted to know why there was no unemployment in the U.S.S.R., and the answer, "Well, you see, they have a Five-Year Plan," did not give universal satisfaction. Of course the truth was that Soviet Russia was just at the beginning of the cycle—now ending in the United States —of development of natural resources and of opening up empty territory. There was also a change in my own attitude since my previous visit. At that time, when anyone said to me, "What do you think about our recognizing Russia?" I used to answer, "That's your affair or the State Department's, not mine. They are doing plenty of business with you already, and they'll do more in the next few years. (This was true; Soviet purchases from the U.S.A. ran about $100,000,000 in 1930 and 1931.) So what does Recognition matter?" But in 1932 I thought differently. To begin with, Soviet-American trade had dropped to a low ebb; I doubt if the total turnover was more than $1,000,000 a month in 1932, at a time when American firms would have welcomed new orders. Although the reasons for this were not wholly political, politics did enter the question. Secondly, there was the question of Japan and the growing menace of war, not only in the far East but in the West, where Hitler was master of Germany. Finally, I was convinced that the Kremlin was the firmest citadel of power in Europe, that the U.S.S.R. would henceforth play a great and growing part in world affairs and that the absence of diplomatic relations between it and the U.S.A. was illogical and absurd. In 1932, therefore, I said as much to all inquirers and added the further argument that relations between the two countries had not been marred by dispute for over 100 years, that both—for different reasons—were intensely and genuinely pacifist (and for that matter both geographically Pacific) and that in the troublous times ahead their combined influence on behalf of peace might be a decisive factor.

When the time came for me to go to Washington Bob Lamont was as good as his word, and I received a most charming letter of invitation from his mother although the Secretary was barely convalescent from a tonsil operation. They were both extraordinarily kind to me and the first night I was there they asked the Under-Secretary of State, Bill Castle, and his wife to dinner. I could not but respect Castle's intellect and obvious integrity, but as far as the U.S.S.R. was concerned he was as intransigeant as I had found Mr. Kellogg, the Secretary of State, and Mr. Hoover, the Secretary of Commerce at the time of my former visit. On that occasion Mr. Hoover, for whom I had had great admiration as "Chief" of the A.R.A., shattered it by repeating his statement, which he perhaps supposed to be an epigram, that Russia was an economic vacuum. He may have known what he meant by it, but I didn't, and I don't yet, unless it was that Russia was a place into which you poured money and did not get it back. This, I fear, was Mr. Hoover's case, for he had been associated with Leslie Urquhart in the celebrated Russo-Asiatic concession. Castle had no such unhappy memories, but he was equally unbending, and after he had gone home I said to my host, "You know the State Department reminds me of one of those little china mandarins, except, of course, that it's larger than life and twice as dignified, whose heads are set on a spring so that they can move them only one way, either wagging from side to side to say no, no, no, or nodding from back to front to say yes, yes, yes—always one or the other; no mandarin is capable of both. The Department is set on the no, no, no motion and they will have to ungum its head before it says yes, yes, yes." Mr. Lamont laughed and perhaps did not wholly disagree with me, for I think he felt that the U.S.S.R. was too big and too important a world factor to be treated any longer as a naughty child who has been stood in the corner for punishment.

I had an interesting talk the next day with the Secretary of the Treasury, Ogden Mills. He was exceedingly busy at the time but managed to find half an hour for me, which extended itself to nearly an hour and a half as the Secretary waxed hot in an effort to show me the error of my ways. He ended a burst of torrid eloquence by thrusting a stubby finger at me across his desk with the words, "I tell you this, Mr. Duranty, the people of this country will never stand for diplomatic relations with a Government of atheists and unbelievers." Some of his arguments were better than that one, and I left the room with no small respect for Mr. Mills as a man and a political figure. I should not be surprised if he is heard of again in the public life of America, despite his inherited wealth.

In July I received an invitation to lunch at Albany with Governor Roosevelt, who had just been chosen Democratic Candidate. I found in the Governor a different type of mind from Messrs. Hoover, Kellogg and Mills. Here were no set opinions nor a mandarin refusal to change nay to yea but a broadminded interest and a profound knowledge of Soviet affairs which showed me that the Governor had paid no small attention to the subject. We talked quite freely because I at least had understood that it was purely a personal conversation and in no sense a newspaper interview. Indeed I was much surprised—and gratified—the following day to see that the Candidate had given the story to the newspapers with some flattering remarks about me. I have often noticed that in talking with public men above the average level of intelligence a reporter gets mighty little from their answers to his questions—unless they have something specific they want to tell him—but often can glean much from the questions they put to him. In this case, I gathered that Mr. Roosevelt was considerably interested in the Soviet capacity to pay for goods they might buy, and more particularly in their gold production. I said that figures on that subject were hard to come by, but that gold production was certainly on the upgrade, would probably reach 60,000,000 roubles or 70,000,000 roubles ($30,000,000 to $35,000,000) that year and as much as 100,000,000 roubles in 1933, which proved to be accurate enough. Apart from this Mr. Roosevelt gave little indication of what he thought about Russia, except that once when I said something about "people who have a sentimental prejudice against the U.S.S.R. and that kind of nonsense," then added quickly, "if you don't mind my using the word nonsense," he replied at once, "On the contrary, I think your word is apt." Before I left we had a few moments' conversation about the Governor's chances for election. I said that in New York they were quoting even odds or at the most five to four in the Governor's favor, but that I had talked a good deal with the Agency crowd in Washington and with other newspaper men whose jobs gave them a nation-wide viewpoint, and that their opinion was that the odds were nearer five to two on Mr. Roosevelt. I ended, "So next time I see you I think I will address you as Mr. President, not as Governor." He smiled his attractive smile and said simply, "I think so too, but I'm glad to hear you say it."

. . . .

The first thing I found in Moscow on my return at the end of August was an outbreak of typhus, although it was still far from the epidemic stage, which it reached in the following year. I know this beyond doubt because my Russian secretary caught it—on a trip to her native village, it is true—and I went to see her in a hospital where there were at least 100 other typhus patients. Nevertheless, nine months later a high official of the Commissariat of Health told me blandly that there had been no typhus in Moscow city, although he admitted that there might

have been a few cases here and there in the Moscow province
I asked him if he thought he was talking to a tourist and left it
at that. So did he. I soon saw, too, that something had gone
wrong with the harvest, although the acreage sown was nominally level with the previous year and the weather had been
good on the whole. The fact was that much of the land had been
sown so "light," a bushel or less to an acre, because the peasants were eating the seed grain, as hardly to count at all, and
that in many sections it had either been choked by weeds or the
peasants were too exhausted to harvest it. That fall the *Economic Life* stated editorially, "On scores and hundreds of collective farms of the North Caucasus part of the harvest is
unreaped and grain has been left to rot in the fields." Yet the
atmosphere of Moscow was not pessimistic; it was clear that Socialism was winning on the industrial front and that despite the
food shortage the Bolshevik slogan of "Finishing the Five-Year
Plan in Four," that is, by the end of 1932, would be approxi-
mately fulfilled. What impressed me most was that there was no
sign of faltering on the part of the Kremlin, none of the rumors
about wobble or change of policy that had been current a year
before. Stalin made this abundantly clear in a speech at a Communist session on January 11, 1933, in which, incidentally, he
laid the blame for what had happened upon Communist errors
and miscalculation of conditions in the villages. No less significant was the announcement by Kaganovich of the formation of
the Political Tractor Sections, which showed that the Kremlin
had realized the true weakness of collectivization to wit, the
mismanagement of collective farms, and now at long last was
taking steps to correct it. In April I made a flying trip through
the Ukraine on my way to Constantinople and saw the new Political Sections in action; thenceforward I had no doubt that the
solution of the agrarian problem had been found and that the
spring sowing would be successfully accomplished.

That spring there occurred the sensational trial of the Metro-Vickers engineers, which caused more ink to flow abroad than anything which had happened in Russia since the case of the Roman Catholic priests ten years before. The six British engineers were accused of sabotaging the turbines and machinery provided by their own firm, which was ridiculous on the face of it, although the charge was supported by a mass of verbal testimony from their Russian fellow-accused, and of espionage for which no scrap of documentary evidence was produced, save a fantastic confession by one of them named Thornton, who had been born in Russia and appears to have yielded to panic. Nevertheless, the trial created an unpleasant impression upon all foreigners who attended it, irrespective of their nationality. The accused men defended themselves in a surprisingly lukewarm way considering the gravity of the charges. Although they had a perfect right to insist on every word being translated into English, which would have given them time to think, and of making their replies in the same language, they allowed proceedings to be conducted in Russian. Still worse, the principal accused, Monkhouse, withdrew during the trial his initial statement to the British Ambassador, Sir Esmond Ovey (which he repeated the following day to the British and American newspaper men) that he had been subject to inquiry during forty of the forty-eight hours which followed his arrest. His avowal in court that instead of forty hours his examination might have been as much as fourteen out of forty-eight caused what might well be termed a "painful sensation" to his foreign hearers. The prevailing impression in foreign circles in Moscow was that voiced to me by a prominent diplomat: "I don't believe they are guilty as charged although their defense was strangely supine at times, *mais*"—he sniffed significantly—"*mais, ça sent mauvais quelque part.*" An equally prominent Bolshevik put it differently, "Well," he said in my hearing before the trial was ended, "they may be guilty or they may be innocent, but all I can say is that if those two, Thornton and McDonald, were Communists on trial before an English court they would be kicked out of the Party for cowardice when they came back to Russia, whether they were acquitted or not."

I spent the early summer in Greece and Central Europe and found when I got back to Moscow that the spring sowing had surpassed expectations and that a good crop was assured unless the weather was exceptionally bad. As a matter of fact, it was the biggest grain harvest on record, although I saw for myself when I visited the North Caucasus in August how the high road from Rostov to the Kuban ran at times for miles through a wilderness of lofty weeds which had been golden wheat fields only three years before. In the Ukraine, where I halted on the way home to Moscow, there was less evidence of damage, but there were empty cottages in the villages that are usually so crowded, and a marked scarcity of animals and poultry. The people looked healthier and more cheerful than I had expected, although they told grim tales of their sufferings in the past two years. One thing that puzzled me at first was that almost all the local officials whom I asked about mortality figures during the hard times replied evasively—they were not quite sure, they had not the data at their finger-tips, and so forth—and it was only gradually that I discovered that they were telling the truth, for the simple reason that nine out of ten of them had not been there at all during the period in question, but had only been appointed in the last six months or so. The Political Sections may have been a tardy discovery on Stalin's part, but there is no doubt that they made a thorough job of it once they were put to work.

I had hardly been back in Moscow a month before suddenly, out of a clear sky, it seemed, came President Roosevelt's invitation to the Soviet Government to discuss the questions pend-

ing between the two countries with a view to the reëstablishment
of diplomatic relations. There was a story afterwards in Washington that the President's action was prompted by the report
from a presumably trustworthy source that the Japanese even at
that late hour were planning a surprise attack on Vladivostok.
This may have had some bearing on events in respect to the
time element, but I think it more probable that the President
had made up his mind to recognize the U.S.S.R., if the latter
was willing to satisfy him on certain points, and that he had not
done so before because he had been too busy with home affairs.
It is one of the sorrows in the life of a conscientious reporter
that sensational stories are always the most interesting but the
drab ones are often the most true. When it was announced that
Litvinov would leave immediately for Washington, I cabled to
my office in New York for permission to accompany him, and
they agreed. We sailed on the *Berengaria* and had an unusually
calm passage for that time of year, much to Litvinov's relief,
because he had heard dark tales of the stormy Atlantic from
some of his fellow-Bolsheviks who had crossed it in smaller vessels and far less auspicious circumstances.

Before leaving Berlin Litvinov had said to the American
newspaper men there that as far as he was concerned all outstanding points between the U.S.A. and the U.S.S.R. could be
settled in half an hour. This was an incautious and undiplo-
matic remark, not merely because it happened to be true, but
because Washington had staged a somewhat elaborate comedy,
the prime purpose of which, I imagine, was to convince the
American public that a patriotic and tenacious Administration
would fight to the last ditch to extract from the Bolsheviks the
uttermost farthing of concession. Within certain limits, as I well
knew, Litvinov would have allowed the Americans to "write
their own ticket" after the half-hour's discussion to which he referred in Berlin. As it was, the agreement reached after ten

days of apparently laborious negotiations, did not overstep those limits anywhere save in one case, for which there existed a precedent. I refer to the paragraph whereby the two Governments mutually undertook to refuse harborage on their territory to any organization or group which aimed at overthrowing the political or social order of the other. On the face of it this appears to imply a disavowal by the Soviet Government of the Communist International. On the other hand there was a similar clause in an agreement reached a few months earlier between the U.S.S.R. and France (which explains Litvinov's readiness to accept it in Washington) and on that occasion the Soviet Foreign Office had declared with satisfaction that it meant that the French were thus pledged to suppress "White" Russians, Ukrainian Nationalists or other anti-Bolshevik organizations on French soil. When I asked about the Comintern the reply then was, "Oh, that is different." Where the difference lies I still am unable to understand, although I do not doubt that Bolshevik casuistry had satisfied itself that a difference existed and that it applied to the Washington agreement as well.

I "covered" the story of the negotiations from the only angle which seemed possible to me, that is as a "horse trade," which was prolonged somewhat unduly, I hinted, by artful fencing between two shrewd dealers, but whose result was more or less a foregone conclusion. As a matter of fact I am afraid that my metaphor was all too apt, and that both sides outsmarted the other and so outsmarted themselves, because when some months later, after an exchange of ambassadors and the establishment of full diplomatic relations, an attempt was made to create a working business arrangement along the lines laid down in Washington, a serious deadlock occurred, in which each side seemed convinced, I believe with full sincerity, that it was right and honest and that the other was wrong and tricky. The deadlock lasted eighteen months and led to much ill-feeling; meanwhile trade between the two countries continued to languish. It was not until July, 1935, that the ice was broken by a commercial agreement signed in Moscow by Litvinov and the American Ambassador, William C. Bullitt. Superficially this agreement appeared a meager substitute for the glowing hopes of economic coöperation that had been entertained eighteen months before, but its political significance doubtless lies in the fact that the question of debts and claims, which had formed the crux of the long deadlock, was not even mentioned and may therefore be presumed to have been dropped.

CHAPTER
26

TIME FORWARD!

I AM often asked what induced me to stay so long in Russia. People abroad have heard so much of the discomforts and difficulties of Soviet life, not to mention its actual danger, that they find it hard to understand why anyone should spend the best years of his life there if he had any choice in the matter. My reply has always been that Moscow is the most interesting place in the world and that as a newspaper man I would not change it for any other assignment. It is interesting politically because there before your eyes is being created something wholly new in human history. Still greater in my opinion is what might be called the natural interest of Russia—its utter difference from anything one has known before and its Alice-in-Wonderland topsy-turviness as compared with the Western world. Except for the direct human qualities of courage, skill, perseverance, integrity, loyalty and intelligence all our standards of values seem to be reversed in the U.S.S.R. Thus, Britain's most honored motto "Fear God and honor the King" (in the United States one might substitute "Honor the President as People's Choice") would be regarded with horror in Soviet Russia; its first half would entail the expulsion from the Communist Party of any Bolshevik who adopted it, and the second half would lead to his arrest for counter-revolution. Respect for the Past or hereditary rank and rights are as discredited in the U.S.S.R. to-day as respect for money. It is no exaggeration to say that the possession of wealth is regarded as a shame; the attempt to use wealth for personal gain or advantage is juridically a crime.

Many foreigners who spend more than a few weeks in Russia are so disgusted by this upset of familiar standards that they hurry away never to return and express their spleen in violent books or speeches. If forced to remain they share the fate of tobacco smokers in Calverley's poem:

> *Who grow by slow degrees*
> *Brainless as chimpanzees,*
> *Meager as lizards,*
> *Go mad and beat their wives,*
> *Plunge after shocking lives,*
> *Razors and carving knives*
> *Into their gizzards.*

On the other hand I find that anyone who can stand a year or more in Russia, however much he may grumble and pretend to dislike or disapprove of it, is henceforth caught by Russia as by a habit-forming drug. The virus, not of Bolshevism but of the novelty, variety and fantasy of Russian life, with its amazing contrasts between the extremes of *laissez faire* and rigid discipline, of inconsequence and the strictest logic, can never be extracted from his blood and drags him back almost against his will to a further plunge in the strange intoxicating waters. When, as in my case, this mysterious charm of Russia is trebled, and quadrupled by a profound interest in politics, there is no need for further explanation why I stay there.

I shall speak of politics later but for the moment let me mention three or four other things I have seen or heard in Russia

which illustrate its strangeness. The first was quite trivial, although its implications were not trivial, but it was bizarre and
arresting because of its departure from the commonplace. It
was no more or less than cats on leashes. I was so struck by this
sight that I wrote another little poem in the e e cummings manner to express my amazement, thus:

ten years in Moscow, ten long years in Moscow,
each year strange sights to whet a taste for stranger sights
indeed a rich pageant of variety spiced with blood if blood is
*   a spice*
or if pageants can be spiced

and i thought of the strangest things id ever seen in this rich
*   and bloody pageant*
youd never guess what it was
a fat old woman in a sheepskin coat and a thin little girl in a
*   blue skirt and jumper*
and a tall young soldier in red army uniform with the peaked
*   hat Scythian archers wore*
when they drove Darius the great king back across the Danube
and each of the three the woman the girl and the soldier all
*   in a row*
was leading a plump white furry cat on a leash
like pekinese on Park Avenue easter sunday
did ever you see such a thing in your life
as three white cats on leashes in soviet Moscow in december
*   1921*

yet the answer was simple like Columbus and the egg
when you knew it
that was the famine year no heat in pipes no fuel for stoves
*   and not much food*

but cats were muffs and meat
and given alas to gallivanting away from home
so prudent cat-fanciers kept their pets on leashes
and didnt allow them to gallivant or procreate their species
save at home.

I was so pleased with this epic when I composed it in 1931
on a dreary winter night that I went on with it and evolved a
long legend in the same manner called *Solomon's Cat,* which
I thought and still think was the finest thing I ever wrote, and I
am not quite sure that it was not the finest thing anyone ever
wrote, so full it was of subtle philosophy about cats and kings
and wealth and women. But I never found anyone to agree with
me or agree to print my masterpiece, much less pay for it. So it
remains in my archives, unhonored save by me.

Then there was the departure of the "Potemkin Trotzky"
from the Kazan station, which I still think an incredibly fantastic performance, and something still more extraordinary which
I did not see but heard. It was the story of a Bolshevik who con-
versed with a corpse. He told it to me himself and undoubtedly
believed it although he was an average tough Bolshevik who
naturally disbelieved in Heaven and Hell and a Life beyond the
Grave. This man was doing "underground" revolutionary work
in St. Petersburg when the War broke out but was caught by the
police and exiled to the far north of Siberia. In the second winter of the War he escaped from his prison camp and reached an
Eskimo village where they gave him shelter until the spring.
They lived, he said, in beastly conditions and the only one
whom he could talk to was the shaman, or medicine man, who
knew a little Russian. The shaman once boasted that he could
foretell the future, which my Bolshevik friend ridiculed. The
next day the shaman took him to a cave in the side of a hill in
which there was a big transparent block of ice enclosing the

naked body of a man—a white man not a native—apparently about thirty years of age with no sign of wound anywhere. The man's head, which was clean-shaven, was outside the block of ice; the eyes were closed and the features were European. The shaman then lit a fire and burnt some leaves, threw powder on them muttering incantations, and there was a heavy aromatic smoke. He said in Russian to the Bolshevik, "Ask what you want to know." The Bolshevik spoke in German; he was sure that the shaman knew no German, but he was equally sure that he saw the lips of the corpse move and heard it answer, clearly, in German. He asked what would happen to Russia and what would happen to him. From the moving lips of the corpse came the reply that Russia would be defeated in war and that there would be a revolution; the Tsar would be captured by his enemies and killed on the eve of rescue; he, the Bolshevik, would fight in the revolution but would suffer no harm; later he would be wounded fighting a foreign enemy but would recover and live long. The Bolshevik did not really believe what he had seen, although he was quite certain that he had seen it, I mean that he explained it by hypnotism or auto-suggestion or something of the kind, but it was true, he said that he passed unscathed through the Revolution and the Civil War and was wounded in the Polish War when the Red Army recovered Kiev.

There were many other fantastic tales that I heard in Russia. The story of the doctor who was supposed to have been visited by the ghost of a little girl and to have talked about it the next day to his class in the Medical School of Moscow University. I met this doctor, whose name was Snegueriov, and asked him what had really happened. He said that nothing had happened, that there had been no ghostly visitant, but that the story which all Moscow was repeating had doubtless been circulated by his rivals for an important post in the Medical School; they thought to discredit him by suggesting that he talked superstitious nonsense to his students. Whether this was true or not I cannot say, but he did not receive the appointment in question. Another astonishing story described the ceremonious burial alive behind a wall of a young couple to the strains of mournful music, while a young girl who had to be a virgin waited to sweep up the débris of bricks and plaster. This story ran like wildfire across Moscow, as a strange and terrible version of the old "Suicide Club" romance, but when I made inquiry of the police they said that they of course had heard of it but that it was utterly untrue.

There was also the gang of crazy poets, all of them dopefiends and alcoholics, who were cajoled by a shrewd rascal to commit mass suicide on the Red Square in order that their souls might fly at once to the star Capella to enjoy eternal happiness in that distant heaven. The form their suicide should take, he suggested, would be that each of them marching in the Red Square Parade should carry two bombs and at a given signal the whole group of ten or twelve should throw one bomb at Lenin's tomb where Stalin and the other Soviet leaders would be assembled to watch the parade, and then the other at their own feet. This, he told them, would be a most startling and successful way to die. He had the bombs, too, and the poets were willing and eager to throw them, but by sheer accident the matter came to the knowledge of the Gay-pay-oo, who saw there was more behind it than mere craziness. The poets were sent to a mental home but the shrewd rascal and his chief accomplice were shot for counter-revolution. And another tale, told earlier in 1922, of the Tsarina Alexandra, wife of Nicholas II, having escaped by some miracle with her son, the Tsarevich, from the firing-squad of Sverdlovsk to appear in a convent in the Province of Penza and there work miracles and cause, incidentally, a great commotion. I do not know whether the nuns believed this woman's story—she was actually the daughter of a schoolmaster in Kovno, who did, it seems, resemble the late Empress to a remarkable degree—but they profited by it sufficiently for the convent to receive in one month forty-eight wagon-loads of food and other gifts from the surrounding peasantry, who believed story and miracles alike. The woman and the boy were arrested and imprisoned in the county town, but their legend had grown so strong that the jailer himself released them. Later they were caught again and brought to trial, when they pleaded that they were only grafters and were let off with a trifling punishment. The convent, however, was suppressed.

Yet all these stories, and a hundred others like them, are less curious to me than the destination of Lenin's body. Before Lenin died he said he wanted no statues or memorials made for him, that instead they should use the money for juvenile education, which he thought would be the greatest tribute to his memory. I am told that he made no specific disposal of his body but took it for granted that it would be burnt. Instead, it was embalmed and placed in a $1,000,000 mausoleum, which is visited every year by hundreds of thousands of pious pilgrims. Surely this would seem the supreme anomaly of Soviet Russia, that the Bolsheviks who believe neither in God nor Resurrection should thus deify their dead Leader and use the utmost of their science to immortalize his mortal clay.

Or it is no anomaly at all but proof positive that the Bolsheviks have full mastery of Russian psychology, which has a background of mysticism yet yields so readily to a visual appeal? The more I think of this point the more I wonder whether the cynical Roman motto of "Bread and Circuses" as an easy means to lead the masses by the nose is not too Western for an Asiatic-minded people like the Russians. Or perhaps it would be fairer to say that cheap food and entertainment might satisfy the degenerate mob-herd of Imperial Rome but that the young virile population of New Russia want something more.

It is incredibly hard for foreign outsiders to gauge the truth in such a matter, however unbiased they may be. It is almost impossible for them to have contact with the vast, dim, voiceless Russian masses, whereas they are always meeting representatives of the old ruling or satisfied minority, which hates the Bolsheviks and all their works. I hesitated long before I could make up my own mind on this important issue, and I think that the spell which Lenin's mausoleum undoubtedly exercises upon the Russian people was to me the determining factor. I could not believe that thousands of people would wait for hours in rain or snow or icy cold to visit Lenin's tomb unless they were inspired by something far more profound and spiritual than curiosity or a desire to acquire merit in the eyes of Authority. For further enlightenment I stood in line myself and talked with the waiting people as they moved forward step by step. That experiment was conclusive; Lenin meant for them something outside themselves—call it uplift or aspiration or religion—and something more important still, which, unless I am vastly mistaken, is the heart and essence of the Bolshevik hold on the varied peoples of the U.S.S.R. For the first time this incoherent mass has a common symbol in Lenin's tomb, one star for all to follow, and from this community of aim and veneration the Bolsheviks have been able to distill a new elixir for their Soviet peoples in the shape of a tremendous and universal pride and a passionate interest in their country and its noble deeds. This may sound extravagant but I believe it is true.

Take first the rescue of the crew and passengers of the steamer *Chelyuskin*, which was caught and crushed in the Arctic ice just north of Behring Straits. They escaped alive from the destruction of their vessel and sent a wireless call for help. Within two weeks fifty aëroplanes were flighting northwards regardless of wind and weather, and the remotest villages of the U.S.S.R. were following their flight by radio from day to day.

The success of that high endeavor did far more than demonstrate the courage and efficiency of Soviet airmen; it thrilled the whole Soviet nation with pride of its own achievement. It was then for the first time that I realized what Bolsheviks had accomplished; when I heard the children in my court-yard and old women in street-cars and workers at a meeting and soldiers in a camp and high officials in their offices all saying exactly the same thing, *"We* have rescued the Chelyuskinites." The thing that hit me was this *"we,"* the fact that all of them felt that they somehow shared in the anxious waiting of a group of men and women on the ice-floe and in their gallant rescue.

Then there was the Soviet stratosphere flight. Despite all the pseudo-scientific nonsense that has appeared in the newspapers of the world about the stratosphere and cosmic rays, I personally refuse to believe that this stratosphere business is anything more than a glorified publicity stunt. If the first balloonist, Montgolfier, had thought of suggesting that above the "ceiling" of his primitive hot-air balloon there existed a mysterious No-Man's-Land between earth and heaven called the stratosphere, he would probably have set it at about 500 meters, that is to say, at the limit of his balloon's ascension. A few years ago an ingenious Belgian scientist set the limit at 10,000 meters or more and built a balloon to plumb these hitherto unmeasured heights and equipped it with instruments to measure the cosmic rays, whatever they may be. I have read with care all the accounts of all the stratosphere flights that have been made, but I defy anyone to tell me what, if any, discoveries about cosmic rays have yet been made by any of them or what they have added to the store of human knowledge save that the higher you go the colder it gets, and the further you see and the darker the sky looks, and the further the higher the colder. In short, I consider these stratosphere flights on a par with round-the-world races, trans-Atlantic or trans-Pacific aviation, and similar ballyhoo. They are doubtless proofs of human courage, but every youngster in the American, British, French or German air force who flew a fighting plane across the Front in 1918 was taking greater risks than Lindbergh or Miss Earheart or Admiral Byrd or Amy Johnson and her husband, and all the rest of them put together, and, what is more, went on taking them every day and made no money out of it, nothing but a choice of crosses, the Distinguished Cross of Valor or a wooden cross above their graves.

Perhaps I am wrong; perhaps the stratosphere flights are more momentous than the voyages of Columbus or Captain Cook. At all events the Russians seemed to think so and set out to make stratosphere flights of their own. One beat all records for high flying; another ended in disaster. But the point I wish to make is that the record-breaking flight thrilled all Russia with an exaltation of "our own" success, and the disaster was mourned by everyone as "our own" loss. It was the same when the giant airplane *Maxim Gorky* crashed in the spring of 1935. The Russian people had been proud of *Maxim Gorky* as the biggest land-plane in the world and when it crashed the whole nation sorrowed and sent its money in tiny dribblets—one, two, five, ten roubles, from boys and girls at school or workers and peasants—to form a colossal fund of 100,000,000 roubles to build new planes of the same type. No propaganda and no fear of Authority can explain mass action on this scale.

Another example is the new subway in Moscow. I saw an old peasant make his first visit to the subway. He had never, he told me, been underground before except to get ice out of the hole in which he stored it in his own back-yard. He went down the stairs through the gleaming tiled passages to the marble station aglow with hidden light. Timidly he stepped aboard the train, the first un-engined train he had ever seen, which to him was as strange and new, perhaps as terrifying, as a cart that ran without a horse. He sat rigid on his seat till he reached the terminus, then walked along the platform and came to the escalator; and paused. He watched the iron steps rising as if by magic out of the ground to carry people upwards; then at last he heaved a deep breath, gripped the side-rail and stood firmly on the step. I watched him as he rode up with popping eyes, but when he stepped off at the top with a sigh of relief his words were to me enormously significant. He said, *"We* have built a fine railroad under the ground and when I go back and tell my comrades in the village about our railroad, they won't believe most of it, but I shall go on telling them until they do believe it, that we Russians have built a finer underground railroad than anyone in the world."

It is only in the last two years that the word *Rodina,* meaning birthplace or homeland, has been allowed in the Soviet Press in speaking of the U.S.S.R. Before that they always used phrases like the "Socialist Fatherland" to emphasize the idea of internationalism, but now they are encouraging not so much the pride of the country where they were born as the feeling that they all have a pride and share in what their country does— the subway is *their* subway; the new buildings that are transforming Moscow from an overgrown village into a magnificent modern city are *their* buildings; the rescue of the *Chelyuskin* is *their* rescue; the *Maxim Gorky* is a disaster for *them.* This, I say, is the greatest achievement of Bolshevism in its eighteen years of existence, to have permeated the lowest depths of the Russian people with a spirit of joint and universal effort.

Few foreigners seem to have realized this phase of the Soviet system. To begin with, there is an absurd confusion in foreign minds between the genuine Socialism of the U.S.S.R. and the pseudo-Socialism, or more correctly war-Socialism, of Germany and Italy. Foreigners seem to think because Karl Marx demanded the possession and control of production and means of production for his Socialist State, that this was the beginning and end of Socialism. Theoretically of course, it is true, but in practice the thing which distinguishes a real working Socialist system from a pseudo-Socialist system is the abolition of the power of money and the profit motive and of the possibility for any individual or group of individuals to gain surplus value from the work of others. This and this alone is the true foundation of Socialism. It does not exist in Germany and it does not exist in Italy, but in Soviet Russia to-day it is a cardinal principle which is absolute and definite and supported by the harshest of laws and rules and regulations. No less an expert in foreign affairs than David Lawrence suggested in an article in the *Saturday Evening Post* of July 20, 1935, that there was no great difference in the systems of the U.S.S.R., Germany and Italy, and said, "In none of these countries is there any semblance to-day of Socialism." This is sheer ignorance. In Germany and Italy there is exactly that, a semblance or surrogate of Socialism, which centralizes and reënforces the power of the State for purposes which are approved by the majority of its citizens or by their dominant sections. This is pseudo-Socialism or war-Socialism, a relinquishing of individual or group interests in order to strengthen the State in a critical period. France and Britain accepted a similar system during the World War, and even the United States was willing to allow a degree of centralized control that it would never have allowed in peace time. This, however, is far from Socialism; it is nothing but a consolidation of power in order to gain an objective. In the U.S.S.R., on the other hand, there is full real Socialism, in that all the dynamic forces of the country, not only the forces of money but the forces of invention, energy, technique, discipline, effort and initiative are applied for and by the community instead of for and by individuals. Just as the interest and enthusiasm of individuals have been taught to follow a common purpose and rejoice over common successes or weep over common failures, so the common energy and effort have been canalized in a single channel; it is no longer a question of what *I* do or what *I* get but of what *we* do and what *we* get. I venture to suggest that there could be no simpler definition of the difference between Socialism and Individualism.

Looking backwards over the fourteen years I have spent in Russia, I cannot escape the conclusion that this period has been a heroic chapter in the life of Humanity. During these years the first true Socialist State, with all that that implies in planned economy, in the ownership of production and means of production, in communal effort as opposed to individual effort and in communal pride and interest in everything that the community rather than the individual accomplished, was constructed and set moving despite incredible difficulties. I am profoundly convinced that the U.S.S.R. is only just beginning to exercise its tremendous potentialities. According to Soviet law a man "comes of age" at eighteen, and this is the eighteenth year of New Russia's existence. The fourteen years which I have seen have been a time of growth and construction, a sort of larval period from which the adult creature is only just emerging. The U.S.S.R. is now economically and financially independent; it has the largest and perhaps the most powerful army in Europe; it has vast territory and resources, which it is learning to develop and use. In short, the U.S.S.R. has recovered the position lost by the Tsarist Empire in 1917 of one of the great world powers. This progress at home and abroad has been paralleled by a remarkable advance of the Soviet leaders in knowledge and wisdom; am I wrong in believing that Stalin is the greatest living statesman and that Litvinov is the ablest foreign minister? Not only these two but other Soviet leaders have grown with the growth of their country and gained in mental capacity to meet the growing magnitude of the problems which they have had to solve.

More important still, Stalin and his associates have carried with them the strongest and most intelligent elements of the Russian people, and have created a national unity and enthusiasm which the Tsarist Empire never knew. They have learnt by their own errors and pulled themselves up by their own bootstraps, and the nation has followed them. Nothing that may be said abroad about the tyranny and high-handedness of the Bolshevik régime can alter the fact that the Russian masses think and speak of "our" Rodina, "our" technicians, "our" successes and "our" failures.

.   .   .   .

I believe that folklore is one of the keys to the character of a nation, and I think there is a kinship, mental or psychological, between the Russians and the Chinese. There is a Chinese folk-story about certain exceptional men who are able to transmit their "life"—which may mean soul or spirit or vital principle, as you care to call it—to an animal or object, and that as long as this animal or object remains unhurt, their vital principle continues. Thus a Chinese may transfer his vital principle to a goldfish and as long as the goldfish swims serene in his little bowl, so long its human "owner" will prosper and defeat his enemies. The human owner may be forced to face a firing-squad but if the goldfish swims unmolested the bullets will miss and the "life" will not be quenched. In Russian folklore there is a similar legend of the giant "Koshchei Bez-smertny," Koshchei the Deathless, who revived smiling after decapitation or a spear-thrust through the heart, until one day there came a young Hero with wit to ask where the "life" of Koshchei the Deathless might be found. They told him this and they told him that, but finally he learned the truth, that in a nest in a distant swamp was a duck, and in the body of the duck was an egg and in the egg was the "life" of the deathless Koshchei. To vanquish the giant all he needed was to find and crush this egg, which he did and Koshchei died.

I once spoke of this story to a Bolshevik whom I knew well. At first he sniffed and sneered at my talk of fairy-tales and old-world superstition but when I persisted he grew interested as Russians will, in anything that is a mental problem—perhaps that is why they are the world's best chess players—and asked me finally, "What has this to do with me or with the U.S.S.R.?"

"I am telling you," I said. "It has to do with the U.S.S.R. in that I want to know where the 'life' of your new jump in human progress is concealed, and it has to do with you in that I want you to tell me." He looked at me very seriously for about a minute, then he said slowly, "Let me understand this right. You want to know where is the life of our young Soviet giant? All right then, I will tell you. The life of our Soviet giant is to be found in the center of a territory far greater than any land unit under any flag. At this center there is a rock of granite and in the heart of the granite a diamond, harder than any stone; on the diamond is written, 'Not mine for me but ours for us.' That is the deathless life of the Union of Soviet Socialist Republics."

INDEX

343

ABOUT THE AUTHOR

WALTER DURANTY, *Moscow correspondent of* The New York Times *since 1920, says that he first heard of Russia at the age of four when his nurse took him to a fair in his native Lancashire and they witnessed a rough-and-tumble Russian comedy. It was a significant omen, for Mr. Duranty's subsequent career both in Russia and elsewhere has been a succession of adventures.*

During the War he served as newspaper correspondent on the Western Front where he got such a baptism of fire that nothing he saw afterwards in the Soviet Union made him turn a hair. In 1919 Mr. Duranty was holding down a dull job as "second man" in the Paris office of The New York Times *when he was suddenly assigned to accompany Commander Gade, the newly appointed American High Commissioner to the Baltic states, as correspondent for that whole area. From the Baltic states he moved to Moscow where, unlike many foreign correspondents, he mastered the language and thus won the friendship of the Soviet leaders.*

Mr. Duranty has twice interviewed Stalin and accompanied Litvinov to the United States when Soviet-American relations were resumed in the fall of 1933. He has covered all the important news stories from Russia since Hoover's American Relief Association ministered to the famine sufferers after the War and Revolution. He has met all the important visitors to Moscow during the past fifteen years, but his best friend and the man he admired most was the late Bill Ryall (William Bolitho) to whom this book is dedicated.

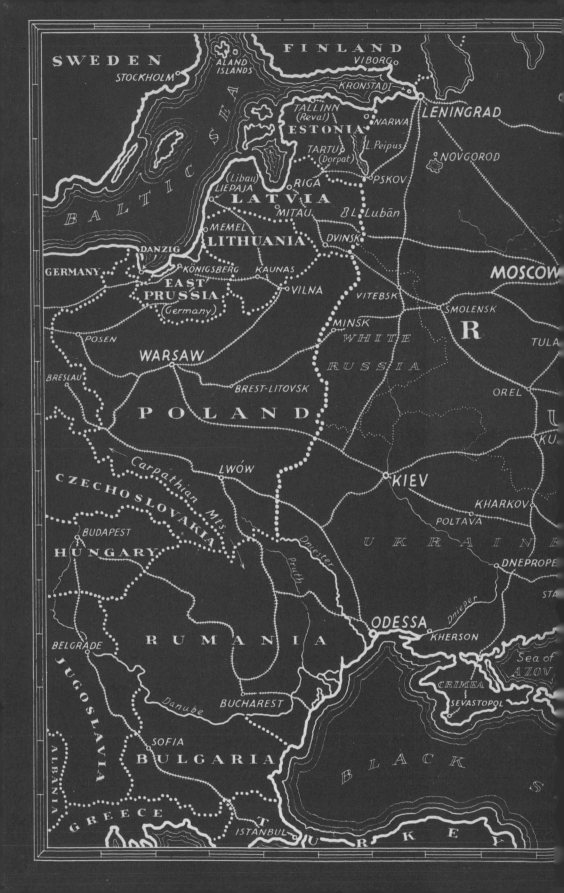